# THE PREGNANCY
# HEALTH GUIDE

# THE PREGNANCY HEALTH GUIDE

PROFESSOR PETER ABRAHAMS

**amber**
BOOKS

First published in 2007 by
Amber Books Ltd
Bradley's Close
74–77 White Lion Street
London N1 9PF
United Kingdom
www.amberbooks.co.uk

ISBN-13: 978-1-905704-41-5

Distributed in the UK by
Bookmart Ltd
Blaby Road
Wigston
Leicester LE18 4SE

Project Editor: Michael Spilling
Design: Hawes Design

Printed in Czech Republic

# Contents

Right: Despite the millions of sperm that are produced and released in each ejaculation, only one can fertilise an egg. The gender of a baby depends on which type of sperm penetrates the egg first – sperm with a Y chromosome will make a boy baby, and sperm with an X chromosome will make a girl.

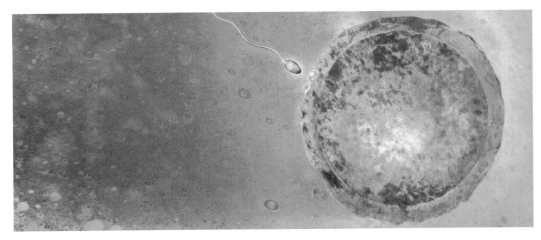

Right: At a time when new parents can often feel overwhelmed by their new responsibilities, support from family and friends is crucial in the first few weeks after the birth.

# Introduction

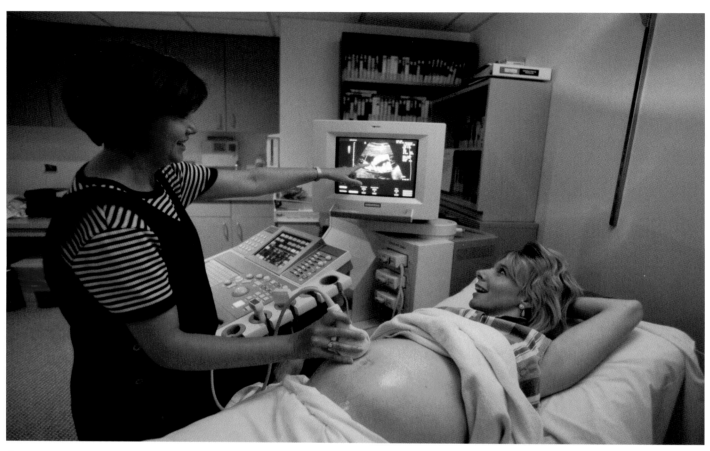

Conception, pregnancy and childbirth are a chain of extraordinary events that lead to the creation of a new human life. These events are highly emotional, but they are also normal physiological processes, controlled by our natural urge to continue the species. Such processes can occasionally go awry, but developments in pre-conception planning, pregnancy monitoring and delivery mean that having a child is now safer than ever. However, would-be parents may feel overwhelmed by the plethora of advice and information on offer. This guide aims to provide women and their partners with straightforward and medically accurate information about childbirth.

## CONCEIVING YOUR CHILD

Over the decades, attitudes towards, and aspects of childbirth have changed dramatically. Efficient contraception means that couples can now delay pregnancy until they feel ready to start a family. A carefully planned pregnancy also enables women and their partners to adopt a healthy lifestyle before conception occurs, and so contribute to the well-being of both mother and baby. Having said that, conception is not necessarily instant – it may take weeks, months or years to become pregnant, and some couples never manage to conceive. Many parents are older – in their 30s and 40s – and have focused on a career before taking the decision to have a child, and at this later stage in life, it may be more difficult to conceive. However, even for prospective parents who are beginning to give up hope, technological advances mean that a simple procedure can often result in a pregnancy.

When conception does

Expectant mothers can have a number of prenatal scans to check the position and health of the baby.

occur, one of the greatest fears is that the child may have a difficulty or abnormality, a possibility that is greater for older women. Modern monitoring techniques, sophisticated tests and skilled health care professionals mean that the majority of pregnancies in the developed world are problem-free. But the ability to intervene during pregnancy and labour can also create anxiety and stress for would-be parents, in which case clear information about any procedures, and how they will affect the mother and unborn child, is essential.

### THE GROWING BABY

It is impossible to describe a 'normal' pregnancy. Every woman has a different experience and while many mothers relate an experience of immense well-being during pregnancy, others will tell of morning sickness, swollen ankles and backache. Of course, similar physiological changes occur in every pregnancy. The baby grows and develops over a period of just over nine months, and to accommodate this the uterus expands to about 20 times its normal size. There are other changes in a pregnant woman's physical appearance. She will notice her breasts enlarging by about 1–1.5 kg (2.2–3.3 lb) in preparation for breast-feeding, and there are skin changes that result from an increased production of hormones, for example.

At around 37 weeks, the baby settles into position for birth and from then on there is a period of waiting, and often understandably impatience. A few weeks later, a pregnant woman will go into labour – the final stage of pregnancy. At this stage, for most prospective parents, there are two primary concerns; they want a healthy baby and a problem-free birth.

Pain relief is often a priority although, once again, women differ enormously in their needs and in their experience of pain. Some prefer to undergo birth without painkillers, and others opt for gas and air or an epidural. Whatever the level of pain, emotional support during labour and birth are vital, and birthing partners have an important role to play.

### AFTER THE BIRTH

When the baby is finally born, emotions are likely to be high, and feelings may well include exhaustion, relief and excitement. Becoming a parent, particularly for the first time, can be a daunting prospect and the first few weeks with the baby will reinforce the sense of new responsibilities and difficulties ahead, but also the prospect of many rewards.

### THIS BOOK

*The Pregnancy Health Guide* takes you through the whole process of starting a family, from making the decision to go ahead to the first few weeks after birth. Clear, straight-forward advice about the normal processes is provided, as well as explanations of possible difficulties and unexpected outcomes.

Several sections describe relevant anatomy and physiology to help provide a clear understanding of the processes that a woman's body goes through during pregnancy and childbirth.

During pregnancy it is vital that an expectant mother eats and drinks healthily.

# Conception

Conception refers to the process of fertilization of the egg by a sperm and its consequent implantation in the uterus (womb) lining. The process of conception can be far from easy.

Although some couples conceive readily, sometimes without even 'planning' a pregnancy, others have no success for months or even years. The statistics, however, are optimistic: six out of ten couples will conceive within six months, two will take up to a year, and by two years, nine out of ten couples will have conceived.

So it is important not to worry if you plan to start a family and do not become pregnant immediately.

Left: Discovering that you are pregnant can be one of the most joyful experiences for a couple.

## OPTIMISING THE CHANCES OF CONCEPTION

Today, a range of easily accessible contraception means that couples can plan pregnancies, and have time to consider the full implications of starting a family. For many people, having a baby involves changes to lifestyle such as giving up smoking and taking drugs, minimising alcohol intake, and eating a healthy diet. People at risk of sexually transmitted diseases may want to have a sexual health check-up, and genetic counselling is advisable for couples who have a family history of inherited diseases. Other measures may include switching from hormonal contraception – 'the pill' – some time before trying to conceive. Ideally, all these factors should be taken into account to make sure that the mother and baby have good health during the pregnancy and afterwards.

## FERTILITY

Most women are fertile – that is, able to conceive a child – from puberty, which can be as early as age 10, until menopause at around forty-five to fifty years of age. However, after age 30 a woman's fertility declines as the 'quality' of her eggs (which have been stored in her ovaries since before she was born) declines. Women start life with up to 2 million eggs, but by puberty only between 40,000 and 400,000 remain.

Each menstrual cycle, which lasts around 28 days, some 20 eggs will start to develop but only one (or two in the case of non-identical twins) is usually released. Ovulation is signified by changes in hormones, body temperature and vaginal secretions, which means that ovulation can be predicted with simple tests.

Men do not start producing sperm until puberty but they do not have a menopause in the same way that women do and are capable of fathering a child much later than women – Charlie Chaplin famously fathered his last child when he was 73.

## THE FERTILIZED EGG

During conception, the man ejaculates 200-400 million sperm, but mere thousands will make the full two-hour journey to the entrance of the fallopian tube in which the egg is located. Of these, only a few hundred make their way up the tube, where they begin to

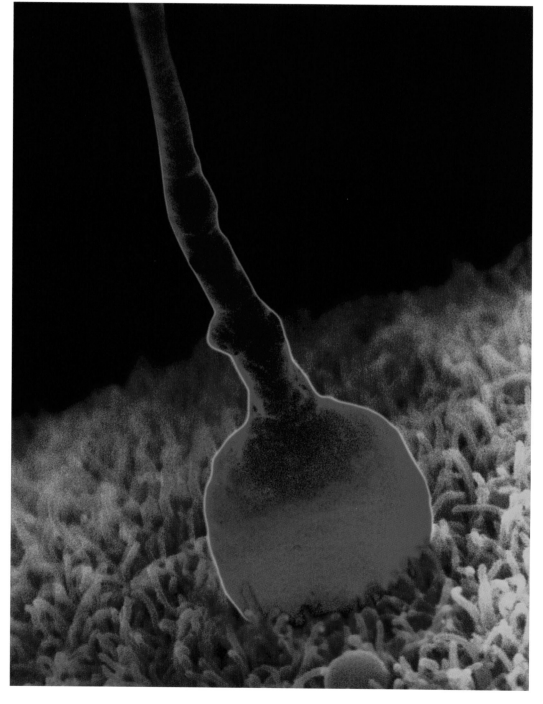

In this computer-enhanced image a human sperm penetrates the wall of a female egg.

If conception proves difficult after six month many couples seek medical advice.

break down the outer coating of the egg. The first sperm to penetrate the egg triggers a mechanism that repels all the other sperm. The combination of genetic material from the head of the sperm and that carried within the egg is the beginning of complex process that results in a fully-grown baby around 40 weeks after conception.

## FAILURE TO CONCEIVE

For some couples, starting a family is not a simple process. A failure to conceive does not necessarily mean that one or the other partner is infertile but it is worth getting some professional advice about whether to start investigations.

There are many reasons for not conceiving readily and some of these are easily resolvable. It may be that simple lifestyle changes are all that's needed to improve fertility (see below). Stress is known to reduce fertility in both women and men, so it is important not to get too anxious, and in particular not to become too focused on the need to become pregnant. This is especially important advice for people who are undergoing infertility investigations or treatment, since a diagnosis of infertility can be traumatic and the treatment itself can represent a real source of stress.

In men, infertility is often due to a low sperm count or poor quality of the sperm. A complete absence of sperm is known as sterility. Many factors can affect sperm production, including infection and inflammation, and these conditions are often easily treated. Female infertility is common and can be due to anything that disrupts or prevents the normal cycle of egg production and ovulation, fertilisation and implantation. If an irreversible problem exists with a couple conceiving, then techniques such as in-vitro fertilisation, or sperm, egg and embryo donation can make it possible for a couple to have a child where once there would have been no possibility.

## MAKING CONCEPTION MORE LIKELY

❧ Reach a healthy weight
❧ Try to stop smoking
❧ Avoid unnecessary drugs (seek advice from your GP about prescription drugs)
❧ Reduce alcohol intake
❧ Take regular exercise
❧ Eat healthily
❧ Get treatment for sexually transmitted infections

# Male reproductive system

The male reproductive system includes the penis, scrotum and the two testes (contained within the scrotum). The internal structures of the reproductive system are contained within the pelvis.

The structures constituting the male reproductive tract are responsible for the production of sperm and seminal fluid and their carriage out of the body. Unlike other organs it is not until puberty that they develop and become fully functional.

### CONSTITUENT PARTS

The male reproductive system consists of a number of interrelated parts:

■ Testis – the paired testes lie suspended in the scrotum. Sperm are carried away from the testes through tubes or ducts, the first of which is the epididymis
■ Epididymis – on ejaculation sperm leave the epididymis and enter the vas deferens
■ Vas deferens – sperm are carried along this muscular tube en route to the prostate gland
■ Seminal vesicle – on leaving the vas deferens sperm mix with fluid from the seminal vesicle gland in a combined 'ejaculatory' duct
■ Prostate – the ejaculatory duct empties into the urethra within the prostate gland
■ Penis – on leaving the prostate gland, the urethra then becomes the central core of the penis.

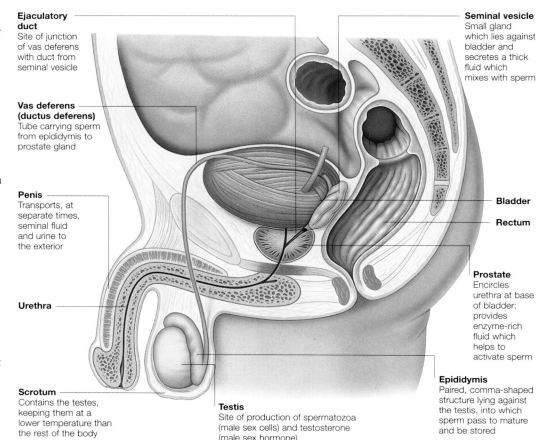

**Ejaculatory duct**
Site of junction of vas deferens with duct from seminal vesicle

**Vas deferens (ductus deferens)**
Tube carrying sperm from epididymis to prostate gland

**Penis**
Transports, at separate times, seminal fluid and urine to the exterior

**Urethra**

**Scrotum**
Contains the testes, keeping them at a lower temperature than the rest of the body

**Seminal vesicle**
Small gland which lies against bladder and secretes a thick fluid which mixes with sperm

**Bladder**

**Rectum**

**Prostate**
Encircles urethra at base of bladder; provides enzyme-rich fluid which helps to activate sperm

**Epididymis**
Paired, comma-shaped structure lying against the testis, into which sperm pass to mature and be stored

**Testis**
Site of production of spermatozoa (male sex cells) and testosterone (male sex hormone)

## External genitalia

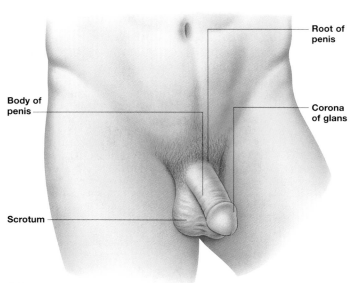

**Root of penis**

**Body of penis**

**Corona of glans**

**Scrotum**

The external genitalia are those parts of the reproductive tract which lie visible in the pubic region, while other parts remain hidden within the pelvic cavity.

Male external genitalia consists of:
■ The scrotum
■ The penis.
In adults, these are surrounded by coarse pubic hair.

### SCROTUM

The scrotum is a loose bag of skin and connective tissue which

*The external male genitalia consist of the scrotum and the penis, which are situated in the pubic area. In adults, pubic hair surrounds the root of the penis*

holds the testes suspended within it. There is a midline septum, or partition, which separates each testis from its fellow.

Although it would seem unusual for the testes to be held in such a vulnerable position outside the protection of the body cavity, it is necessary for sperm production for them to be kept cool.

### PENIS

Most of the penis consists of erectile tissue, which becomes engorged with blood during sexual arousal, causing the penis to become erect. The urethra, through which urine and semen pass, runs through the penis.

# Prostate gland

The prostate gland forms a vital part of the male reproductive system, providing enzyme-rich fluid, and produces up to a third of the total volume of the seminal fluid.

About 3 cm (1.2 in) in length, the prostate gland lies just under the bladder and encircles the first part of the urethra. Its base lies closely attached to the base of the bladder, its rounded anterior (front) surface lying just behind the pubic bone.

### CAPSULE
The prostate is covered by a tough capsule made up of dense fibrous connective tissue. Outside this true capsule is a further layer of fibrous connective tissue, which is known as the prostatic sheath.

### INTERNAL STRUCTURE
The urethra, the outflow tract from the bladder, runs vertically through the centre of the prostate gland, where it is known as the prostatic urethra. The ejaculatory ducts open into the prostatic urethra on a raised ridge, the seminal colliculus.

The prostate is said to be divided into lobes, although they are not as distinct as they may be in other organs:
■ Anterior lobe – this lies in front of the urethra and contains mainly fibromuscular tissue
■ Posterior lobe – this lies behind the urethra and beneath the ejaculatory ducts
■ Lateral lobes – these two lobes, lying on either side of the urethra, form the main part of the gland
■ Median lobe – this lies between the urethra and the ejaculatory ducts.

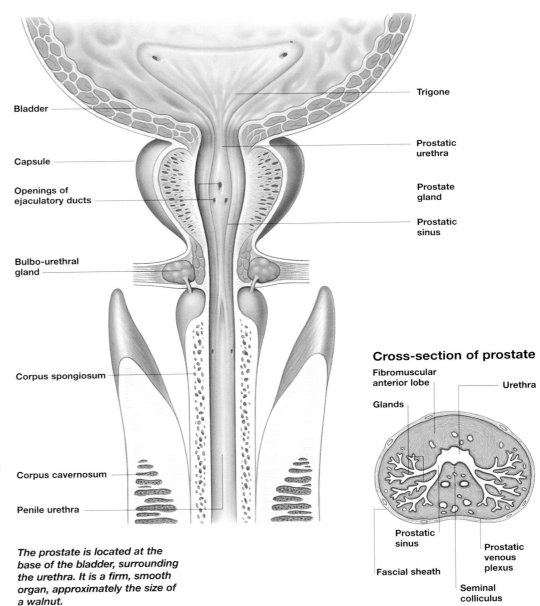

**Location of the prostate gland**

Trigone

Bladder

Prostatic urethra

Capsule

Prostate gland

Openings of ejaculatory ducts

Prostatic sinus

Bulbo-urethral gland

Corpus spongiosum

Corpus cavernosum

Penile urethra

*The prostate is located at the base of the bladder, surrounding the urethra. It is a firm, smooth organ, approximately the size of a walnut.*

**Cross-section of prostate**

Fibromuscular anterior lobe

Urethra

Glands

Prostatic sinus

Prostatic venous plexus

Fascial sheath

Seminal colliculus

## Seminal vesicles

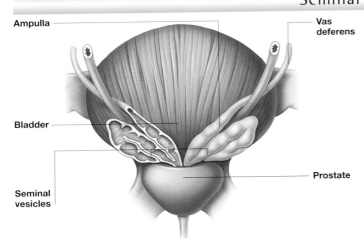

Ampulla

Vas deferens

Bladder

Prostate

Seminal vesicles

The paired seminal vesicles are accessory glands of the male reproductive tract and produce a thick, sugary, alkaline fluid that forms the main part of the seminal fluid.

### STRUCTURE AND SHAPE
Each seminal vesicle is an elongated structure about the

*The seminal vesicles are situated at the back of the bladder. Secretions pass into the vas deferentia, which empty into the prostatic urethra.*

size and shape of a little finger and lies behind the bladder and in front of the rectum, the two forming a V-shape.

### PROSTATE VOLUME
The prostate gland is sac-like, with a volume of approximately 10–15 millilitres. It consists internally of coiled secretory tubules with muscular walls.

The secretions leave the gland in the duct of the seminal vesicle, which joins with the vas deferens just inside the prostate to form the ejaculatory duct.

15

# Female reproductive system

The role of the female reproductive tract is twofold.
The ovaries produce eggs for fertilization, and the uterus nurtures
and protects any resulting fetus for its nine-month gestation.

The female reproductive tract is composed of the internal genitalia – the ovaries, uterine (Fallopian) tubes, uterus and vagina – and the external genitalia (the vulva).

### INTERNAL GENITALIA

The almond-shaped ovaries lie on either side of the uterus, suspended by ligaments. Above the ovaries are the paired uterine tubes, each of which provides a site for fertilization of the oocyte (egg), which then travels down the tube to the uterus.

The uterus lies within the pelvic cavity and rises into the lower abdominal cavity as a pregnancy progresses. The vagina, which connects the cervix to the vulva, can be distended greatly, as occurs during childbirth when it forms much of the birth canal.

### EXTERNAL GENITALIA

The female external genitalia, or vulva, is where the reproductive tract opens to the exterior. The vaginal opening lies behind the opening of the urethra in an area known as the vestibule. This is covered by two folds of skin on each side, the labia minora and labia majora, in front of which lies the raised clitoris.

*The female reproductive system is composed of internal and external organs. The internal genitalia are T-shaped and lie within the pelvic cavity.*

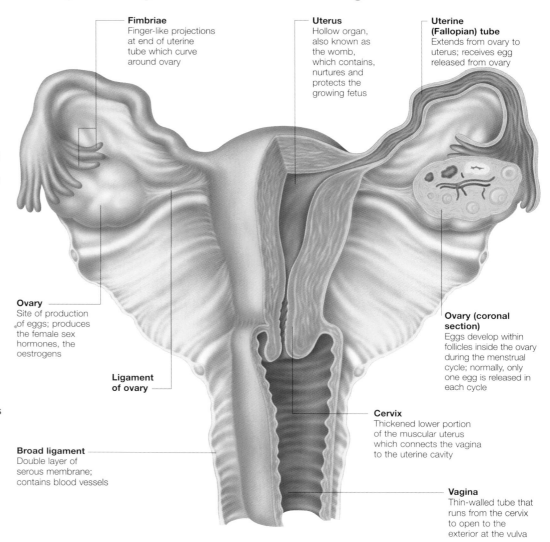

**Fimbriae**
Finger-like projections at end of uterine tube which curve around ovary

**Uterus**
Hollow organ, also known as the womb, which contains, nurtures and protects the growing fetus

**Uterine (Fallopian) tube**
Extends from ovary to uterus; receives egg released from ovary

**Ovary**
Site of production of eggs; produces the female sex hormones, the oestrogens

**Ligament of ovary**

**Broad ligament**
Double layer of serous membrane; contains blood vessels

**Ovary (coronal section)**
Eggs develop within follicles inside the ovary during the menstrual cycle; normally, only one egg is released in each cycle

**Cervix**
Thickened lower portion of the muscular uterus which connects the vagina to the uterine cavity

**Vagina**
Thin-walled tube that runs from the cervix to open to the exterior at the vulva

## Position of the female reproductive tract

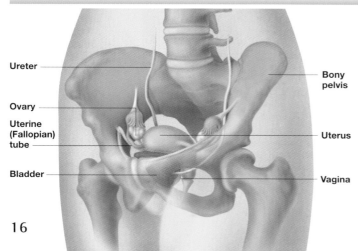

**Ureter**

**Ovary**

**Uterine (Fallopian) tube**

**Bladder**

**Bony pelvis**

**Uterus**

**Vagina**

In adult women the internal genitalia (which, apart from the ovaries, are basically tubular in structure) are located deep within the pelvic cavity. They are thus protected by the presence of the circle of bone which makes up the pelvis.

This is in contrast to the

*The internal reproductive organs in adult women are positioned deep within the pelvic cavity. They are therefore protected by the bony pelvis.*

pelvic cavity of young children, which is relatively shallow. A child's uterus, therefore, like the bladder behind which it sits, is located within the lower abdomen.

### BROAD LIGAMENTS

The upper surface of the uterus and ovaries is draped in a 'tent' of peritoneum, the thin lining of the abdominal and pelvic cavities, forming the broad ligament which helps to keep the uterus in its position.

# Blood supply of the internal genitalia

The female reproductive tract receives a rich blood supply via an interconnecting network of arteries. Venous blood is drained by a network of veins.

The four principal arteries of the female genitalia are:

■ **Ovarian artery** – this runs from the abdominal aorta to the ovary.

Branches from the ovarian artery on each side pass through the mesovarium, the fold of peritoneum in which the ovary lies, to supply the ovary and uterine (Fallopian) tubes. The ovarian artery in the tissue of the mesovarium connects with the uterine artery

■ **Uterine artery** – this is a branch of the large internal iliac artery of the pelvis. The uterine artery approaches the uterus at the level of the cervix, which is anchored in place by cervical ligaments.

The uterine artery connects with the ovarian artery above, while a branch connects with the arteries below to supply the cervix and vagina

■ **Vaginal artery** – this is also a branch of the internal iliac artery. Together with blood from the uterine artery, its branches supply blood to the vaginal walls

■ **Internal pudendal artery** – this contributes to the blood supply of the lower third of the vagina and anus.

### VEINS

A plexus, or network, of small veins lies within the walls of the uterus and vagina. Blood received into these vessels drains into the internal iliac veins via the uterine vein.

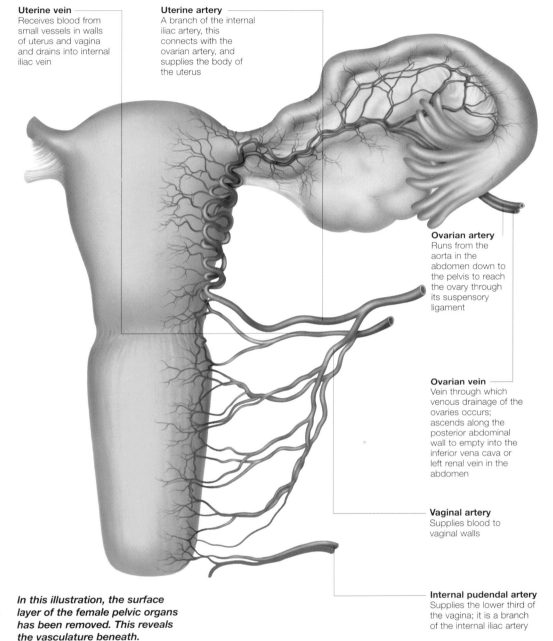

**Uterine vein**
Receives blood from small vessels in walls of uterus and vagina and drains into internal iliac vein

**Uterine artery**
A branch of the internal iliac artery, this connects with the ovarian artery, and supplies the body of the uterus

**Ovarian artery**
Runs from the aorta in the abdomen down to the pelvis to reach the ovary through its suspensory ligament

**Ovarian vein**
Vein through which venous drainage of the ovaries occurs; ascends along the posterior abdominal wall to empty into the inferior vena cava or left renal vein in the abdomen

**Vaginal artery**
Supplies blood to vaginal walls

**Internal pudendal artery**
Supplies the lower third of the vagina; it is a branch of the internal iliac artery

*In this illustration, the surface layer of the female pelvic organs has been removed. This reveals the vasculature beneath.*

## Visualizing the female reproductive tract

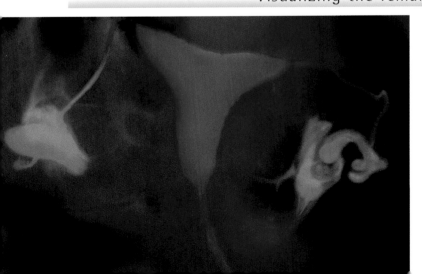

The tubal or hollow parts of the female reproductive tract can be outlined by performing a hysterosalpingogram.

In this procedure a special radio-opaque dye is passed up into the uterus through the cervix, while X-ray pictures of the area are taken. The dye fills the uterine cavity, and enters

*This hysterosalpingogram shows the uterine cavity (centre) filled with dye. Dye is also seen in the uterine tubes and emerging into the peritoneal cavity.*

the uterine tubes. It then runs along their length until it flows into the peritoneal cavity at their far end.

### ASSESSING TUBES

A hysterosalpingogram is sometimes carried out in the investigation of infertility to determine whether the uterine tubes are still patent (unobstructed). If the tubes have been blocked, as may happen after an infection, the dye will not be able to travel along their full length.

# Menstrual cycle

The menstrual cycle is the regular process by which an egg is released from an ovary in preparation for pregnancy. This occurs approximately every four weeks from the time of a woman's first period right up to the menopause.

The menstrual cycle is characterized by the periodic maturation of oocytes (cells that develop into eggs) in the ovaries and associated physical changes in the uterus. Reproductive maturity occurs after a sudden increase in the secretion of hormones during puberty, usually between the ages of 11 and 15.

## CYCLE ONSET

The time of the first period, which occurs at about the age of 12, is called the menarche. After this, a reproductive cycle begins, averaging 28 days. This length of time may be longer, shorter or variable, depending on the individual. The cycle is continuous, apart from during pregnancy. However, women suffering from anorexia nervosa or athletes who train intensively may cease to menstruate.

## MENSTRUATION

Each month, if conception does not occur, oestrogen and progesterone levels fall and the blood-rich lining of the uterus is shed at menstruation (menses). This takes place every 28 days or so, but the time can range from 19 to 36 days.

Menstruation lasts for about five days. Around 50 ml (about an eggcup) of blood, uterine tissues and fluid is lost during this time, but again this volume varies from woman to woman. Some women lose only 10 ml of blood, while others lose 110 ml.

Excessive menstrual bleeding is known as menorrhagia; temporary cessation of menstruation – such as during pregnancy – is called amenorrhoea. The menopause is the complete cessation of the menstrual cycle, and usually occurs between 45 and 55.

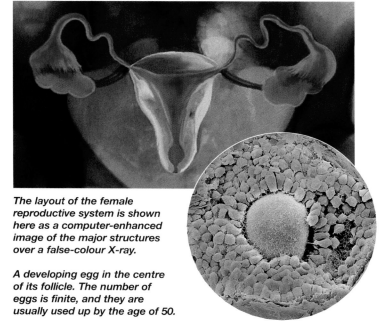

*The layout of the female reproductive system is shown here as a computer-enhanced image of the major structures over a false-colour X-ray.*

*A developing egg in the centre of its follicle. The number of eggs is finite, and they are usually used up by the age of 50.*

## Monthly physiological changes

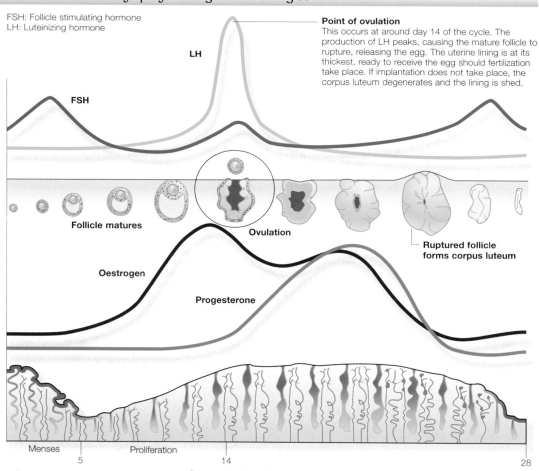

*This diagram illustrates the ongoing changes during the cycle. Between days one and five, the lining is discharged, while another follicle is developing. The uterine lining thickens, and around day 14, the egg is released, at the point called ovulation.*

**Gonadotrophic hormones**
Released by the pituitary gland to promote the production of the egg and of sex hormones in the gonads (ovaries)

**Ovarian activity**
Each month, one follicle develops to maturity, then releases an egg at ovulation; the surviving tissue in the ovary forms the corpus luteum, a temporary hormone-producing gland

**Ovarian hormones**
Secreted by the ovary to encourage the lining to grow; extra progesterone is produced by the corpus luteum after ovulation to prepare the uterus for pregnancy

**Lining of uterus**
Progressively thickens to receive the fertilized egg; if the egg does not implant, the lining is shed (menses) during the first five days of the cycle

FSH: Follicle stimulating hormone
LH: Luteinizing hormone

LH

FSH

**Point of ovulation**
This occurs at around day 14 of the cycle. The production of LH peaks, causing the mature follicle to rupture, releasing the egg. The uterine lining is at its thickest, ready to receive the egg should fertilization take place. If implantation does not take place, the corpus luteum degenerates and the lining is shed.

Follicle matures

Ovulation

Ruptured follicle forms corpus luteum

Oestrogen

Progesterone

Days
Menses
5
Proliferation
14
28

One menstrual cycle

# Egg development

The process of developing a healthy egg for release at ovulation takes around six months. It occurs throughout life until the stock of oocytes is exhausted.

Two million eggs (oogonia) are present at birth, distributed between the two ovaries, and 400,000 are left by the time of the first period. During each menstrual cycle, only one egg – from a pool of around 20 potential eggs – develops and is released. By the time menopause is reached, the process of atresia (cell degeneration) in the ovaries is complete and no eggs remain.

Eggs develop within cavity-forming secretory structures called follicles. The first stage of follicle development occurs when an oogonium becomes surrounded by a single layer of granulosa cells and is called a primordial (primary) follicle. The genetic material within the egg at this stage remains undisturbed – but susceptible to alteration –

until ovulation of that egg occurs, up to 45 years after it first developed. This helps to explain the increase in abnormal chromosomes in eggs and offspring of women who conceive later in life.

Primordial follicles develop into secondary follicles by meiotic (reductive) division and then into tertiary (or antral, meaning 'with a cavity') follicles. As many as 20 primary follicles will begin to mature, although 19 will eventually regress. If more than one follicle develops to maturity, twins or triplets may be conceived.

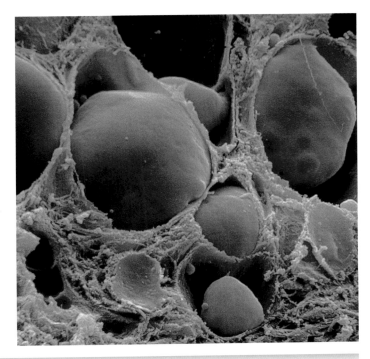

*The follicles are located in the cortex of the ovary. This micrograph shows the follicle separated by connective tissue.*

## Ovulation

The final 14 day period of follicular development takes place during the first half of the menstrual cycle and depends on the precise hormonal interplay between the ovary, pituitary gland and the hypothalamus.

The trigger for selecting a healthy egg for development at the start of each cycle is a rise in the secretion of follicle stimulating hormone (FSH) by the pituitary gland. This occurs in response to a fall in the hormones oestrogen and progesterone during the luteal phase (second 14 days) of the previous cycle if conception has not occurred.

### EGG SELECTION
At the time of the FSH signal, there are about 20 secondary follicles, 2–5 mm (0.1–0.2 in) in diameter, distributed between the two ovaries. A single follicle is selected from this pool, while the others undergo atresia. Once a follicle is selected, the development of further follicles is prevented. A typical 5 mm (0.2 in) secondary follicle will then require 10–12 days of sustained stimulation by FSH to grow to a diameter of 20 mm (0.8 in) before rupturing, releasing the

*Under a light microscope, a secondary oocyte (mature egg) can be seen surrounded by the cells of the corona radiata that support it during development.*

egg into the uterine (Fallopian) tube. As the follicle enlarges, there is a steady rise in oestrogen production, triggering a mid-cycle rise in luteinizing hormone (LH) by the pituitary, which in causes release and maturation of the egg. The interval between the LH peak and ovulation is relatively constant (about 36 hours). The ruptured follicle (corpus luteum) that remains after ovulation becomes a very important endocrine gland, secreting oestrogen and progesterone.

### HORMONE REGULATION
Progesterone levels rise to a peak about seven days after ovulation. If fertilization takes place, the corpus luteum maintains the pregnancy until the placenta takes over at about three months' gestation. If no conception takes place, the gland has a lifespan of 14 days, and oestrogen and progesterone levels decline in anticipation of the next cycle.

In the first half of the cycle, oestrogen secreted by the developing follicle (stage before corpus luteum) enables the lining of the uterus (endometrium) to proliferate and increase in thickness ready to nourish the egg should it become fertilized. Once the corpus luteum is formed, progesterone converts the endometrium to a more compact layer in anticipation of an embryo implanting.

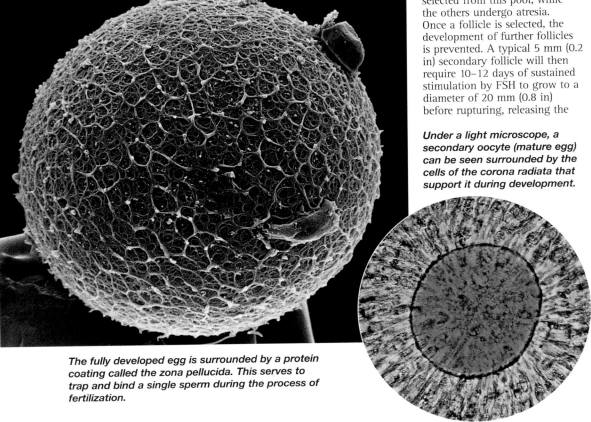

*The fully developed egg is surrounded by a protein coating called the zona pellucida. This serves to trap and bind a single sperm during the process of fertilization.*

# How ovulation occurs

The total supply of eggs for a woman's reproductive years is determined before she is born. The immature eggs are stored in the ovary until puberty, after which one is released every month.

An ovum (egg) is the female gamete, or sex cell, which unites with a sperm to form a new individual. Eggs are produced and stored in the ovaries, two walnut-sized organs connected to the uterus via the uterine (Fallopian) tubes.

### THE OVARY
Each ovary is covered by a protective layer of peritoneum (abdominal lining). Immediately below this layer is a dense fibrous capsule, the tunica albuginea. The ovary itself consists of a dense outer region, called the cortex, and a less dense inner region, the medulla.

### GAMETE PRODUCTION
In females, the total supply of eggs is determined at birth. Egg-forming cells degenerate from birth to puberty and the timespan during which a woman can release mature eggs is limited from puberty until menopause. The process by which ova are produced is

known as oogenesis, which literally means 'the beginning of an egg'. Germ cells in the fetus produce many oogonia cells. These divide to form primary oocytes which are enclosed in groups of follicle cells (support cells).

### GENETIC DIVISION
The primary oocytes begin to divide by meiosis (a specialized nuclear division) but this process is interrupted in its first phase and is not completed until after puberty. At birth, a lifetime's supply of primary oocytes, numbering between 700,000 and two million, will have been formed. These specialized cells will lie dormant in the cortical region of the immature ovary and slowly degenerate, so that by puberty only 40,000 remain.

*This micrograph shows an ovary with several large follicles (white). During ovulation, up to 20 follicles begin to develop, but only one matures to release an egg.*

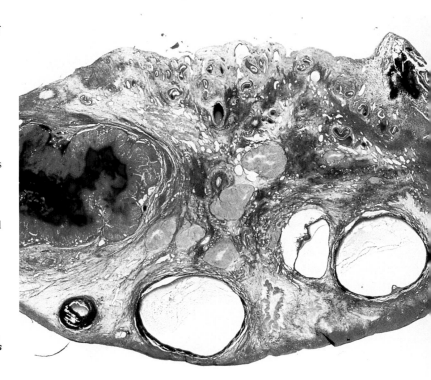

## Egg development

### How an egg develops

**BEFORE BIRTH** — Primordial follicle

**CHILDHOOD**

Zona pellucida — Follicular development arrested

**AT PUBERTY** — Primary follicle

Granulosa cells — Developing secondary follicle

Cumulus mass — **Graafian follicle**
Although several primary follicles develop with each menstrual cycle, only one Graafian follicle is formed; the other follicles regress

— Ruptured follicle

*Follicular development begins in the fetus, stops during childhood and is stimulated to continue each month by the onset of the ovarian cycle at puberty.*

— Released egg

Before puberty the primary oocyte is surrounded by a layer of cells (the granulosa cells), forming a primary follicle.

### PUBERTY
With the onset of puberty, some of the primary follicles are stimulated each month by hormones to continue development and become secondary follicles:
■ A layer of clear viscous fluid, the zona pellucida, is deposited on the surface of the oocyte.
■ The granulosa cells multiply and form an increasing number of layers around the oocyte.
■ The centre of the follicle becomes a chamber (the antrum) that fills with fluid secreted by the granulosa cells.
■ The oocyte is pushed to one side of the follicle, and lies in a mass of follicular cells called the cumulus mass.

A mature secondary follicle is called a Graafian follicle.

### Meiosis

The first meiotic division produces two cells of unequal size – the secondary oocyte and the first polar body. The secondary oocyte contains nearly all the cytoplasm of the primary oocyte. Both cells begin a second division; however, this process is halted, and is not completed until the oocyte is fertilized by a sperm.

*Meiosis, a specialized nuclear division, occurs in the ovaries, giving rise to a female sex cell and three polar bodies.*

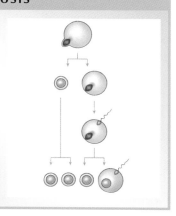

# Egg release

Ovulation occurs when a follicle ruptures, releasing a mature oocyte into the uterine tube. It is at this stage in the menstrual cycle that fertilization may occur.

As the Graafian follicle continues to swell, it can be seen on the surface of the ovary as a blister-like structure.

### HORMONAL CHANGES
In response to hormonal changes, the follicular cells surrounding the oocyte begin to secrete a thinner fluid at an increased rate, so that the follicle rapidly swells. As a result, the follicular wall becomes very thin over the area exposed to the ovarian surface, and the follicle eventually ruptures.

### OVULATION
A small amount of blood and follicular fluid is forced out of the vesicle, and the secondary oocyte, surrounded by the cumulus mass and zona pellucida, is expelled from the follicle into the peritoneal cavity – the process of ovulation.

Women are generally unaware of this phenomenon, although some experience a twinge of pain in the lower abdomen. This is caused by the intense stretching of the ovarian wall.

### FERTILE PERIOD
Ovulation occurs around the 14th day of a woman's menstrual cycle, and it is at this time that a woman is at her most fertile. As sperm can survive in the uterus for up to five days, there is a period of about a week when fertilization can occur.

In the event that the secondary oocyte is penetrated by a sperm cell and pregnancy ensues, the final stages of meiotic division will be triggered. If, however, the egg is not fertilized, the second stage of meiosis will not be completed and the secondary oocyte will simply degenerate.

The ruptured follicle forms a gland called the corpus luteum that secretes progesterone. This hormone prepares the uterine lining to receive an embryo.

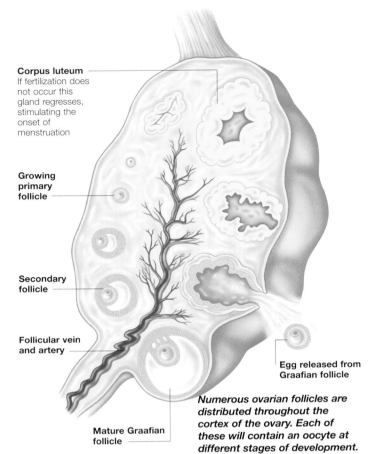

**Corpus luteum**
If fertilization does not occur this gland regresses, stimulating the onset of menstruation

**Growing primary follicle**

**Secondary follicle**

**Follicular vein and artery**

**Mature Graafian follicle**

**Egg released from Graafian follicle**

*Numerous ovarian follicles are distributed throughout the cortex of the ovary. Each of these will contain an oocyte at different stages of development.*

## The menstrual cycle

*This graph shows the fluctuation of anterior pituitary and ovarian hormones during the menstrual cycle, together with structural changes within the ovary and uterus.*

The oestrus, or menstrual cycle, refers to the cyclical changes which take place in the female reproductive system during the production of eggs.

These changes are controlled by hormones released by the pituitary gland and ovaries: oestrogen, progesterone, luteinizing hormone and follicle-stimulating hormone.

### UTERINE CHANGES
Following menstruation the endometrium thickens and becomes more vascular under the influence of oestrogen and follicle-stimulating hormone.

During the first 14 days of the menstrual cycle a Graafian follicle matures. Ovulation occurs around day 14 when the secondary oocyte is expelled and swept into the uterine tube.

The ruptured follicle becomes a hormone-secreting body called the corpus luteum. This secretes progesterone, stimulating further thickening of the uterine lining (endometrium) in which the fertilized ovum will implant.

If fertilization does not occur, the levels of progesterone and oestrogen decrease. This causes the endometrium to break down and be excreted into the menstrual flow.

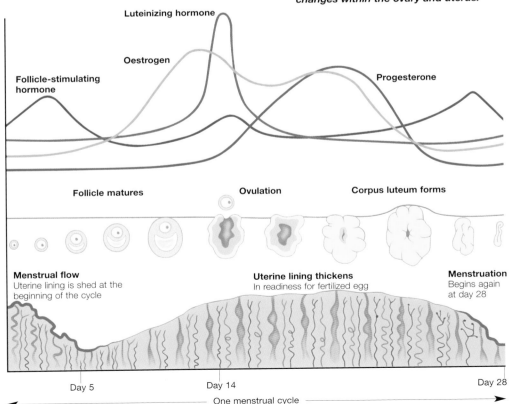

**Luteinizing hormone**

**Oestrogen**

**Follicle-stimulating hormone**

**Progesterone**

**Follicle matures**

**Ovulation**

**Corpus luteum forms**

**Menstrual flow**
Uterine lining is shed at the beginning of the cycle

**Uterine lining thickens**
In readiness for fertilized egg

**Menstruation**
Begins again at day 28

Day 5

Day 14

Day 28

One menstrual cycle

21

# Male reproductive years

A man's journey towards sexual maturity begins with adolescence.
But even after this milestone is reached, emotional development
continues and there are several distinct stages throughout adulthood.

The physical changes that characterize puberty generally take place between the ages of 10 and 15, making males both fertile and attracted to the opposite sex. Most importantly, there is a surge in the level of testosterone, which is the most important of male sex hormones and is responsible for the development of most of the male secondary sexual characteristics.

### ADOLESCENCE
During early adolescence, sexual thoughts and feelings become increasingly prominent and teenage boys usually begin their journey towards sexual maturity by forming friendships with girls. During middle and late adolescence, physical contact becomes more important; holding hands, kissing and heavy petting may lead to a desire for sexual intercourse.

### FIRST-TIME DECISION
Deciding when to have sexual intercourse is one of the most important decisions that an adolescent can make. Research shows that teenage boys usually feel pressurized by their peers, or by cultural expectations of male sexuality.

### RELATIONSHIPS
It is usually in his late teens that the average man will experience sexual intercourse for the first time. Around this time,

*Many men in their late 20s and early 30s settle down in a stable relationship. Many will start a family and get involved in bringing up the children.*

*When first asserting their sexuality, men focus on the physical aspect of the relationship. For women, emotional bonding is stronger.*

men tend to be at their sexual peak and often undergo a period of promiscuity. For many men, sexual intercourse is seen as a sufficient goal in itself; emotional fulfilment to one partner may not be deemed so necessary at this stage in their lives.

Later on in life, most men will settle into a longer-term relationship, as they increasingly require emotional support to help them through life's tribulations. Others may prefer to remain unattached throughout their lives, enjoying the sexual freedom that a single life offers.

### MIDDLE AGE
Men in their 30s may notice that their sexual responses begin to slow down slightly as testosterone levels begin to decline. Lack of libido as a result of work or family-related stress is not uncommon at this time.

Men in their 40s and 50s may notice a few changes in their sexual responses, but none of these has a serious impact on their ability to make love. However, having intercourse more than once a day may present more of a challenge at 50 than at 20.

### EMOTIONAL FULFILMENT
As men mature, the emphasis upon physical gratification shifts in favour of emotional

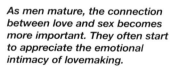

*As men mature, the connection between love and sex becomes more important. They often start to appreciate the emotional intimacy of lovemaking.*

fulfilment. Many men report that sexual enjoyment reaches a peak in middle age because they have gained an intimate knowledge of both their own and their partner's sexual responses.

Some men also note that the link between love and sex has become more important to them, and that they enjoy the emotional intimacy that lovemaking involves.

*Excessive stress can have a serious effect on health, and even cause impotence. This, in turn, can put a great strain on personal relationships.*

### MALE MENOPAUSE
For men who feel that their roles as provider, husband and father are eroding, midlife can be a difficult and insecure time.

A man may compare himself to younger men and feel that he is no longer sexually attractive. At work, he may experience feelings of rivalry with younger colleagues. At home, his wife or partner may be suffering from menopausal symptoms that affect not just the couple's sex life, but their entire relationship.

A man's role as a father may

*For many older men, long-term relationships give them an advantage of knowing their partner's and their own sexual response. Thus, lovemaking becomes a fulfilling experience.*

also diminish as his children grow up and leave home. In addition, health difficulties may make him aware of his own mortality. Resulting stress and low self-esteem can lead to impotence which, in turn, can put great strain on relationships.

### MID-LIFE AFFAIRS
Stress in mid-life marital relationships sometimes causes men to seek sex outside of marriage. It is not uncommon for a man to try to recapture his youth by having an affair with a woman many years his junior. Such affairs can reassure men of their virility and provide the energy and sexual tension lacking in long-term relationships with a wife or partner.

*With advancing age, libido may be diminished as a result of health problems. This does not necessarily mean the end of sexual fulfilment, though.*

### SEXUAL ACTIVITY
Three physical factors affect sexual activity in older people: the hormonal changes that affect desire and cause the ageing of the urogenital tract; muscle weakness and lower energy levels due to age; and the increased probability of medical conditions. In men, lower production of testosterone decreases sexual desire and genital sensitivity. At this age, many men may find that

*In their middle years, some men are adversely affected by intense pressures at work. Others, however, relish the challenges that this age brings.*

arousal takes much longer and that their sexual performance is diminished.

### SEX AFTER 60
One study of male sexual behaviour reported that 57 per cent of men between the ages of 61 and 75 said that their desire for sex either increased with age or remained the same. When asked how age affected their enjoyment of sex, only 11 per cent of them reported a decline.

### SENSUAL EXPERIENCE
The best prediction of an active sex life after 60 is the high level of desire and activity of men in their youth. Couples in their later years are able to take advantage of their slower sexual responses by spending more time on foreplay, so that sex becomes a more sensual experience for both partners.

# Female reproductive years

A woman's reproductive years begin at adolescence and last through to the menopause. The experiences women have of sexuality and relationships change throughout the different stages of their lives.

Between the ages of nine and 15 most girls reach puberty. The first sign is usually breast budding, which occurs around the age of 11, with the first menstrual period usually starting a year or more later. Puberty is considered established when menstrual periods begin to occur at regular, predictable intervals.

During puberty girls may experience anxiety about their body image. In addition, they may fantasize about unobtainable men, such as famous pop stars, who they may regard as less threatening than men they know.

### SOCIAL PRESSURES

There are undoubtedly more cultural pressures for girls than for boys to remain chaste. In particular, parents are more concerned about their daughters having sexual intercourse at a young age than their sons. The obvious reason for such concern is that sex can result in girls getting pregnant. Media and peer pressures to be sexually active are believed to contribute to teenage pregnancy.

### DATING

Often it is boys who ask girls out for dates. The date is often conducted so that it is known to the rest of their peer group. On dates boys and girls may engage in sexual activity such as kissing or petting.

Parents are generally becoming more permissive about allowing relationships to be conducted in the family home. However, they are concerned about HIV and other sexually

*Adolescent girls often worry about their body image. Anxieties may focus on weight or breast size, and girls may feel pressured to be sexually active.*

transmitted diseases, so they want to ensure that their children are using condoms.

### SEXUAL EXPERIENCES

More women nowadays are undergoing periods of promiscuity before settling down with their life partners. The wide array of modern contraceptive methods available has acted to separate sex from reproductive

function. However, as they grow older, many women come to recognize that love and sex within committed relationships provide a special sense of emotional security.

Single people are no longer predominantly in the 18 to 25-year-old age group; they are more likely to be older adults. Many women in this older group are conscious of their biological clocks and anxious that they are running out of time to find a mate and have children.

### HAVING CHILDREN

Increasingly couples are putting off starting families until their 30s and 40s, while the woman establishes a career. However, often when women do start trying to conceive many experience problems.

An estimated 20 per cent of

*Girls usually become interested in the opposite sex during their teens. This often takes the form of fantasies about unobtainable men, such as pop or film stars.*

couples have difficulty becoming pregnant. It is not unusual for couples who have infertility problems to secretly blame each other, withdraw from interactions with friends who have children or develop stress-related sexual problems due to the need to schedule intercourse on fertile days.

Pregnancy can signal a change in women's sexual relationships. Some pregnant women are not interested in having sex; some are, but only at certain points of the pregnancy.

*Adolescent girls often engage in activities such as kissing when they go out with boys. This can lead to tension between parents and their teenage daughters.*

*Mothers often have to combine bringing up young families with working. This can mean that women with children have less time to spend with their partner.*

*In the first few months of motherhood the desire for sex may decline. Intercourse can be physically painful for women immediately after childbirth.*

## MOTHERHOOD

After giving birth, women may have vaginal tears that take time to heal, and women who are breast feeding may find that their reduced vaginal lubrication makes sex painful. In such circumstances couples may wish to use other sexual activities until intercourse becomes comfortable again.

In addition, psychological factors such as fatigue and focusing on the new role of motherhood, may reduce a woman's interest in sex.

Women with young families who work and carry the major share of the household tasks

*For many older couples, physical intimacy is an important part of a successful relationship. Contact with family and friends is also a source of pleasure.*

may find that they have little time or energy left for themselves or sexual behaviour.

Many couples find that they settle back into a more frequent sexual pattern once their children have grown older.

A satisfying sex life may encourage a couple to stay together. It also acts to provide pleasure, bolster self-esteem and reduce tension and anxiety.

## LONG-TERM RELATIONSHIPS

It is often reported that after the first year or two of living together or being married, the average couple has intercourse two or three times a week during their 20s and 30s, and then

gradually less often after that. Although women may be having less sex, the quality improves.

Women enjoy a sexual peak later than men, experiencing their highest numbers of orgasms from their mid-20s to mid-40s. This may be because women need to learn to have orgasms and take time to feel secure about their sexuality and relationships.

For women, sexual pleasure is not dependent on fertility. Furthermore, human genital anatomy is specialized for pleasure no less than procreation – for example, the sole function of the clitoris is the generation of sexual pleasure.

Even in a long-established relationship, women tend to be less likely to initiate sex. If they do so it can be an extremely subtle cue, such as putting on a particular nightdress to signal that the partner's attentions would be welcomed.

## THE MENOPAUSE

A woman's menstrual cycle will gradually become irregular in her 40s and 50s. Menopausal symptoms such as vaginitis (dryness, perhaps with bleeding) and a thinning of the skin in the vagina can cause sexual discomfort. In general, such symptoms are helped by hormone replacement therapy (HRT).

Older couples often find that they still enjoy sex. Women having sex in their 70s and beyond report that sex is as gratifying as ever.

However, problems can occur when male partners suffer from physical difficulties, such as impotence caused by cardiovascular problems, and are unable to maintain an erection.

*In long-term relationships couples may find that they have sex less often than at the outset. This may contribute to other difficulties in the relationship.*

# Planning a family

Deciding to have children is one of the most important decisions a couple can make together. Many different factors influence when people start a family, and how many children they would like.

Couples often see the desire to become parents as signifying a very important stage in their relationship. Whether subconsciously or consciously, many men and women see having children as the ultimate purpose in life.

As contraception is so efficient, couples now have the opportunity to plan their families as never before. They can choose when to have their children, how many to have and the time interval to leave between having each child. They may even choose not to have any children. However, children are often not planned at all.

### DECIDING WHEN TO HAVE CHILDREN

There is a natural drive in people to have children, although this is variable between individuals. For couples who meet when they are young and want to plan a family, the first decision to be taken is when they should start a family. They can decide to have children when young and healthy, but not financially secure; or wait until they are older and better off financially, but perhaps with less energy.

### DECIDING HOW MANY CHILDREN TO HAVE

Once they have one child, couples need to decide whether they want more. If the answer is yes, they may then decide

*One consideration involved in planning when to have children is sibling rivalry. Hostility may be more intense between children who are close in age.*

whether to have them at close intervals, or whether they should space them out. One reason for the latter is that time between births allows a period of recovery each time.

Some couples only have one child. They may feel that they can devote more time to that child, or there may be medical reasons not to have any more children, such as post-natal depression or being physically unable to have more children, so having no other option.

*Some couples decide to have children when they are relatively young. While not as financially secure as older parents, they generally have more energy.*

### LARGE FAMILIES

Other couples feel that only children tend to be spoilt, and that it is a better preparation for life to be part of a large family. Older siblings can contribute to the emotional and social growth of a child. however, some studies suggest that children from large families do not perform as well at school.

Often the sex of the second child is the deciding factor in the number a couple will eventually have. Some people desire a male-female balance, and if they continue having children of the same sex will persevere until a child of the other sex is born.

Family size is also influenced by cultural factors and socio-economic status. The increased use of assisted conception for older mothers can also have an impact on the number of children a couple eventually has.

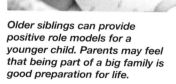

*Older siblings can provide positive role models for a younger child. Parents may feel that being part of a big family is good preparation for life.*

### SIBLING RIVALRIES

Psychologists have observed certain patterns for sibling rivalry. It appears to be more intense the closer the children are in age. A respected older sibling may serve as a role model. But when there is hostility between siblings, the older one can become a model not for emulation, but for rebellion against.

## PARENTHOOD

Having a child changes a couple's priorities and brings with it new responsibilities. Parents find they have to deal with the child's needs before their own: when planning to go out they have to arrange a sitter first. They may also feel tired by the exhausting task of looking after children and stressed by new financial pressures.

Early in a relationship many couples see parenthood as a narrowing rather than a

*A couple's life together will change dramatically with the arrival of a baby. The demands of the child may make the father feel supplanted in affections.*

widening of their prospects. Many young couples want time to explore their relationship and enjoy themselves.

But having children is often a question of timing. What can seem like a life sentence at one stage in life, at another point becomes much less threatening.

## MOTHERHOOD

Pregnancy is a natural state in biology, but it also has natural limits, from the menarche (onset of menstruation) to the menopause. The ability to avoid having children at either extreme reduces the chances of hazards to maternal and fetal health. Women in their mid- to late 30s are often aware that their biological clock is ticking and time is running out.

For women with careers the timing of when to have a baby can be particularly difficult. Many discover that there is no 'right time' to start a family. Some find that having a break from work at a crucial stage in their career can spoil their chances of ever getting beyond a certain level in their chosen profession.

However, this can lead to conflicts when their partners, who can father children throughout their lives, do not appreciate the woman's sense of urgency. The result may be a compromise which suits one partner more than the other.

*Finding the right time to start a family can be very difficult for women with careers. Mothers often have to juggle bringing up their children with working.*

## DECIDING NOT TO HAVE CHILDREN

Reasons for deciding against having children include fear of commitment, bad experiences as a child, and fear of not being a good parent. Some people may prefer to nurture their careers with the same level of involvement that they would have devoted to offspring.

## PREPARING FOR A BABY

Planning for a healthy baby should begin months before conception. Women are generally advised to:

■ Stop smoking and stop taking any recreational drugs
■ Reduce alcohol intake
■ Start taking folic acid supplements to prevent neural tube defects, such as spina bifida
■ Check that they have had a rubella vaccination to avoid contracting German measles
■ Avoid taking the contraceptive pill for several months before conception is desired.

## GETTING PREGNANT

To optimize their chances of conception, it is recommended that couples have intercourse every other day during the most fertile time of each menstrual cycle. This fertile time begins approximately eight days before ovulation is expected to occur and continues up to the day after ovulation has occurred.

*Parenthood brings with it a need for responsibility and planning. For example, childcare needs to be arranged before going out for the evening.*

# Prenatal genetic counselling

One to two per cent of babies have a major congenital malformation. Genetic counselling is offered to couples thought to be at high risk of having a baby with a major abnormality.

Genetic counselling may be offered to a couple before pregnancy, in the first few weeks of pregnancy or following an abnormal screening test.

### AT-RISK COUPLES

If a couple is thought to be at high risk of having a baby with problems it is much better that the couple is seen prior to pregnancy, since at that stage all possible options can be discussed with them.

Couples at high risk of having a baby with an abnormality are those where:
■ Both parents-to-be are known carriers of a disease, such as cystic fibrosis and sickle-cell disease, and so both could pass on the abnormal gene to the child – the child will then develop that disease (autosomal recessive disease)
■ One of the parents-to-be has a genetic disease, such as neurofibromatosis and myotonic dystrophy, that can be passed directly from one generation to another (autosomal dominant disease)
■ The woman is at risk of being,

or is confirmed as being, a carrier of an X-linked recessive disease (a disease that can affect males and is carried by females, such as haemophilia)
■ There is a known chromosome change (chromosome translocation) within the family.

### UNKNOWN DIAGNOSIS

The diagnosis within a family may not be known. This is especially common when there is a history of non-specific learning difficulties.

In these circumstances the chance of a couple having a further child with similar problems is given as an empiric risk; this figure being based on the relatedness of the affected child to the couple in question. Hence the risk of having an affected child will be much greater if a previous sibling has been affected, as opposed to, say, a niece or nephew.

*Genetic counselling is available to couples who are at risk of passing on a genetic condition. It may also be offered after an abnormal screening test.*

## Options for high-risk couples

Options open to couples at high risk of fetal abnormality who wish to prevent the birth of a handicapped child include:
■ Not having further children

■ Undertaking prenatal diagnosis with a view to aborting the abnormal fetus
■ Artificial insemination by donor (AID). In couples who are

at risk of having a baby with an autosomal recessive disease, either donor egg or sperm could be used. In an X-linked recessive disease, donor eggs would need to be used and in an autosomal dominant disease, donor gametes would be needed to replace either the egg or the sperm that is at high risk of carrying the disease
■ Pre-implantation diagnosis – *in vitro* fertilization is required for this process. This option is only open for a very select group of diseases and enables sex selection to be made for medical reasons.

*A donor's semen sample is pipetted for analysis before use in artificial insemination. This technique may be used to avoid certain genetic conditions.*

*An amniocentesis test may be performed during pregnancy at 16 weeks' gestation. Amniotic fluid surrounding the fetus is withdrawn through a needle.*

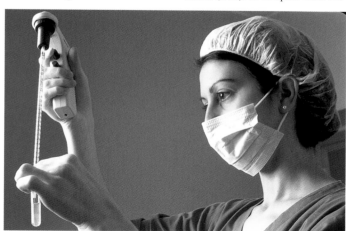

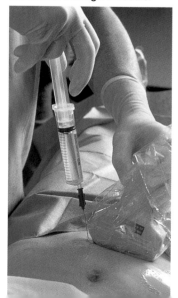

# Prenatal diagnosis

Prenatal diagnosis confirms the likelihood of occurrence of a genetic disease. Diagnostic procedures may be carried out prior to conception or during pregnancy, enabling couples to make informed decisions.

Pre-pregnancy genetic counselling will first allow confirmation of the clinical disease diagnosis; this will be followed by confirmatory diagnostic tests either enzymatically, molecularly or chromosomally.

Diagnosis can be confirmed during pregnancy but it is often a time-consuming process and it is therefore better if diagnosis can be made prior to conception.

### PRE-CONCEPTION TREATMENT

The risk of having a further affected child can be discussed. Occasionally, pre-pregnancy treatment may reduce this risk. For example, treatment with folic acid reduces the risk of a recurrence of spina bifida.

Women who are on treatment for epilepsy may need their drug treatment altered prior to pregnancy, as some anti-epileptics have a higher risk of causing fetal abnormality than others.

Prenatal treatment is available for very rare diseases, such as congenital adrenal hyperplasia – in such cases, treatment needs to be started very early in the pregnancy. This is, therefore, another reason for seeing couples for pre-pregnancy counselling.

### RISK OF MISCARRIAGE

The couple's views on prenatal diagnosis must be explored; there are always concerns about the risk to the baby of any intervention. All invasive

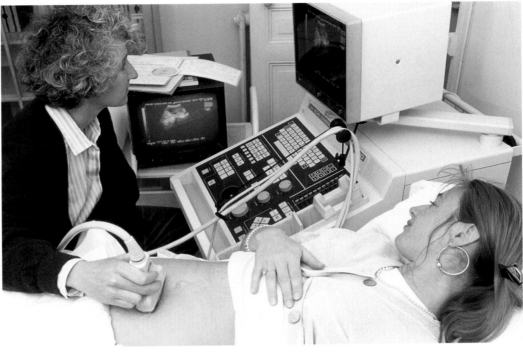

methods of prenatal diagnosis have a miscarriage risk associated with them and this needs to be balanced against the risk of having an affected child.

Many couples would not consider prenatal diagnosis if the only management option was a termination of pregnancy, either because they feel the disease in question is not serious enough or because their personal ethics do not allow this option to be explored further.

Some couples opt for prenatal diagnosis even though they would not consider abortion. As

the method of prenatal diagnosis may lead in rare cases to miscarriage (one per cent), this option must be considered with great caution.

### IMPORTANCE OF TIMING

Timing of prenatal diagnosis is crucial. Chorionic villus sampling (CVS) can be carried out from 11 weeks' gestation. Amniocentesis can be carried out soon after this time but is generally performed at 16 weeks. Ultrasound diagnosis tends to be carried out later than CVS but many diseases can now be

*New ultrasound technology means that ultrasound scans can be carried out in early pregnancy. These scans can detect fetal abnormalities.*

diagnosed earlier due to improved ultrasound technology and the skill of the operators.

If results of the prenatal diagnosis are available before 13 weeks' gestation, an abortion can be safely carried out under general anaesthetic. If, though, the gestation has passed the 14 week point, labour needs to be induced.

## Role of the genetic counsellor

The genetic counsellor's role is to facilitate a couple's decision-making process. The counsellor is not there to make decisions for a couple, but to enable the couple to make the best possible decision for themselves and their family.

The personal opinion of the counsellor should not be sought. Couples need the freedom to carry out their own decisions, not those of the counsellor.

*The genetic counsellor should encourage a couple to reach their own decision. Counselling should be non-directive – the counsellor's own opinions are not relevant.*

### GIVING SUPPORT

Support needs to be given after the prenatal diagnosis has been made and the couple have taken their decision. If the pregnancy has been terminated, further counselling may be required. This may well be carried out more successfully by some of the excellent support groups available, whose contact details should always be given to the couple whether they feel they need it at the time or not.

Coping strategies vary, and one member of the couple may not share the same strategy as the other – different forms of help may thus be required at different times.

# How conception occurs

Millions of sperm cells travel up the female reproductive tract in search of the oocyte (egg). It takes hundreds of sperm to break down the outer coating of the oocyte, but only one will fertilize it.

Fertilization occurs when a single male gamete (sperm cell) and a female gamete (egg or oocyte) are united following sexual intercourse. Fusion of the two cells occurs and a new life is conceived.

### SPERM
Following sexual intercourse, the sperm contained in the man's semen travel up through the uterus. Along the way they are nourished by the alkaline mucus of the cervical canal. From the uterus the sperm continue their journey into the uterine (Fallopian) tube.

Although the distance involved is only around 20 cm (8 in), the journey can take up to two hours, since in relation to the size of the sperm the distance is considerable.

### SURVIVAL
Although an average ejaculation contains around 300 million sperm cells, only a fraction of these (around 10,000) will manage to reach the uterine tube where the oocyte is located. Even fewer will actually reach the oocyte. This is because many sperm will be destroyed by the hostile vaginal environment, or become lost in other areas of the reproductive tract.

Sperm do not become capable of fertilizing an oocyte until they have spent some time in

the woman's body. Fluids in the reproductive tract activate the sperm, so that the whiplash motion of their tails becomes more powerful.

The sperm are also helped on their way by contractions of the uterus, which force them upwards into the body. The contractions are stimulated by prostaglandins contained in the semen, and which are also produced during female orgasm.

### THE OOCYTE
Once it has been ejected from the follicle (during ovulation) the oocyte is pushed towards the uterus by the wave-like motion of the cells lining the uterine tube. The oocyte is usually united with the sperm about two hours after sexual intercourse in the outer part of the uterine tube.

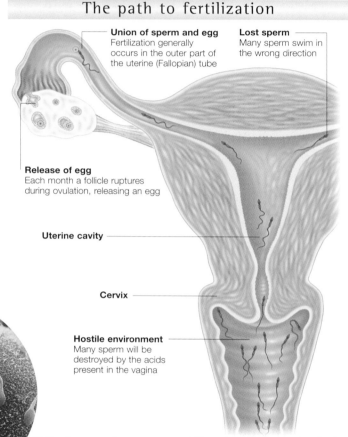

## The path to fertilization

**Union of sperm and egg**
Fertilization generally occurs in the outer part of the uterine (Fallopian) tube

**Lost sperm**
Many sperm swim in the wrong direction

**Release of egg**
Each month a follicle ruptures during ovulation, releasing an egg

**Uterine cavity**

**Cervix**

**Hostile environment**
Many sperm will be destroyed by the acids present in the vagina

*Following sexual intercourse, millions of sperm cells make their way up the reproductive tract in search of the oocyte.*

*Although many sperm begin the journey towards the oocyte, only a fraction reach the uterine tube. The majority are destroyed or become lost on the way.*

## Reaching the oocyte

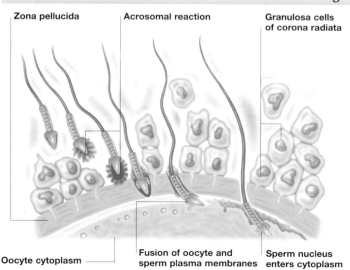

**Zona pellucida**

**Acrosomal reaction**

**Granulosa cells of corona radiata**

**Oocyte cytoplasm**

**Fusion of oocyte and sperm plasma membranes**

**Sperm nucleus enters cytoplasm**

On the journey towards the oocyte, secretions present in the female reproductive tract deplete the sperm cells' cholesterol, thus weakening their acrosomal membranes. This process is known as capacitation, and without it fertilization could not occur.

Once in the vicinity of the oocyte, the sperm are chemically attracted to it. When the sperm cells finally come in to contact with the oocyte, their acrosomal membranes are completely

*When sperm cells reach the oocyte they release enzymes. These enzymes break down the protective outer layers of the ovum, allowing a sperm to enter.*

stripped away, so that the contents of each acrosome (the enzyme-containing compartment of the sperm) are released.

### PENETRATION
The enzymes released by the sperm cells cause the breakdown of the cumulus mass cells and the zona pellucida, the protective outer layers of the oocyte. It takes at least 100 acrosomes to rupture in order for a path to be digested through these layers for a single sperm to enter.

In this way the sperm cells that reach the oocyte first sacrifice themselves, to allow penetration of the cytoplasm of the oocyte by another sperm.

# Fertilization

When a single sperm has entered the oocyte, the genetic material from each cell fuses. A zygote is formed, which divides to form an embryo.

Once a sperm has penetrated the oocyte, a chemical reaction takes place within the oocyte, making it impossible for another sperm to enter.

### MEIOSIS II
Entry of the sperm nucleus into the oocyte triggers the completion of nuclear division (meiosis II) begun during ovulation. A haploid oocyte and the second polar body (which degenerates) are formed.

Almost immediately, the nuclei of the sperm and oocyte fuse to produce a diploid zygote, containing genetic material from both the mother and father.

### DETERMINATION OF SEX
It is at the point of fertilization that sex is determined. It is the sperm, and therefore the father, that dictates what sex the offspring will be.

Sex is determined by a combination of the two sex chromosomes, the X and the Y. The female will contribute an X chromosome, while a male may contribute either an X or a Y. Fertilization of the oocyte (X), will either be by a sperm containing an X or a Y to give a female (XX) or a male (XY).

### CELL DIVISION
Several hours after fertilization the zygote undergoes a series of mitotic divisions to produce a cluster of cells known as a morula. The morula cells divide every 12 to 15 hours, producing a blastocyst comprised of around 100 cells.

The blastocyst secretes the hormone human chorionic gonadotrophin. This prevents the corpus luteum from being broken down, thus maintaining progesterone secretion.

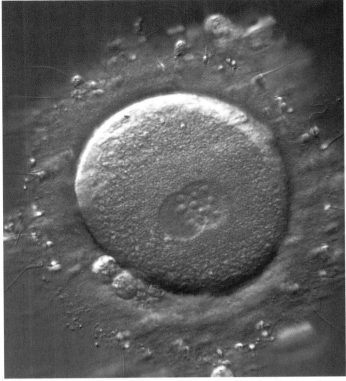

*Once a sperm has penetrated the oocyte, the nuclei of both cells fuse. A diploid zygote forms, containing both the mother's and father's genes.*

## Implantation and development

*As it travels down the uterine tube, the zygote divides. A blastocyst is formed, which implants itself in the lining of the uterine wall.*

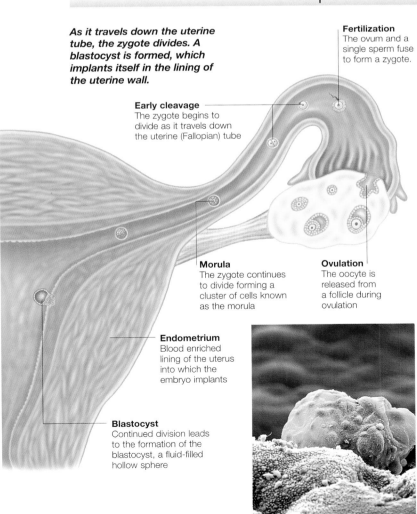

**Early cleavage**
The zygote begins to divide as it travels down the uterine (Fallopian) tube

**Fertilization**
The ovum and a single sperm fuse to form a zygote.

**Morula**
The zygote continues to divide forming a cluster of cells known as the morula

**Ovulation**
The oocyte is released from a follicle during ovulation

**Endometrium**
Blood enriched lining of the uterus into which the embryo implants

**Blastocyst**
Continued division leads to the formation of the blastocyst, a fluid-filled hollow sphere

Around three days after fertilization, the blastocyst will begin its journey from the uterine (Fallopian) tube to the uterus.

Normally the blastocyst would be unable to pass through the sphincter muscle in the uterine tube. However, the increasing levels of progesterone triggered by fertilization cause the muscle to relax, allowing the blastocyst to continue its journey to the uterus.

A damaged or blocked uterine tube preventing the blastocyst from passing at this stage would result in an ectopic pregnancy in which the embryo starts to develop in the uterine tube.

### MULTIPLE BIRTHS
In most cases a woman will release one oocyte every month from alternate ovaries.

Occasionally however, a woman may produce an oocyte from each ovary both of which are fertilized by separate sperm, resulting in the development of non-identical twins. In this case, each fetus will be nourished by its own placenta.

*When the zygote reaches the uterus it will adhere to the endometrium. Nourished by the rich blood supply, it begins to develop.*

Very occasionally a fertilized oocyte may split spontaneously in two to produce two embryos. This will result in identical twins that share exactly the same genes, and even the same placenta.

Siamese twins occur when there is an incomplete split of the oocyte several hours after fertilization.

### IMPLANTATION
Once it has reached the uterus, the blastocyst will implant itself in the thickened lining of the uterine wall.

Hormones released from the blastocyst mean that it is not identified as a foreign body and expelled. Once the blastocyst is safely implanted, gestation will begin.

### IMPERFECTIONS
About one third of fertilized oocytes fail to implant in the uterus and are lost.

Of those that do implant, many embryos contain imperfections in their genetic material, such as an extra chromosome.

Many of these imperfections will cause the embryo to be lost soon after implantation. This can occur even before the first missed period, so that a woman will not even have known that she was pregnant.

# Fertilization

Fertilization is the first moment of life. It is the process by which the genetic material in the male sperm and the female egg fuse to create a new life. In normal circumstances this takes place about 12 hours after sexual intercourse.

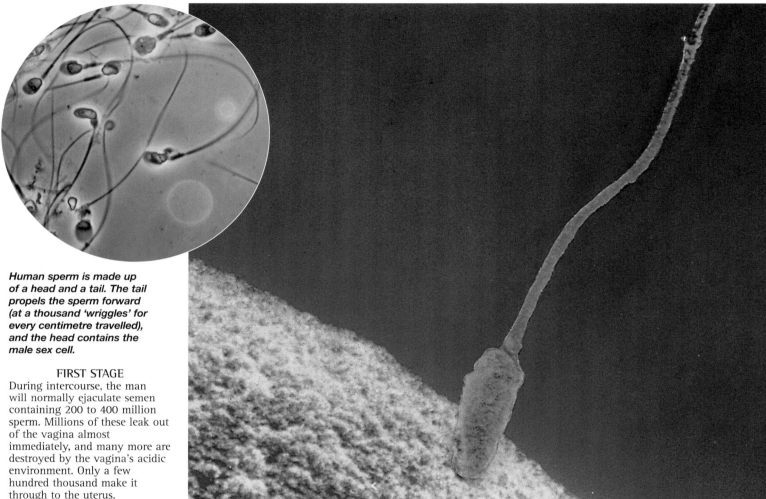

*Human sperm is made up of a head and a tail. The tail propels the sperm forward (at a thousand 'wriggles' for every centimetre travelled), and the head contains the male sex cell.*

*A sperm (shown in this false-colour electron micrograph image in blue) is about to penetrate the egg (pink). To get to this stage, the sperm has completed a long journey, outswimming millions of other sperm to reach the egg.*

### FIRST STAGE
During intercourse, the man will normally ejaculate semen containing 200 to 400 million sperm. Millions of these leak out of the vagina almost immediately, and many more are destroyed by the vagina's acidic environment. Only a few hundred thousand make it through to the uterus.

In the uterus, the sperm are subjected to forceful uterine contractions that help to disperse them through the uterine cavity (womb), where thousands more are destroyed by special types of white blood cell that are normally present. Eventually, just a few thousand, and often only a few hundred, reach the fallopian tube to meet the egg moving towards the uterus.

### CAPACITATION
To make this trek possible, sperm are equipped with powerful tails that allow them to swim towards the egg, a journey that can take over 10 hours. During this time, the sperm must undergo a process called capacitation to enable them to fertilize the egg.

Although the process of capacitation is not well understood, it appears to involve special chemicals being produced by the uterine tissue to remove chemicals that are present on the sperm's surface.

This weakens the outer protective coating, or membrane, that covers each sperm's head. The membranes must become weakened and fragile so that the inner layer, called the acrosome, can be exposed. Until this outer layer has been removed, a sperm is unable to fertilize the egg. Capacitation also allows the sperm to become more active, enabling them to reach the egg more quickly and efficiently.

### AT THE EGG
Once the sperm have reached the egg, they must get extremely close for the next stage to take place. At this stage, the egg is surrounded by the corona radiata, a mass of cells and gelatinous material from the ovaries. The sperm must penetrate this to reach the egg.

The sperm do this by producing an enzyme that dissolves this material and disperses the corona. Both the corona and the zona pellucida, the outer layer of the egg, must be breached before the egg itself can be penetrated.

### When can fertilization happen?

Sperm are capable of fertilization for about 12 to 48 hours after ejaculation. After being released from the ovary, eggs can be fertilized for up to about 12 to 24 hours. For successful fertilization to take place, intercourse must occur no more than 72 hours before ovulation and no later than about 24 hours afterwards, at which point the egg is approximately one-third of the way down the length of the fallopian tube.

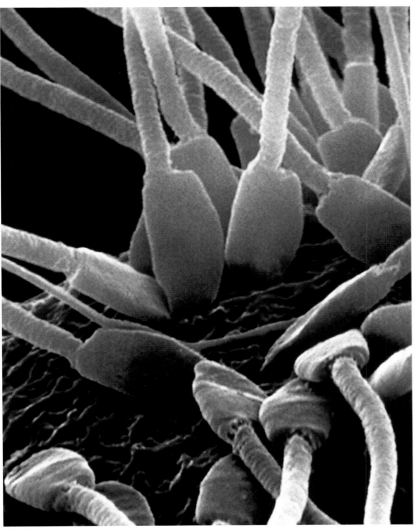

## Entering the egg

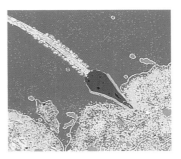

**1** This human sperm is at an early stage in the process of fertilization. It is beginning to penetrate the corona radiata, a layer of protective cells surrounding the female sex cell (the oocyte). Many other competing sperm cells will also be attacking this protective outer layer of the egg, and many will make it through.

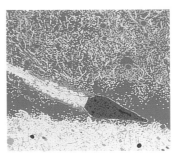

**2** At the next stage of their journey into the egg, most of the sperm are in a space between the corona radiata and the upper zona pellucida. The sperm attack the thick membrane of the zona pellucida, and attempt to burrow through this barrier towards the outer coating of the egg. Only one will make it through successfully.

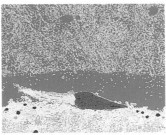

**3** Once past the zona pellucida, the single sperm penetrates the oocyte. This triggers a rapid chemical change in the egg, causing the membrane surrounding the oocyte to thicken and prevent the entry of competing sperm. The other sperm still attached to the zona pellucida fall away and die.

**4** The oocyte has now been fully penetrated by the successful sperm. The tail of the sperm falls away, and the arrow-shaped head, which contains the 23 male chromosomes, is attracted towards the nucleus of the egg, where it will eventually be united with the female genetic material. When this happens, the making of a new life begins.

### EGG CONTACT

The first sperm to breach the zona pellucida makes contact with the egg itself (known as the *oocyte*). When this happens, the outer coating of the egg fuses with the single sperm. Then, for successful fertilization to occur, no other sperm are allowed to enter.

To prevent this happening, a reaction takes place in the zona pellucida. At the point at which the successful sperm reaches the oocyte, granules in the egg release a chemical into the space beneath the zona pellucida that thickens this protective layer. This causes all the competing sperm still in contact to become detached and fall away, preventing them from fusing with the egg.

The entry of several sperm into a single egg does occur in some animals, but not normally in humans. For successful human fertilization only a single sperm is allowed to penetrate the egg. If two sperm do achieve fertilization, there will be too much genetic material present, and unfortunately the embryo will probably die at an early stage of development.

*Head first, a mass of sperm is attached to the egg (blue). The thick surface of the egg attracts the sperm and enables them to attach themselves to it. Only one of the many sperm here may penetrate the egg and fuse with the egg nucleus.*

## The moment of fertilization

Shortly after the egg's inner membrane has been penetrated, the sperm loses its tail and body, which drop off, while its head enlarges and migrates towards the centre of the egg. The nuclei, which contain the genetic material (the chromosomes) of sperm and egg, meet somewhere near the centre of the egg, and fuse. This is generally considered to be the moment of fertilization, when the maternal and paternal genetic material combine to produce a zygote – the cell that contains all the genetic material for the new individual. The entire process, from the moment the fertilizing sperm reaches the egg to the moment the nuclei fuse, takes about 30 minutes.

*This is a recently fertilized egg. Inside, the genetic material from the male sperm and the female egg are combining. The 23 chromosomes from the male and 23 chromosomes from the female are pairing up to make up the full 46 chromosomes that are found in each human cell.*

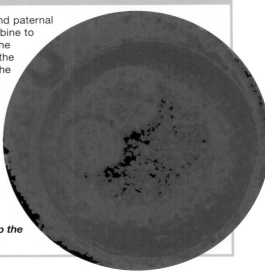

# Implantation

Fertilization is only the beginning of the development of a baby. The fused egg and sperm, now called a zygote, has to travel back down the Fallopian tube and into the uterus, retracing the path taken earlier by the sperm.

Once it arrives in the uterus, the fertilized egg needs to find a place on the wall of the uterus to implant itself, where it will receive nourishment from the mother's blood supply. However, before reaching the uterus, the cells have to negotiate the journey through the Fallopian tube.

### SOPHISTICATED CELL

Immediately after fertilization, the zygote measures about 0.15 mm (0.005 in). Barely visible to the naked eye at this stage, it is still the largest cell in the human body, and probably the most sophisticated.

This tiny mass contains all the genetic information that determines the manner in which the baby will develop physically, such as colour of the hair and eyes. It also contains information that contributes to the personality, mental ability and emotional character of the young child.

### CELL DIVISION

As the zygote passes along the Fallopian tube, the division of cells – known as cleavage – begins. Looking at the zygote under a microscope, the first

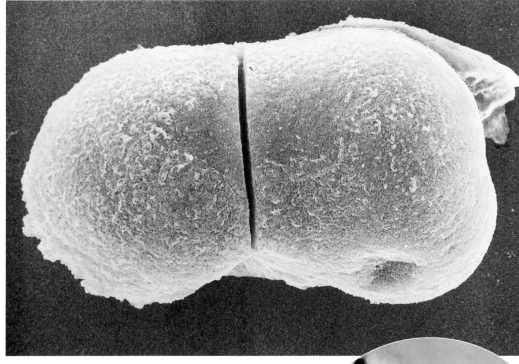

*A division line down the centre of the zygote heralds the start of the cell division process. The zona pellucida (pink) would normally still surround the egg.*

*A coloured light-micrograph image taken at about 30 hours after fertilization reveals the two-cell stage. The red area is a mass of corona cells that once surrounded the unfertilized egg.*

*This view of the two-cell stage has been taken using an electron microscope. It clearly shows the two blastomeres. After this stage, the divisions speed up, coming every half day.*

sign of this process is a groove around the middle of the cell. This leads to a split in the cell, with equal numbers of maternal and paternal chromosomes passing to each of the 'daughter' cells, or blastomeres. The first

few cells that divide are much bigger than ordinary cells and have to shrink to reach normal size.

Each cell contains a central nucleus, which is surrounded by a fluid called cytoplasm. When the original cell first divides, it creates a second nucleus which houses the chromosomes, but no new cytoplasm.

Half of the fluid from the first cell enters each of the new daughter cells, so the overall size of each cell is reduced. This happens several times, with each division producing smaller cells using the same cytoplasm.

Once the cells reach the normal size for a human cell, a mechanism is triggered that causes cytoplasm as well as the nucleus to be formed in every subsequent cell division.

### THE BLASTOCYST

This division process takes place every 12 hours or so. After about four days, the original zygote has increased in size to between 16 and 20 cells and formed a solid ball known as the morula.

As the divisions continue, there is a gradual accumulation of fluid within the morula. This shapes the morula into a hollow ball of cells, known as the blastocyst.

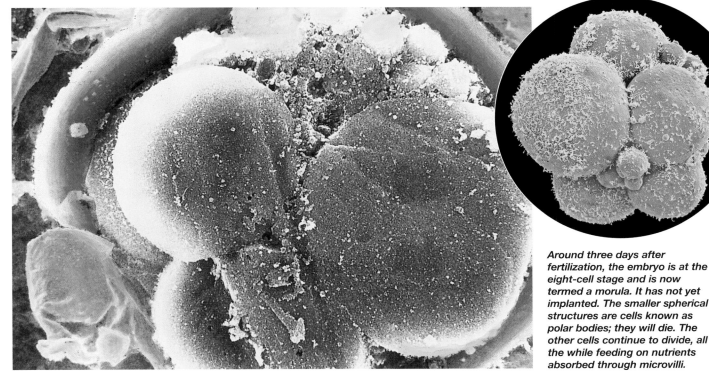

*Around three days after fertilization, the embryo is at the eight-cell stage and is now termed a morula. It has not yet implanted. The smaller spherical structures are cells known as polar bodies; they will die. The other cells continue to divide, all the while feeding on nutrients absorbed through microvilli.*

## ARRIVING AT THE UTERUS

Between five and seven days after fertilization, the cells have travelled through the Fallopian tube and reached the uterus. Once the blastocyst reaches the uterus, it sits in the uterine cavity as it continues to grow and develop.

So far, all the cell divisions have taken place within the outer casing of the zygote, the zona pellucida. For the embryo to develop further, this layer has to be removed, and secretions from the lining of the uterus help to dissolve the zona.

## IMPLANTING

Two to four days after reaching the uterus, the implantation process takes place, usually somewhere along the back wall of the uterus. The blastocyst burrows down into the endometrium (the lining of the uterus) using special enzymes to digest the surrounding cells.

The oxygen, fluids and nutrients that are released from the endometrium are absorbed by the embryo and used as nourishment. If all goes well, the blastocyst will be securely implanted, constantly secreting hormones to signal to the mother's body that pregnancy has occurred.

This is important, as otherwise the mother would continue to ovulate each month. And if the process of menstruation were to continue, the womb lining would peel away as part of its normal monthly cycle, taking with it

*Here the layers of a 4–6 cell embryo can be seen. The blastomeres (large and yellow) are the cells formed from divisions of the fertilized egg. Surrounding the embryo is a membranous envelope, the zona pellucida (pink).*

the newly implanted blastocyst. This would cause what doctors call a natural miscarriage.

By this stage of development, there are two distinct groups of cells in the blastocyst. A mass of round cells at the centre are separated from an outer wall of flattened cells by fluid. This central mass of cells will soon form the embryo; the outer layer of flattened cells will become the placenta, which will supply nutrients to the growing embryo.

**Fertilization**

**Two-cell stage** (30 hours after fertilization)

**Fallopian tube**

**Morula** (3 days)

**Blastocyst** (5 days)

**Implantation** (6–8 days)

**Uterus**

**Ovary**

*After fertilization, the embryo changes – each cell dividing into two. After three days, it is a body of 8–16 cells called the morula. Upon reaching the uterus, it is a hollow ball of cells called the blastocyst. Cells of the blastocyst attach to the lining of the uterus – the endometrium. At this stage, pregnancy has truly begun.*

## Implantation problems

Sometimes the embryo implants in the wrong place. If it implants in the uterus but close to the opening where it joins the cervix – the os – it can lead to a condition known as placenta praevia. As the placenta develops and grows, it can cover up the os. Sometimes this causes no problems, but in other cases it can lead to heavy bleeding in the later stages of pregnancy when the placenta separates from the uterus.

Ectopic – 'out of place' – pregnancy results from the embryo implanting somewhere other than the uterus. This most commonly occurs in the Fallopian tube but occasionally takes place in the ovary, the cervix or the abdominal cavity.

Ectopic pregnancy is a serious condition, for as the embryo develops it can cause surrounding tissue to become damaged or to rupture, leading to heavy bleeding and severe pain.

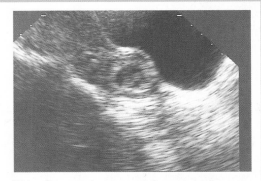

*This ultrasound scan reveals an ectopic pregnancy in the right Fallopian tube. In pregnancies such as this, the fetus will damage the Fallopian tube and cause pain.*

35

# Diagnosing male infertility

Male infertility is diagnosed when a normal, healthy couple have failed to conceive over a year, without taking contraceptive precautions, and the female partner's fertility has been found to be normal on investigation.

## DEFINING INFERTILITY

Infertility describes a state that exists between two people, but the term requires further definition of the other partner's fertile state before causation can be attributed directly to either the male or female partner.

Male infertility cannot be defined by sperm counts alone, unless the sperm count and the sperm quality revealed in that count is so low, or indeed absent, that it is counted as zero.

## ABSENCE OF SPERM

In the case of a sperm count result returning as zero, a sterile rather than an infertile state is described. A complete absence of sperm is known as azoospermia, and this will require further investigation to determine its cause.

A reduced sperm count (oligospermia) may be indicative of a fertility problem, but this also needs to be investigated further, as described below.

### Male reproductive organs

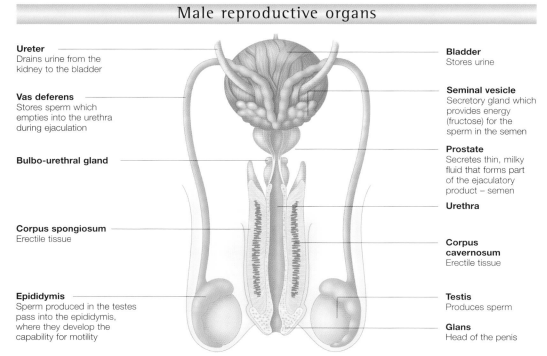

**Ureter**
Drains urine from the kidney to the bladder

**Vas deferens**
Stores sperm which empties into the urethra during ejaculation

**Bulbo-urethral gland**

**Corpus spongiosum**
Erectile tissue

**Epididymis**
Sperm produced in the testes pass into the epididymis, where they develop the capability for motility

**Bladder**
Stores urine

**Seminal vesicle**
Secretory gland which provides energy (fructose) for the sperm in the semen

**Prostate**
Secretes thin, milky fluid that forms part of the ejaculatory product – semen

**Urethra**

**Corpus cavernosum**
Erectile tissue

**Testis**
Produces sperm

**Glans**
Head of the penis

## Sperm analysis

Most couples consulting a specialist about presumed male factor infertility have already undergone female partner investigations. Often, the male is found to have a 'low' sperm count. This is a sample in which the number of sperm (density) is lower than the normal range, or its quality, as described by sperm motility (ability to move in a purposeful way), and morphology (shape), is found to be in some way lacking.

### SUPPLYING A SAMPLE

A man should have three specimens taken on different occasions after a standard period of abstinence from any form of ejaculation, usually three days. This produces some uniformity in the timing of the sperm production because as the period of abstinence extends beyond 24 hours, so the sperm density increases. However, after 72 hours the quality of the sperm may decline.

When three consecutively measured sperm counts have been deficient, either in terms of density, morphology or motility, then the infertile state can be ascribed to the male partner.

The doctor will inform the patient of the sperm numbers, the percentage motility, the percentage of normal sperm and the quality of the motility, graded from one to four. It is important to realize that these numbers are not absolutes, but merely give a point of reference from which further investigation can start.

These baseline measurements only serve to predict the likelihood of pregnancy if no treatment was undertaken over the subsequent year. It is often

incorrectly assumed that if a couple attends a fertility centre with established male infertility, the fertility unit will offer the couple a better chance of pregnancy than they might have on their own.

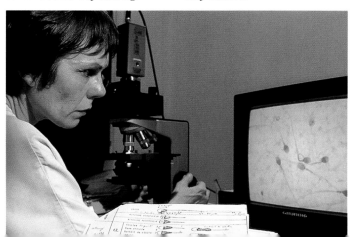

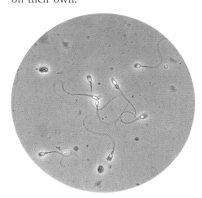

*Microscope analysis is used to examine sperm samples. The major cause of male infertility is a failure to produce sufficient numbers of healthy sperm.*

*An average sperm count is evident under a light microscope. The shape and movement of the sperm will be examined from three samples.*

## ALTERNATIVE TECHNIQUES

Patients should be made aware that there are other techniques that may be employed, either at the time of the vasectomy reversal operation or afterwards, to try to enhance their chances of fertility. This may involve taking sperm from the storage tubules that lie on the outside of the testicle – the epididymis – and freezing them before going on to reverse the vasectomy. This is an 'insurance policy': if there are motile (active) sperm that can be frozen, the couple may have to rely on these for IVF treatment should the vasectomy reversal operation fail.

The usual vasectomy reversal procedure involves general anaesthesia and an incision in the scrotum. The testicles are then delivered through the scrotum, and the gap in the vas deferens that was created during the vasectomy operation can be identified. The two previously cut ends can then be joined back together.

The operation is carried out under a microscope, and may take two hours or more, particularly if the procedure involves retrieving sperm for freezing. The recovery period is principally related to the duration of the general anaesthesia; an overnight stay in hospital is common after a vasectomy reversal.

### RECOVERY

Recovery is not particularly painful, unless there was a wide gap between the ends

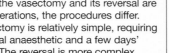

# Vasectomy and reversal procedures

Although the vasectomy and its reversal are simple operations, the procedures differ. The vasectomy is relatively simple, requiring only a local anaesthetic and a few days' recovery. The reversal is more complex, requiring general anaesthetic and a longer recovery period.

### ▶ VASECTOMY

The surgeon palpates (feels) for the vas, finding the point where it is closest to the skin. For each testicle, a small incision is made and about 3 cm (1.2 in) of vas is drawn out. It is then clamped at two points and segmented. The cut ends are then tied, and the incision is stitched closed.

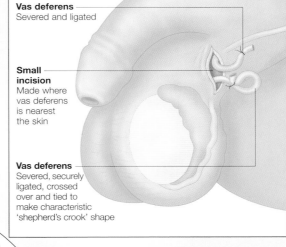

**Vas deferens**
Severed and ligated

**Small incision**
Made where vas deferens is nearest the skin

**Vas deferens**
Severed, securely ligated, crossed over and tied to make characteristic 'shepherd's crook' shape

**Stitches**
A series of tiny stitches has to be put around the severed vas to ensure that sperm can pass through

**Vas deferens**

**Internal suture**

### ◀ VASECTOMY REVERSAL

Under a general anaesthetic, a slit is made in the scrotum and the testicles are drawn out. The cut and ligated ends of the vas are located. The two ends are then rejoined in an operation called a vasovasostomy. This involves temporarily clamping the cut ends and placing a single suture in the inner wall of the vas. This helps to keep the two ends together while they are securely joined with a series of sutures at the outer edge of the vas. The testicles are replaced, and the patient is advised to avoid ejaculation for three weeks.

of the vas tubes created by the original vasectomy. In this case, the testicles might adopt a new, higher position, which can be

uncomfortable for the first two or three weeks. The doctor will advise the patient to rest at home for a week to 10 days, and to avoid sport and strenuous work for a month after that.

### POST-OPERATIVE CARE

The return of sperm to the ejaculate is dependent upon the technical success of the procedure and the interval between vasectomy and its reversal. Sperm should return to the ejaculate after 12 weeks, but may not return for six or even nine months. Generally, in an older patient with a longer interval between vasectomy and reversal, there would be an absolute limit on follow-up of one year. After that time, patients may be best advised to use any sperm that was stored at the time of the vasectomy reversal operation.

Some gynaecologists running fertility units with active IVF programmes may take the view that it would be

much easier merely to aspirate the sperm from the epididymis (using a hollow needle) or even directly from the testicle, rather than opting for a reversal. This may appeal to men who want the quickest solution to their problem or who wish to avoid surgery. However, the success is dependent on actually finding sperm using the aspiration technique, which may not always be successful.

### GETTING APPROVAL

Any man who has had a vasectomy can undergo a reversal, unless he is unfit for general anaesthesia or the surgical procedures involved. These conditions may be serious enough to preclude the possibility of paternity by this means.

It is becoming increasingly difficult to receive this procedure under the National Health Service. Programmes adopted by most health authorities involving 'priority scoring' for surgical procedures, are beginning to produce a low priority for – or even exclude altogether – sterilization reversal procedures, whether they be for men or women.

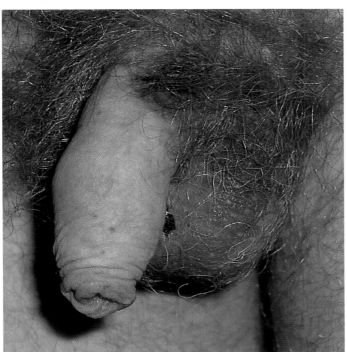

*Although the scrotum is bruised after the reversal, it will return to normal within a few days. It then remains to be seen whether natural fertilization can result.*

# Causes of female infertility

Infertility is common and affects one in six couples at some time.
As part of an ongoing analysis, there are several procedures that can
be performed to investigate why a woman cannot conceive.

Although women often wait up to a year after failing to conceive before seeing their doctor, women over 35 should consider being investigated sooner. This is because egg quality declines with age, and success rates, particularly with IVF treatment, are much lower as women approach 40.

A woman usually sees her GP first for simple hormone tests, and her partner will be asked to provide sperm for analysis. The woman is then referred to a gynaecologist for further investigations and treatment.

## OVULATION FAILURE

Each month, a healthy egg needs to be released from the ovary (ovulation). One of the first tests the doctor will arrange is a blood test seven days before the period is due, to measure the level of progesterone produced by the corpus luteum formed in the ovary after the egg is released.

The commonest cause of infertility, and the easiest to treat, is failure of ovulation (anovulation) and is typically found when the cycle length varies more than five days from one month to the next.

## POLYCYSTIC OVARIES

Many women with anovulation have polycystic ovaries (PCO) and these can be identified on a pelvic ultrasound scan. Although some women with polycystic ovaries have regular cycles and ovulate, most have irregular periods or no periods at all. Other symptoms include increased body and facial hair or hair loss and weight gain. A hormone test may show a raised level of luteinizing hormone (LH) and of the male hormone testosterone.

Being stressed or over- or underweight can also disrupt the cycle and cause anovulation.

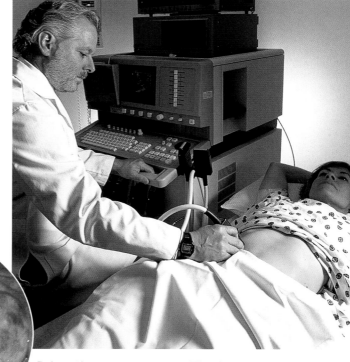

*Polycystic ovary syndrome (PCOS-) is a hormonal disorder whereby ovulation fails to occur. Without ovulation, conception can not occur.*

*The ultrasound probe can either be passed over the lower abdomen or through the vagina. Both methods allow visualization of the reproductive organs and diagnosis of fertility problems.*

## Hormonal reasons for infertility

As a woman gets older, her egg quality and numbers start to fall. This is reflected in a rise in FSH (follicle stimulating hormone) levels in the blood. Ideally, this should be measured in the first few days after the period starts as FSH levels in the early part of the cycle reflect a woman's 'body clock'.

Even if ovulation is taking place, high FSH levels imply a reduced number of eggs and poor egg quality and hence a low chance of conceiving.

Premature menopause is when periods cease completely before the age of 40, indicating that the egg supply in the ovary is exhausted. Women so affected can only become pregnant using donated eggs from another woman under an IVF programme.

Another cause of infrequent periods and anovulation is excessive secretion of prolactin by a benign tumour of the pituitary gland. Excessive prolactin interferes with the production of FSH, which is the hormone signal that drives the ovary to make an egg each month. Over- or underactivity of the thyroid gland can also disrupt the cycle and lead to infertility. Both conditions are easily treatable and thyroid hormone and prolactin levels are routinely checked if a woman's cycle has become irregular.

*A blood sample will be taken in cases of infertility. Hormone imbalances and diseases which may make conception difficult or impossible can thus be identified.*

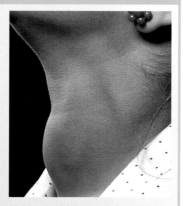

*This goitre (swelling) is caused by an overactive thyroid gland. This condition can disrupt the normal production of eggs.*

# Investigating female infertility

Several tests can be performed to investigate infertility. Some require invasive surgery, while others use X-ray or ultrasound technology.

### LAPAROSCOPY

One method to assess whether the uterine (Fallopian) tubes are working properly is to perform a laparoscopic investigation. This is a minor operation often carried out as a day case.

The patient is given a local, regional or general anaesthetic, and the surgeon makes a small incision near the navel. The peritoneal cavity (which lines

*Laparoscopy allows direct visualization of the reproductive organs. The laparoscope is introduced through an incision in the abdomen.*

the inside of the abdomen) is then inflated with carbon dioxide gas to 'separate' the internal organs to allow better visualization of the various structures.

A special endoscope called a laparoscope is passed through the incision, and the uterus, Fallopian tubes and ovaries are visualized. Dye is then passed through the neck of the womb into the tubes, via a uterine cannula, to check that they are not blocked or constricted.

The surgeon will be able to see abnormal growths or other problems – occasionally these

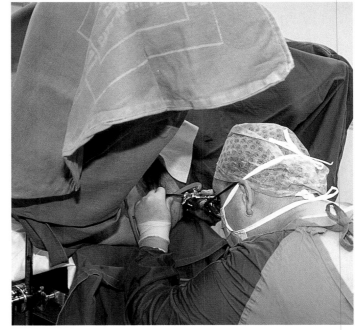

can be corrected at the time, or a biopsy (tissue sample) can be obtained, which will be analysed. This can then be used to decide on further surgery or investigations.

### HYSTEROSCOPY

A hysteroscopic investigation is similar to laparoscopy, except that no incision is made and the investigation is carried out as an outpatient procedure, but still using anaesthesia. The technique is increasingly used to investigate causes of infertility.

*A hysteroscope – a type of endoscope – is passed into the uterine cavity via the vagina. This can provide accurate diagnosis of infertility problems.*

The hysteroscope – a type of endoscope – is introduced through the neck of the womb into the uterus to check the uterine cavity is of normal shape. This method allows more accurate diagnosis of intrauterine adhesions (such as scar tissue, for example) than other investigative methods.

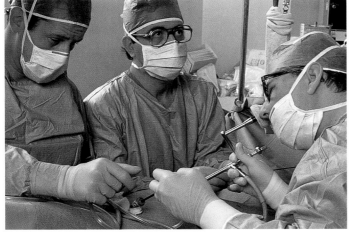

## Other methods of investigating infertility

### HYSTEROSALPINGOGRAPHY

An alternative to laparoscopy is X-ray hysterosalpingography (HSG). This provides an image (called a hysterosalpingogram) of the uterine tubes and uterus. It is an X-ray technique that employs a contrast (radio-opaque) medium injected into the uterus to outline the reproductive organs. This allows detailed visualization of possible blockages in the uterine tubes,

which are a potential cause of female infertility.

The test is carried out at an early point of a woman's menstrual cycle (usually in the first 10 days) when she is least likely to be pregnant. This is because X-ray radiation can damage a developing fetus. The dye flows along the tubes, and blockages can be seen. It is estimated that this visualization method identifies 75 per cent of

tubal blockages.

The passage of the dye through the reproductive organs can sometimes aid pregnancy by 'flushing' the uterus and uterine tubes. However, disadvantages include pelvic discomfort, allergy to the dye and the danger of radiation exposure.

### HYSTEROSALPINGO-CONTRAST SONOGRAPHY

Another related method for investigating infertility is hysterosalpingo-contrast sonography (HyCoSy). This involves a contrast medium injected in to the neck of the womb. A transvaginal ultrasound scan (TVS) is then performed, whereby a probe is

introduced into the vagina. The contrast medium and ultrasound probe allows detailed visualization of the internal organs with minimal discomfort or side effects to the patient.

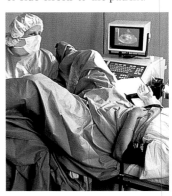

*Transvaginal ultrasonography uses a higher frequency than abdominal ultrasound. This means that clearer resolution of the pelvic anatomy is possible.*

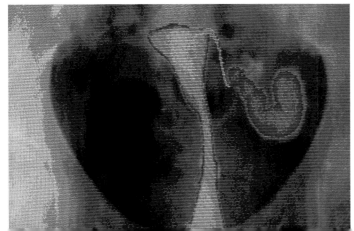

*In this false-colour hystero-salpingogram, the blue contrast medium has failed to flow into the right (left on image) uterine tube, indicating a blockage.*

# In vitro fertilization

Of all the techniques developed to help childless couples conceive, IVF treatment is the best-known. In only 20 years, it has transformed the lives of many by offering the chance of artificially aided conception.

In vitro fertilization (usually shortened to IVF; the literal meaning is 'in-glass' fertilization) was developed through the inspiration and skills of gynaecologist Patrick Steptoe and scientist Robert Edwards. Steptoe pioneered the use of the laparoscope for direct visualization of the pelvic organs during abdominal surgery. The technique allows a doctor to see the ovaries, enabling them to collect eggs with minimally invasive surgery.

Edwards specialized in reproductive physiology, and had undertaken years of research into in vitro fertilization using mice, before moving to work on humans.

Their first success was the much-publicized birth of Louise Brown in Oldham, Lancashire, in 1978. This heralded one of the most outstanding developments of modern medicine: the possibility of so-called test-tube babies.

### BLOCKED TUBES

Initially, IVF was developed for the treatment of infertility in women whose Fallopian tubes were blocked, thus preventing the meeting of sperm and egg. IVF bypassed the block by removing the egg from the body, fertilizing it in vitro, and returning the developing embryo to the uterus. Soon IVF was extended to the treatment of infertility of any specific cause, although until quite recently, the treatment of severe male factor infertility with IVF remained unsuccessful.

Over the two decades since the first successful live birth, there have been relatively few major advances in the original treatment that have had any impact on the success rate of IVF. However, at the same time, there have been numerous subtle changes in clinical management that have made the treatment received by couples today infinitely more streamlined and less disruptive, with the emphasis on outpatient, ultrasound-based treatment rather than on inpatient, invasive procedures under general anaesthetic.

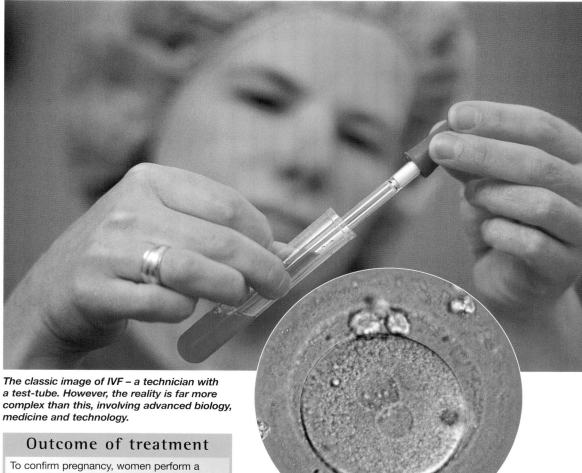

*The classic image of IVF – a technician with a test-tube. However, the reality is far more complex than this, involving advanced biology, medicine and technology.*

## Outcome of treatment

To confirm pregnancy, women perform a urine test two weeks after embryo transfer. Doctors will confirm this three weeks later by viewing a beating fetal heart using ultrasound. Once the pregnancy is established, the chances of it continuing to term are just the same as with natural conception – as are the chances of fetal abnormality.

The chance of the embryo implanting successfully varies according to, among other factors, the woman's age (over 37 years of age the success rate declines dramatically) and whether or not she has previously had a full-term IVF pregnancy; if she has, her chances of a subsequent success are doubled. Overall in the UK, the chance of successful pregnancy following IVF is about 15 per cent per treatment cycle.

*The male and female pronuclei (the two circles at the centre) make contact with each other thanks to IVF. Fertilization takes place in a culture medium, and the resulting embryo will be transferred into the uterus.*

*This false-colour scan of a woman's abdomen uses a contrast medium to outline the uterus (upper triangular feature) and fallopian tubes. The woman's left fallopian tube (right on image) is blocked where the light blue turns to darker blue.*

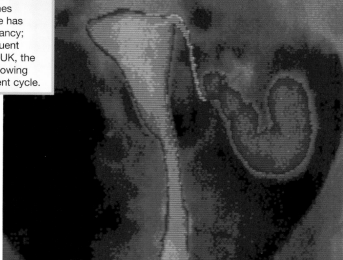

# Breakthroughs in IVF

Since the birth of the first test-tube baby, Louise Brown in 1978,
there have been a number of breakthroughs in medical science that have
made in vitro fertilization a relatively straightforward procedure.

## Cryopreservation

*Cryopreservation may be used at several stages of the IVF treatment cycle. Collected sperm are quickly frozen and stored until they are needed, as can the resulting embryos.*

Commonly, several embryos are generated, of which up to three are transferred to the woman. If the remaining embryos are of sufficiently good quality, they

*Micro-tubules of frozen embryos are placed in a canister of liquid nitrogen. This cryopreservation allows 'good quality' embryos from one treatment cycle to be retained for future cycles, without the need for collecting more eggs and sperm, then fertilizing these new eggs.*

can be cryopreserved (frozen in liquid nitrogen) for use in a subsequent cycle. Thus, the likelihood of a successful outcome from a single cycle of stimulation, egg collection and IVF is increased, as the couple are given several chances.

However, while some centres report success rates with frozen embryos as high as those with fresh embryos, others find the chances of pregnancy with frozen-thawed embryos are reduced by about 50 per cent.

## Vaginal ultrasonography

While the ovaries are being stimulated to produce ripe eggs, they need to be checked. The visualization is now usually carried out using a vaginal rather than an abdominal probe, making the monitoring of the ovarian response to

stimulation, as well collection of the eggs, easier and more accurate.

Vaginal ultrasonography (a form of ultrasound) does not require the bladder to be full, so patients suffer less discomfort, and clinics can run efficiently.

## LHRH analogues

Another major advance is the development of luteinizing hormone releasing hormone (LHRH) analogues. These drugs act by artificially suppressing pituitary activity, and by controlling the production of luteinizing hormone (LH), which triggers a woman's ovulation.

Before the advent of LHRH analogues, treatment was timed according to the woman's natural, unpredictable LH surge. Women had to undergo daily blood tests for hormone levels,

and even four-hourly tests to detect the LH surge, which required them to be admitted to hospital. Up to 20 per cent of cycles were abandoned due to spontaneous ovulation.

The use of LHRH analogues benefits patients and doctors by allowing programmed treatment. Procedures may be planned in advance and hospital visits kept to civilized times. The IVF success rate has now increased because fewer treatment cycles have to be abandoned.

## Intracytoplasmic sperm injection (ICSI)

The most recent, and possibly most dramatic, advance in IVF has been the development of ICSI. With this technique, which was first performed successfully in 1992, it is possible to inject a single sperm into the egg in order to facilitate fertilization.

Prior to ICSI, men who produced sperm that were unable to fertilize eggs – even when the sperm were placed in the immediate vicinity of the egg in vitro – or men who were azoospermic (having no sperm at all in their ejaculate) would have been told they were unable to father a child, and would have to accept either childlessness or the use of donor sperm.

Now, however, provided it is possible to find a single sperm, whether from the ejaculate, the epididymis or the seminiferous tubules, it is possible to achieve fertilization

using ICSI. The fertilization rate following injection, and the pregnancy rate following the transfer of the embryo are about the same as with conventional IVF treatment.

*The micro-needle containing a single sperm recovered from the father is just about to penetrate the egg. The chance of successful fertilization is greatly increased by this method.*

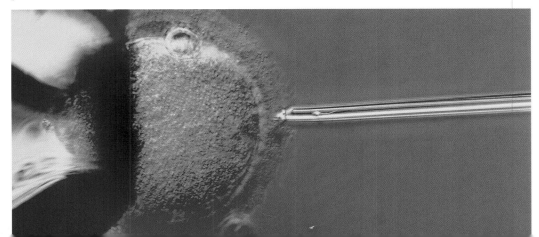

# IVF treatment

The cycle of IVF treatment requires much commitment, both from the couple involved and the medical staff at the fertility clinic. The procedures are complex, and there is no guarantee of success.

Although each IVF clinic will vary in the details of treatment, the general principles will be the same at all centres. Treatment is divided into a number of stages, and is the same for all couples.

The only exception is intracytoplasmic sperm injection (ICSI) for the treatment of male factor infertility (caused by insufficient or deficient sperm). With ICSI, the in vitro part of the treatment is different, but this does not affect the patients' management.

### OVARIAN STIMULATION

The aim of ovarian stimulation is to collect sufficient eggs from the ovaries to maximize the chances of generating several embryos, from which up to three can be selected for transfer to the uterus; some may even be selected for cryopreservation.

Currently, the drug regimens used entail an initial phase of 'down-regulation', or pituitary suppression, using an analogue (a drug sharing the same characteristics as the natural compound) of luteinizing hormone releasing hormone (LHRH). This is followed by a phase of stimulation, with follicle stimulating hormone (FSH). The appropriate dose will be gauged carefully, according to various factors, such as the age of the woman, and her basal serum FSH (her own natural level of FSH production).

Older women, and women with elevated FSH levels receive higher doses of FSH, since they are likely to have a lower ovarian reserve. Too high a dose could lead to an over-response, which might lead to a serious complication known as ovarian hyperstimulation syndrome (OHSS; see below).

### MONITORING

Egg development is monitored using ultrasound, with the use of a vaginal probe. Women are usually seen after eight to ten days of FSH stimulation, and the number and size of the ovarian follicles, in which the eggs are developing, can be measured.

## Four stages within in vitro fertilization

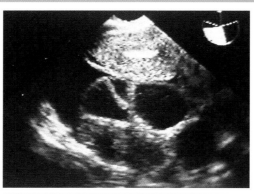

**ULTRASOUND MONITORING**
After about 10 days on ovary-stimulating drugs, the egg-producing follicles are monitored using ultrasound to check that the woman's body is reacting normally. Follicles can be seen on the scan, each of which contains a single egg.

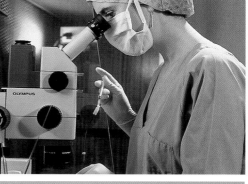

**EGG ASPIRATION**
After IVF treatment, a technician aspirates (draws out) a number of embryos with a syringe, under a microscope. Between one and three of the embryos will later be transferred to the woman's uterus by a gynaecologist.

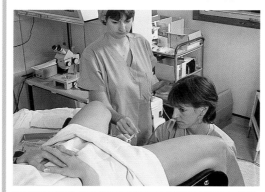

**EMBRYO TRANSFERRAL**
Once the harvested eggs are fertilized, up to three of the resulting embryos are transferred to the uterus to increase the probability of implantation. To do this, a gynaecologist uses a speculum to hold open the vagina.

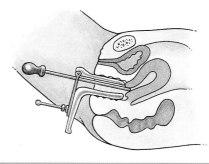

**TRANSFERRAL TECHNIQUE**
The fertilized embryos are injected via a syringe and catheter into the uterine cavity. The embryos then embed themselves in the uterine wall, exactly as they would do if they had arrived naturally.

If, at this stage, the response and consequently the risk of OHSS is considered to be dangerously high, the cycle may be abandoned and no more FSH is administered. For the majority of patients who continue with treatment, further scans will be arranged, the number and frequency varying at different centres around the country.

When a follicle reaches an appropriate size (the optimum size is about 17 mm (0.65 in) in diameter, but this varies from centre to centre) the time of the egg collection will be fixed. Some centres will include additional monitoring by measuring the levels of serum estradiol, as this may give an indication of the risk of developing OHSS (although this is not proven), and of the quality of the eggs that are developing.

Once the timing of the egg collection has been decided, administration of FSH ceases, and a final injection of human chorionic gonadotrophin (hCG) is given 34–36 hours prior to the planned procedure. This last hormone is the trigger for ovulation, and mimics the action of the surge of luteinizing hormone (LH) that occurs in the normal menstrual cycle.

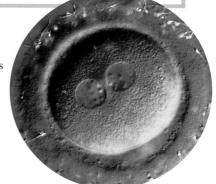

*Once the sperm sample has been prepared and added to the harvested egg, fertilization can take place. This will be confirmed by the presence of two pronuclei.*

## Egg collection

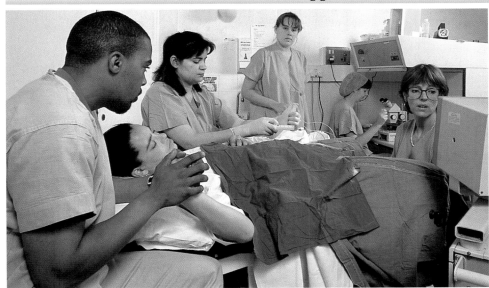

During egg collection, the fluid containing the eggs is aspirated (drawn out) from each follicle in the ovary using a hollow needle, under ultrasound guidance. Although collection can be carried out under sedation and local anaesthetic, some centres may perform the procedure with the patient fully anaesthetized. The eggs are too small to be seen by the naked eye (0.1 mm (0.003 in) diameter), but the surrounding mass of cells can be seen relatively easily. The eggs are collected and transferred to laboratory dishes containing culture medium for incubation prior to insemination.

*Using a trans-vaginal probe, a surgeon collects eggs from the woman's ovaries. Guided by an ultrasound monitor (right), the doctor passes a hollow needle through the vagina to the ovaries.*

## Fertilization

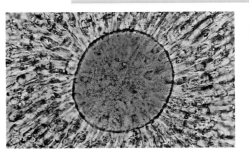

*A mature egg (pink) is seen on this coloured light micrograph. Around the egg is a protective layer, the zona pellucida. Outside this are layers of cells forming the corona radiata (yellow) which nourishes the egg.*

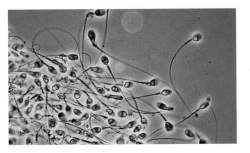

*A field of swimming sperm are shown on this light micrograph. Sperm cells contain a head and a tail. The tail enables the sperm to reach the egg and the head contains the male genetic material.*

Insemination is performed very simply by adding a small volume of sperm suspension to the culture dishes containing eggs. Semen samples are usually prepared using a technique that washes away the seminal plasma, removes debris and concentrates the active sperm.

Successful fertilization cannot be detected until about 18 hours later, when two pronuclei are visible within the cytoplasm. At this, the pronucleate stage, all the embryos look very similar. With normal sperm, about 60 per cent of eggs will become fertilized. Presumably, the remainder do not develop appropriately for normal fertilization to take place, despite being exposed to the same hormonal environment.

## Developing embryo

In a normal pregnancy, fertilization would take place in the woman's Fallopian tube up to 48 hours after intercourse. The fertilized egg, or zygote, would then make its way to the uterus to implant, developing as it proceeds. From fertilization to the two-cell stage takes about 30 hours.

In IVF, the embryo follows the same process of development, thanks to incubation in the culture medium, which serves to replicate the environment of

the Fallopian tube. The first division results in two cells, or blastomeres, each of which will then continue to divide, forming the embryo.

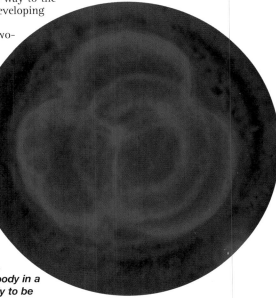

*Now at the four-cell stage, and around 2 days old, this human embryo, grown outside the body in a culture dish, is ready to be transferred to the uterus.*

## Transferring the embryo to the uterus

Embryo transfer is usually performed two days after egg collection, when the embryos have reached the two- to four-cell stage, even though the embryo would not naturally reach the uterus until about five days after fertilization in vivo (during natural conception).

The transfer can be performed on any day between day one (pronucleate stage) and day five (the blastocyst stage) after fertilization, but day two transfers are still the most

frequent. The culture conditions developed for human embryos are not yet ideal, and it is advisable to transfer the embryos into their natural environment as soon as possible.

The second day is the earliest time at which the morphology (appearance) of the embryos can give some indication as to their potential viability. Only about 15–20 per cent of human embryos that are generated in vitro have the potential to

continue their development. The assessment of viability is made by close examination of the shape and size of the cells, and the extent of cellular fragmentation as the cells of the embryo continue to divide and multiply.

The actual transfer procedure is very straightforward and does not require any sedation or anaesthesia for the woman. A fine catheter is passed through the cervical os (the opening of the cervix), and up

to three embryos are injected into the uterine cavity, along with a small volume of the medium in which they were cultured. The procedure allows them to implant in the uterine wall as a normal embryo would.

Hormonal support is often given to aid the implantation. The variety of factors involved means that most couples have about a one-in-six chance of achieving pregnancy in each treatment cycle.

# Sperm donation

Donor sperm is used mainly by couples who have problems in conceiving due to the poor quality of the man's sperm. Donor screening and counselling are essential to the assessment process.

Most couples take it for granted that they are both fertile, and that their gametes (sperm and egg) are compatible.

### ARTIFICIAL INSEMINATION

In some couples, however, the man may be found to have no sperm in his ejaculate (azoospermia). Furthermore, it may not be possible to recover any sperm from a biopsy of his epididymis or testes. In this case, the only chance for conception is for his partner to be inseminated with semen from an anonymous donor.

This option may also be chosen in cases where the man has a family history of a specific inherited disease (such as Huntington's disease, which causes abnormal movements and dementia in adulthood) and the couple do not want to risk having children that may be affected.

### POTENTIAL DONORS

Men who wish to be considered as sperm donors should be fit and healthy and preferably of proven fertility. Most donors are aged between 20 and 40.

Potential donors must first

produce a semen sample for analysis. The semen will be accepted if it is of sufficient quality: it should have a sperm count of over 60 million per millilitre and motility of around 70 to 80 per cent.

All donor samples are frozen for some time before use, so sperm samples must also be tested to ensure that they can survive freezing and thawing.

### FREEZING PROCESS

This is carried out by mixing the sample with a cryoprotectant and then cooling it very slowly to about -80 °C before placing it in liquid nitrogen (-196 °C) for long-term storage.

The sample will be thawed out the following day to determine the survival rate. Only men whose samples contain at least 5–10 million motile sperm upon

*Fertility is affected by a number of factors. If the man's sperm is not suitable, insemination with donated sperm is one way to achieve conception.*

thawing are accepted as donors for artificial insemination.

A poor sperm freezing characteristic is the most common reason why potential donors are rejected.

## Screening donated sperm

*Donor sperm is frozen for up to 12 months before use. This enables the donor to be screened for infections and sexually transmitted diseases.*

It is necessary to freeze donor semen samples for up to a year before they can be used for treatments.

This allows the physician sufficient time to determine whether or not the donor is harbouring any infections (such as hepatitis, HIV, chlamydia, syphilis and genital warts) that might be passed on to the patients who will finally be inseminated.

### STD SCREENING

All donors are screened for sexually transmitted diseases (STDs) at the start of the donation period and all the samples that they donate are frozen and kept in quarantine.

Three months after the last

sample has been quarantined, the donor is screened again; his samples are released for use only if he is clear of all infections.

### MEDICAL HISTORY

As part of the assessment process, the donor's medical history and those of his immediate family members are examined. This is to identify whether there are any obvious medical problems with a strong genetic component that could be passed on to the offspring. For this reason, potential donors who have been adopted – and have little or no knowledge of their genetic parents – cannot be accepted as donors.

For those conditions where a genetic test is available (such as cystic fibrosis), donors are asked to provide a blood sample for testing. At the same time, the man's karyotype (the number of chromosomes) is examined and his blood group is noted.

# Artificial insemination

The woman's menstrual cycle is monitored to determine the best time for insemination. Donor sperm is then injected into her cervix through a catheter.

After appropriate counselling, a couple receiving donor sperm will sign a consent form.

A physical examination will then be carried out by a doctor to ensure that the woman receiving the donor sperm is healthy, and that at least one of the uterine (Fallopian) tubes is patent (open). In some cases, the woman may be given fertility drugs to ensure ovulation.

### MONITORING OVULATION
Daily vaginal ultrasound scans will be carried out from the 11th day of the cycle to monitor the development of the egg and determine the optimum time for insemination – when the egg is released from the follicle.

A sperm sample taken from a donor who best matches the husband's physical traits – such as height, build, hair colour and eye colour – is selected and examined under a microscope to ensure that the sperm are active.

The donor sperm is then injected via a catheter into the woman's cervix. The patient will need to remain still for around 10 minutes, after which time nature takes over. The partner will be encouraged to remain present for the full procedure to enable him to feel involved in the conception.

*Ovulation is closely monitored to determine the best time for insemination. The sperm is then injected into the woman's cervix through a catheter.*

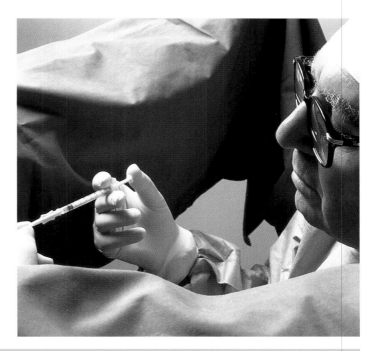

## Success rate

After the insemination has been carried out, there is generally a two-week waiting period before the couple learn whether or not the procedure has been successful. This can be a very stressful time for couples.

### RESULTS
The statistics for success are slightly less than those of a normal pregnancy – 10 per cent in one cycle in a 25-year-old woman – so a number of

*Couples usually have to wait for two weeks to find out whether conception has occurred after insemination. Pregnancy is confirmed by the usual methods.*

treatment cycles may need to be carried out before the woman conceives. The chances of success are highest if the female partner is young, and has no fertility problems.

A pregnancy test is carried out using a standard urine sample to confirm pregnancy. The test measures the presence of HCG, a hormone specifically produced during pregnancy.

### PREGNANCY
Once the woman has conceived, the pregnancy will not be any different from that of a normal pregnancy, with the same chances of miscarriage and birth defects.

## Counselling

Professional counselling is a critical part of the donor assessment process. It verifies that the donor fully understands the procedure and that he has thought about how his samples will be used as well as the possibility that babies may be born as a result of his donations.

### DONOR ANONYMITY
In many countries, the law protects a donor's identity. However, in some countries, couples and/or offspring who were born as a result of that treatment are permitted to contact the donor. Moreover, couples are often encouraged to find a donor that is known to them.

### RECIPIENTS
The couple receiving a sperm donation must also receive counselling before embarking upon artificial insemination with donor sperm.

It is important that the man comes to terms with his own infertility. He must also be encouraged to air his views about the fact that the child will not actually be his biological child. Without adequate professional counselling, the man may grow resentful towards the child or even his partner.

Both parties must be emotionally prepared for the procedure, as well as for any disappointment if the artificial insemination fails.

## Legal restrictions

The donation of sperm is highly regulated in most countries as there are complex ethical issues to consider.

### Safeguards
Legal safeguards are in place to:
■ Protect the identity of both donors and recipients
■ Restrict the number of times that the sperm from a donor can be used in treatment. This is to reduce the possibility that individuals born from treatment with donor sperm in different families might meet in later life and reproduce.

The payment of donors for their sperm donations varies from country to country.

*Sperm donation is a carefully regulated procedure. Legal restrictions ensure the anonymity of both donors and recipients.*

# Egg donation

Some couples may be unable to achieve conception due to the woman's failure to produce healthy eggs. *In vitro* fertilization using donated eggs offers these couples the chance to have children.

Some women are unable to conceive naturally because they are unable to produce eggs. This may occur if the ovaries are not properly developed, if a woman has undergone premature menopause, or if surgery or chemotherapy have rendered her sterile.

### GENETIC REASONS
Some fertile women opt to use donor eggs if they are carriers of genetic disorders, such as haemophilia, which could be passed on to the child. Rather than risk giving birth to a child who may suffer greatly and die young, egg donation offers the chance of a healthy child.

### DONORS
Egg donors should be fit and healthy and preferably already have a family of their own.

Their medical histories are assessed in a similar way to those of sperm donors. Doctors look for any evidence of genetic disorders and diseases that could be transmitted to the recipient or the offspring.

### COUNSELLING
Donors also receive counselling to make sure that they fully understand the process of egg donation and any implications to them or their family.

Egg donation is a far more complicated and expensive procedure than sperm donation. This is due to the combination of the egg retrieval procedure and the donor's need to take stimulatory drugs.

## Preparing donors

As most women only produce a single egg each month during ovulation, egg donors need to undergo stimulation of their ovaries to provide enough eggs to make donation worthwhile; a recipient who receives only a single egg would have a minimal chance of success.

### STIMULATION
The ovaries are stimulated by giving the donor hormone-containing drugs. The drugs are given daily in the form of a nasal spray or injections. The drugs are given in two stages to serve two separate roles:
■ Suppression of the normal menstrual cycle
■ Stimulation of the ovaries to hyperovulate (production of several eggs at once).

During the stimulation process, the ovaries will be monitored closely by ultrasound. Once an adequate number of eggs is seen to be maturing, a final set of drugs is given to complete the maturation process.

This final injection must be carefully timed so that it is given around 34 to 38 hours before collection of the eggs, when they are mature but have not left the ovary.

### SIDE EFFECTS
Unfortunately, the drugs can have some unpleasant side-effects, including hot flushes, headaches, mood swings and depression, as well as tenderness around the ovaries. The symptoms usually pass once the second-stage drugs are given.

### STORAGE
Unlike sperm, donated eggs cannot be frozen and successfully thawed for future treatment.

The donated eggs can be fertilized, however, and the resulting embryos frozen for transfer to the recipient at a future date.

### SYNCHRONIZATION
Alternatively, the ovarian cycle of the donor and the recipient can be synchronized in the month leading up to treatment so that embryos can be transferred to the recipient.

*This technician is removing frozen embryos from storage prior to transfer to the recipient. The embryos have been frozen in liquid nitrogen at -196 °C.*

# Retrieval and incubation of eggs

Unlike sperm donation, the recovery of donor eggs is a complex procedure. Stimulatory drugs must be taken before the eggs can be harvested via the cervix under local anaesthetic. The eggs will then be fertilized and implanted into the recipient.

Eggs, unlike sperm, cannot easily be obtained from donors. The eggs must be recovered from the donor in the same way as that used to obtain eggs from women having *in vitro* fertilization (IVF).

### RETRIEVAL OF EGGS

Egg retrieval involves aspiration (withdrawal by suction) of the egg from each follicle in the ovary. This is performed by first introducing a probe into the vagina. A fine needle is inserted along the probe and, under ultrasound, directed into the ovary to aspirate the eggs.

The eggs are then incubated with sperm from the recipient's partner (or from a sperm donor if her partner is infertile). Incubation lasts for several days.

*A surgeon removes eggs from a woman's ovaries using a fine needle. Ultrasound helps to guide the needle via the vaginal wall into the ovary.*

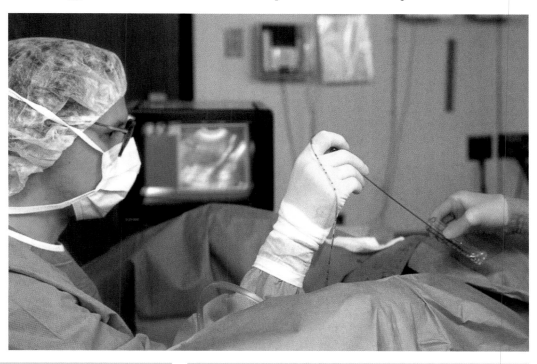

## Embryo transfer

Each day the embryologist will check the eggs and observe those which have been successfully fertilized and are developing into embryos.

### EMBRYO TRANSFER

Transfer of the embryos is usually carried out two days after the eggs have been harvested. Before transfer, the embryos will be closely examined under a microscope to ensure that they are healthy.

Embryo transfer is fairly straightforward and does not require any sedation. A fine catheter is passed through the opening of the cervix, and up to three embryos are placed in the uterine cavity. There is a one in five chance of a pregnancy occurring.

### EMBRYOS FROZEN

Any embryos that are not used may be frozen so that they can be used in future treatment cycles should the first attempt fail. These embryos may also be used for donation to other couples, if so desired.

*Embryos are usually frozen at the eight-cell stage (after three divisions). They are thawed when required and transferred to the recipient's uterus.*

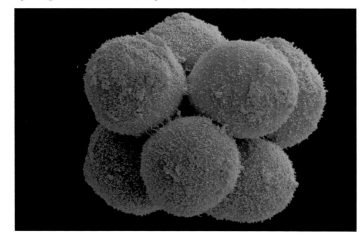

## Preparing the recipient

The hormones progesterone and oestrogen are given to the recipient to prepare her uterine lining for the embryos. The recipient's blood hormone levels will be checked regularly and the uterine lining is monitored by ultrasound. It needs to be enriched with blood and at an optimum level of thickness for embryo implantation to occur.

Ideally, the ovulatory cycle of the recipient will be synchronized with that of the donor. The embryos can then be transferred without the need for freezing.

Recipients must be prepared for disappointment as it may take several treatment cycles before a successful pregnancy is achieved.

*Prior to artificial insemination, the doctor examines the recipient. Her blood hormone levels and uterine lining will also be carefully monitored.*

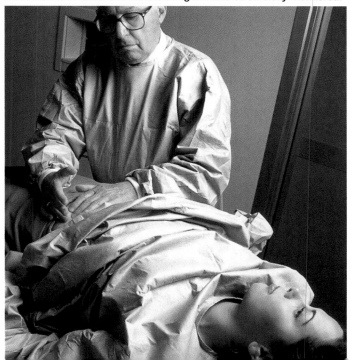

# Embryo donation

Couples who are unable to produce healthy sperm or eggs, and thus cannot conceive naturally, may opt to use a donated embryo. This gives them an opportunity to experience pregnancy and childbirth.

In rare cases, a couple may find that they require both sperm and egg donation in order to start a family. This might occur when a man is found to produce no sperm (azoospermia) and his partner has ovarian failure or a premature menopause.

One option is to be the recipients of both sperm and egg donations; another option is to receive a donated embryo.

### EMBRYOS FROM IVF
When undergoing *in vitro* fertilization (IVF), many couples find that they have too many embryos to be implanted safely at the time of their treatment.

To reduce the chances of multiple births, doctors usually only place two or three embryos in the uterus of women in a single treatment cycle.

In some centres, the couple have the option of freezing spare embryos and these will be kept for them should the treatment cycle fail or should they wish later to have another baby.

However, some couples may decide not to use their frozen embryos and may opt to donate them to another couple.

Although a baby born from a donated embryo will not be genetically related to its parents, many couples still would prefer to undergo pregnancy and childbirth rather than adopt.

### COUNSELLING
Recipient couples undergo rigorous counselling to make sure that they understand the processes involved and that they have thought through the issues that might confront them.

*Sometimes, couples may need the donation of both sperm and eggs for the chance to have a baby. Embryo donation is an option for such couples.*

*A limited number of embryos will be used during IVF. Couples may choose to donate any remaining embryos to others wishing to undergo this form of treatment.*

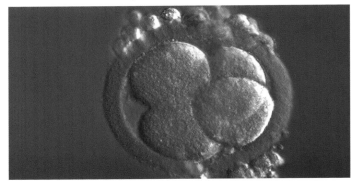

---

## Storage of embryos

Embryos are stored routinely while couples are undergoing the IVF process. The embryos are frozen for up to five years, after which time couples are asked to indicate whether they wish them to be stored for a further period, or discarded.

### MAXIMUM STORAGE
The regulatory body in the UK, the Human Fertilization and

*Embryos are frozen for up to 10 years, during which time their condition remains unchanged. After this time, the embryos are donated or discarded.*

Embryology Authority (HFEA), states that embryos may be stored for a maximum of 10 years. There is no evidence to suggest that freezing harms embryos during this period.

### DONOR MATCHING
The physical characteristics of the donors (for example, height, build, eye and hair colour) are registered with the HFEA and used for matching with those of the recipient couple if possible.

The woman donating the embryos is usually aged 35 or under at the time the embryos were frozen.

# Embryo transfer

Up to three embryos will be transferred into the recipient's uterus. For each embryo inserted, there is a 10 per cent chance that pregnancy will occur.

If the recipient is not undergoing a menstrual cycle (which is common in ovarian failure), she will be given hormone replacement therapy (HRT) to prepare her body for a pregnancy. This therapy is often started many months before treatment begins.

The quality of the recipient's endometrium (uterine lining) will be monitored closely by ultrasound scanning in order to determine the optimum time for embryo transfer.

### TRANSFER
If a healthy endometrium is achieved, then two or three embryos will be inserted into the recipient's uterus. The embryos are transferred painlessly into the uterus via a fine catheter which is passed through the cervix.

### SUCCESS RATE
Like any other woman who is trying to become pregnant, the recipient must then wait to see if she misses her menstrual period and has a positive pregnancy test. Any resulting pregnancy is then allowed to continue in the normal way.

The chance of successful embryo implantation is about 10 per cent per embryo transferred.

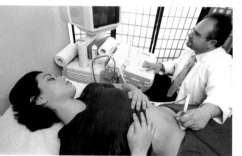

*An ultrasound scan will reveal the quality of the recipient's uterine lining. This will help to determine the best time for insertion of the embryos.*

*A catheter is used to transfer the embryos into the recipient's uterus. Up to three embryos are transferred to maximize the chances of success.*

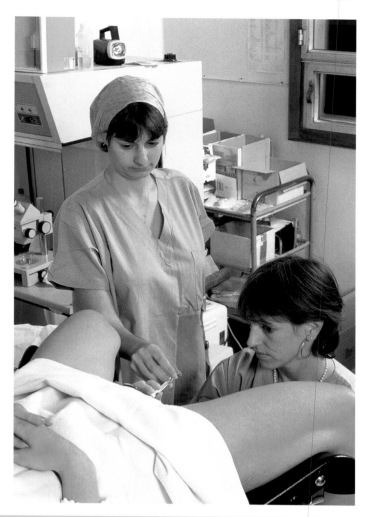

## Donor counselling

Unlike egg and sperm donors, couples who donate their embryos will already have undertaken infertility treatment of their own. They will therefore already have received extensive counselling about their treatment and the possibility that any spare embryos could be donated to other couples at a later stage.

When a couple decide to donate their embryos, however, it may be several years after their treatment took place. They would therefore normally be invited to see a counsellor again to discuss their decision.

**Personal decision**
It is entirely a matter of personal choice as to whether those couples with embryos in storage decide to donate their embryos. Indeed, many embryos are donated for research purposes or are simply destroyed if they are not wanted.

Some countries have very strict rules surrounding embryo donation and the use of embryos in medical research; in a number of countries, both are strictly forbidden.

**Medical research**
Where the use of embryos for medical research is possible, it is tightly regulated and strict controls are placed upon the scientists regarding what the embryos can be used for.

Legal restrictions currently state that embryos cannot be stored for longer than 10 years.

**Legal considerations**
The counsellor will explain the legal situation with regard to the embryo donation and will ascertain the couple's feelings on the idea of genetic siblings of their own children growing up in other families.

Discussions will also inquire into how the couple's own children might feel about the existence of siblings when they grow older, if indeed the couple decide to tell them about their donation.

*Embryo donors will already have received fertility counselling. When they wish to donate, however, they may be invited to have further counselling.*

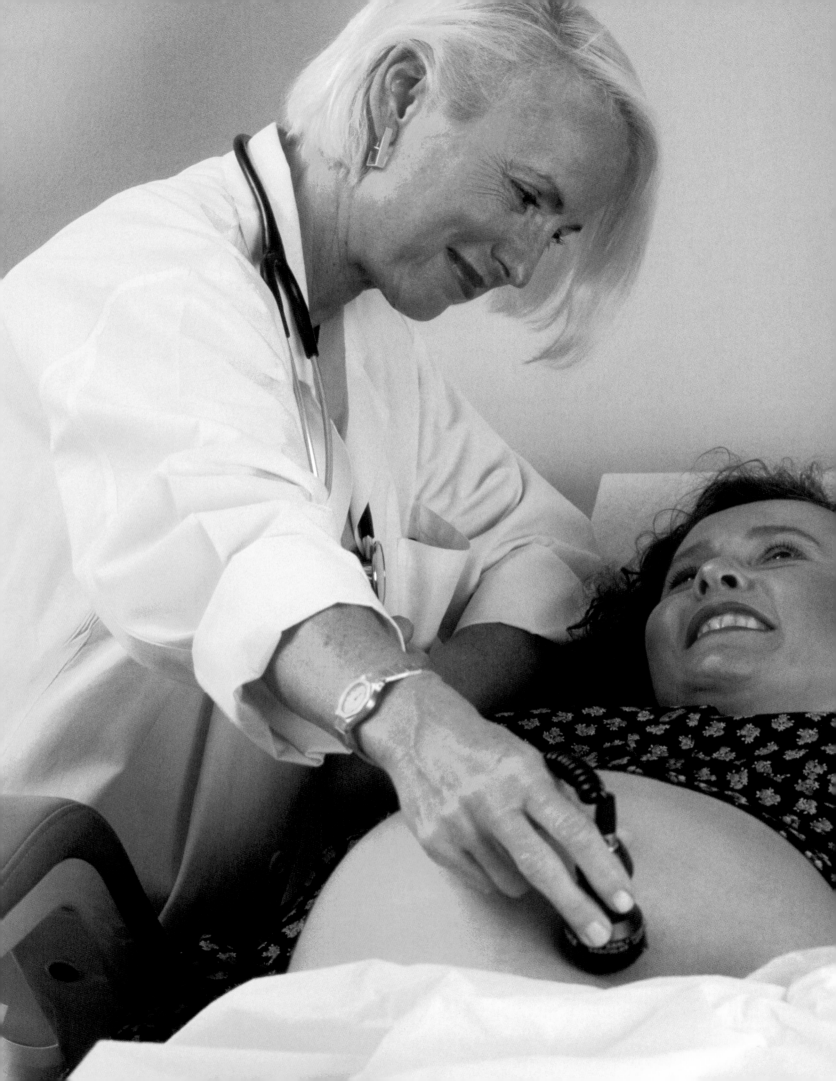

# Pregnancy

Pregnancy is a time of great change – a number of physical, emotional and social adjustments are necessary even before the baby is born.

A couple must cope firstly with the idea of becoming parents and then with the reality of pregnancy, as the woman's body changes to nurture the developing baby.

This can be a time of high emotions, often positive, but it is perfectly normal to feel anxiety and even sadness and fear, for example over the loss of body image or of independence.

Left: Regular checks during the final weeks of pregnancy are vital to avoid any dangerous complications. Medical staff can check the baby's heartbeat.

## THE DISTINCT PHASES OF PREGNANCY

The changes that accompany pregnancy begin with subtle physical alterations, although many women instinctively know that they are pregnant in the days immediately following conception. But ultimately, the changes are enormous. Many of the body's organs and systems, including the pelvic organs and breasts, the heart and blood vessels (cardiovascular system), immune system, and several hormonal systems adapt in obvious ways. These changes are divided into three distinct phases, or trimesters, of about three months each, until labour starts between 38 and 42 weeks.

## THE FIRST 12 WEEKS

The first trimester, up to 12 weeks, is characterized by a number of 'familiar' symptoms, including tiredness, morning sickness, aches and pains and altered taste sensation. The baby is developing rapidly at this point and growing fast, although he or she will remain relatively small and underdeveloped until the second trimester. Most miscarriages occur during these weeks, so many people choose not to discuss their pregnancy until the first trimester is over. During this time, some woman may not feel well or even excited about the pregnancy, and there is little visible evidence of the pregnancy to encourage a couple to plan for a new family member.

Many women choose to live as healthy a lifestyle as possible during pregnancy, but such changes, like stopping smoking and reducing alcohol and caffeine intake, may seem restrictive at first.

## PREPARING FOR THE BABY

The middle trimester of pregnancy is often a time of stability. The irritating symptoms of the first trimester usually pass, and although other body changes occur, they are usually not troubling and can be exciting. In particular, after three months or so, the growing baby starts to reveal itself as a visible 'bump'. At this stage too, the mother can usually feel the baby begin to move. Inside the uterus, the baby is beginning to look like a tiny human being and initially grows quickly, although the growth rate generally slows down after the fourth month.

For the mother, skin changes may occur, breasts enlarge further and she often feels full of energy and relaxed. This trimester may be the right time to start preparing for the baby's arrival, including collecting together practical equipment and becoming an expert in childbirth and parenting.

## COUNTDOWN TO BIRTH

By the final trimester, which begins at 28 weeks, the baby's body systems are almost fully developed, and he or she will now grow steadily and change subtly to prepare for birth. This can

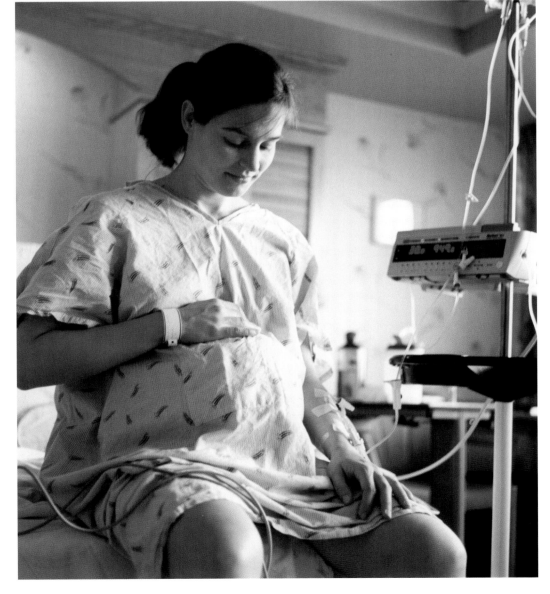

An overdue baby can cause frustration and anxiety, especially for first-time parents.

### WOMEN'S FEARS

During the first trimester some women have a strong sense of their body being invaded and of losing control. Others are disturbed by their changing body image and feel concerned that their partners will no longer find them desirable. Many fears are triggered by old wives' tales that bear little relation to reality.

Many women hide their pregnancy for the first three months. This may be because the pregnancy was unplanned, or because they do not want family, friends or employers to know about their condition, or they may be concerned about the possibility of miscarriage.

Thus women in early pregnancy often have to carry on as normal with everyday tasks, such as commuting to

*Many women experience tiredness during pregnancy. This can be exacerbated if they already have other children who need constant attention.*

*A woman who is pregnant for the first time will undoubtedly have some apprehension about the birth. This may be due to*

work, when they are feeling exhausted and nauseous.

Pregnant women who already have other children may find caring for these children particularly trying during the first trimester.

### MISCARRIAGES

Most miscarriages occur in the first 12 weeks of pregnancy. A miscarriage can be a shattering experience for the couple, who grieve for the baby they have lost and for themselves as parents.

### UNPLANNED PREGNANCY

Unplanned pregnancy is a common occurrence. In the UK, nearly one in three pregnancies is unplanned, and one in three women have an abortion at some time in their lives.

Unplanned pregnancy presents couples with a practical problem they are going to need to resolve quickly. Even couples who know what they want are likely to feel guilty and frightened of the consequences. Abortion is still a relatively taboo subject, so couples will be dealing with difficult feelings in an atmosphere of secrecy or disapproval.

A woman who has had an abortion may grieve for the lost opportunity for motherhood as well as for her child. She could also have fantasies about what her child would have been like.

For many couples, however, an unexpected pregnancy can turn out to be a blessing in disguise, relieving them of the burden of making the decision of when to start a family.

### EFFECT ON FATHERS

All too often male partners get forgotten in the first trimester. Prospective fathers may take some adjusting to the idea of parenthood. Some will have particular worries about their incomes not being sufficient to support their growing family. Others detach themselves from

*Unplanned pregnancies are common, and women who find themselves pregnant unexpectedly may find it difficult to accept that they are carrying a new life.*

the situation because they feel that there is nothing they can do to help.

Some men go through a range of physical changes during their partner's pregnancies, including nausea, heartburn, fatigue, backache and weight gain. These are thought to stem from the emotional conflicts of impending fatherhood.

It is not just parents who will need to adjust to pregnancy. Grandparents too may need time to adjust to the realization that they are entering a new phase of their lives.

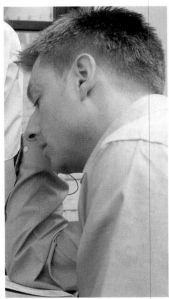

*Some men do not relish the prospect of parenthood. A father-to-be may feel jealous of the attention that his pregnant partner receives.*

# Second trimester of pregnancy

The second trimester is the period of the pregnancy from week 13 to week 28. This is a time of stability: the pregnancy is well established and both parents have a chance to consider the impact of a baby.

In the second trimester of pregnancy women are becoming more used to the idea of motherhood and more confident in their abilities to cope with a baby. Since the birth is still relatively remote, they do not feel unduly anxious about the impending experience.

### FEELING AND LOOKING HEALTHY

By the end of the 14th week many of the minor complaints associated with the pregnancy will have passed. Morning sickness will have disappeared and mothers tend to feel an upsurge of energy.

Women often look healthy with noticeable improvements in their skin and hair. Hormones start to settle down and women feel much less emotionally unbalanced and vulnerable.

This does not mean that feelings of apprehension do not still occur from time to time. Anxiety can be particularly pronounced around the time when tests are performed.

### ROUTINE SCANS

Women are routinely offered two ultrasound scans – the first at 11 to 13 weeks to confirm dates and to screen for Down's syndrome, and the second at 18

*The breasts change substantially in the first half of pregnancy. The pictures below show a breast before pregnancy (left) and at four months (right).*

to 20 weeks to check that the fetus is growing well. Women over 35 and those with a family history of abnormalities are offered amniocentesis to check for genetic abnormalities.

The first scan is the time when some parents discover they are expecting twins, or even triplets. Such information will be a shock and compound parents' anxieties about their financial situation, coping skills and the birth. Parents may also be told

that the fetus is malformed or has a genetic abnormality, and be required to make decisions about whether they will continue with the pregnancy or have a termination.

A bad result at this time is devastating for any couple. They are likely to have formed a relationship with the fetus and once past the danger period of the first trimester expect to produce a living baby.

### EXPECTANT FATHERS

For fathers – who may have felt left out of the experience in the early months of the pregnancy – the baby will become a reality when they see it for the first time on the ultrasound screen. For women, bonding is strengthened around the same time, when they feel the first sensations as the baby starts to move.

### PHYSICAL CHANGES

Around week 16 some women start to notice changes in skin

*Routine ultrasound scans provide parents-to-be with the first opportunity to see their baby. This may increase the*

pigmentation. Their nipples and the surrounding skin may darken and a dark line (the linea nigra) may appear down the centre of the abdomen, through the navel. At around 18 weeks the pregnancy will begin to show, with women finding their abdomen becoming more rounded and that they are losing their waistline.

How big women become during pregnancy depends on many factors, including their height and particular build. Another factor is whether the pregnancy is their first or not, because the uterine muscle tends to get stretched after the first child.

Women may find their changing figures disconcerting and need plenty of reassurance from their partners.

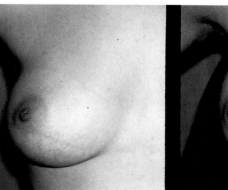
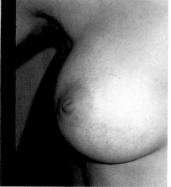

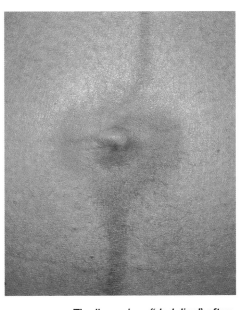

*The linea nigra ('dark line') often appears on the abdomen in the fourth or fifth month. It is a result of hormone changes, but disappears after birth.*

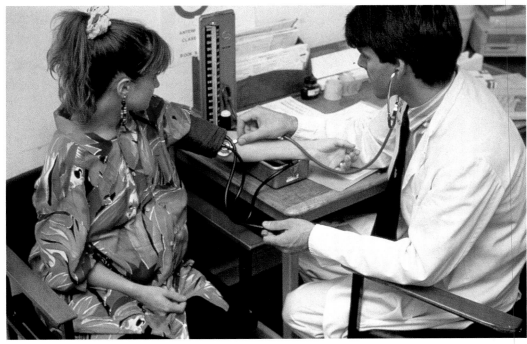

*Pregnant women are monitored regularly; checks performed by a doctor or midwife include blood pressure testing. This can help diagnose pre-eclampsia.*

### SEXUAL ACTIVITY

For women, lovemaking can be particularly enjoyable because they become aroused more easily as a result of increases in their hormone levels. Some women report experiencing orgasm for the first time when they are pregnant. Couples find that it is the one time they can make love more spontaneously without any need for contraception.

Many couples use pregnancy as a time to make the most of the potential for deepening their relationship with their partners, in readiness to include the child in the love that they share. For other couples there can be fears about the safety of having sex and that they might hurt the baby. If this is the case it is important that they express their love in different ways.

### RESOLVING FAMILY ISSUES

Pregnancy can be a good time for parents-to-be to clear up any unresolved issues they have from their past, and in particular their relationships with their own parents. It is a time for becoming aware of the patterns from the past so that they have the freedom and self-awareness to change them.

### CHILDBIRTH DECISIONS

Most women have their first antenatal check between 12 and 16 weeks. After that they see their doctor or midwife every four weeks until 28 weeks. Routine tests include taking blood pressure, measuring weight gain and listening to the baby's heartbeat.

It is during this period that couples start to make decisions about the birth they want, such as whether they want to have the baby in hospital or at home, whether they want pain relief and who they want to be present. Some fathers may not want to attend the birth.

### CHILDBIRTH CLASSES

Many first-time parents find childbirth classes helpful. By teaching prospective parents about the physiological changes that occur during pregnancy and labour, and offering exercises to ease and avoid tension, they offset many of the fears women have about childbirth.

They also offer couples the opportunity to meet others in a similar situation and can help women to create valuable social networks that will bear them in good stead when they stop work.

### PREPARING FOR THE BABY

The period towards the end of the second trimester, when women are feeling full of energy, can be the ideal time to make preparations for the baby. These involve sorting out the baby's room and shopping for the essential clothes, bedding and toiletries (collectively known as the baby's layette), and baby equipment. If pregnant women leave such tasks to the end of the third trimester they may find themselves feeling too tired.

### MAKING DECISIONS

Some couples find that pregnancy puts them on the receiving end of much advice from family and friends and perhaps some criticism too. The important thing is for the couple themselves ultimately to decide what is right both for them and their baby.

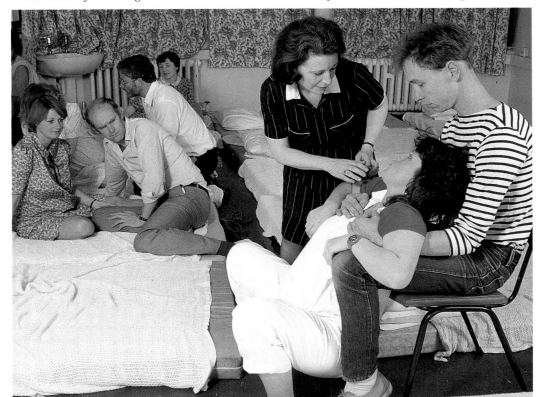

*Antenatal classes give parents an opportunity to learn what to expect at birth and afterwards. Contact with other expectant couples is also beneficial.*

# Third trimester of pregnancy

The third trimester runs from the 29th week of the pregnancy up to the birth of the baby. This is a period when women can take time to prepare themselves for the forthcoming birth.

The third trimester is the period when women start to experience many of the discomforts of pregnancy. For example, it can be difficult for them to find a comfortable position for sleeping; dreams often become more frequent and vivid. Dreams about losing the baby or having a stillbirth are a subconscious psychological preparation for an unwanted outcome and are a way of bringing these fears to the surface.

### PHYSICAL CHANGES

Owing to alterations in the centre of gravity, caused by an enlarged uterus and a slight loosening of the pelvic joints, mothers often experience backache.

In the last few weeks of pregnancy it is common for women to notice Braxton Hicks contractions – the uterus hardening and contracting as a 'trial run' for labour. They only last for 30 seconds and some women are unaware of them. When the baby's head drops down into the pelvis at around 36 weeks, the mother will start to feel more comfortable and her breathing will become easier.

### FREE TIME

For many employed women the interval between stopping work – often around the 32nd week of the pregnancy – and the birth of their baby is the only time they have for themselves. Some use it creatively to try out new hobbies or read books that they have not had time for before.

It is also a time when couples can make the most of going out and enjoying the last opportunity to spend time with each other before the arrival of the baby.

### BONDING WITH THE FETUS

More free time allows women the opportunity to spend time thinking about their baby. This is an important part of the bonding process. By the sixth month, a fetus has fully developed hearing and some parents try to stimulate their unborn child by reading, music and talking to them.

### OTHER CHILDREN

During the third trimester couples who are already parents will need to prepare other children for the new arrival. Young children need careful, sensitive preparation if they are to come to terms with the addition to the family.

Children should be allowed to feel involved in the pregnancy, perhaps putting their hands on the mother's abdomen as it gets bigger to feel the baby kicking.

Single children who have enjoyed the undivided attention of both parents can feel ignored.

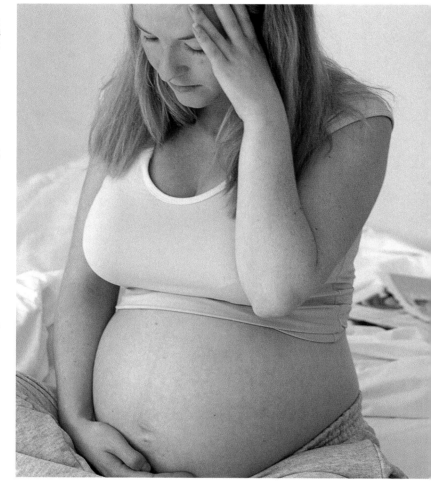

The result can be regression – when toddlers revert to babyish behaviour, such as not talking or using nappies, in order to gain their parents' attention.

### PRACTICAL PREPARATIONS

Towards the end of the pregnancy many women experience the so-called nesting instinct, when they feel a sudden surge in energy and enthusiasm and will prepare the house ready for the new arrival.

*In the later stages of pregnancy women often have a burst of energy and want to prepare the home for the baby's arrival. This is referred to as 'nesting'.*

*Women in the third trimester of pregnancy often experience discomfort and fatigue. Sleep may be disrupted by back pain and vivid dreams.*

Projects such as ensuring that the nursery is ready and buying equipment (such as car seats and cots) and essential clothes, may be undertaken at this time if they have not already been seen to and if the mother has enough energy. To avoid fatigue, women should try to make their preparations in short bursts. It is also important for the father to be involved so that he is also prepared for the changes that are about to take place.

*Fathers can often feel neglected during their partner's pregnancy. Attending antenatal classes together will help the father to feel more involved.*

### JOINT DECISIONS

Parents-to-be have important joint decisions to make – for example what they will call the baby. They need to find a name that they both agree upon that will be suitable for the child at all stages throughout his or her life. For many people, a name conjures up a particular image or character and parents may expect the name they eventually decide upon to suit the child.

At this time, couples may wish to discuss parenting together and the division of future childcare tasks. Fathers may need to talk to their employers about possible paternity arrangements, so that they can spend some time at home helping their partner after the baby is born.

### CONCERNS

As the due date approaches it is only natural that first-time mothers will feel apprehensive about the experience ahead of them; second-time mothers who had a distressing experience of birth may also be nervous.

Common worries among first-time mothers are about whether they will be able to cope with the pain and whether they will lose control and scream or defecate. They can also have serious concerns about whether they will need an episiotomy (an incision into the tissues surrounding the opening of the vagina to make delivery easier).

It is difficult to imagine what the contractions will feel like, and despite helpful descriptions these cannot adequately convey to the reality of the experience itself. Other concerns include doubts over having maternal instincts and worries over knowing how to handle a baby.

### PREPARING A BIRTH PLAN

Getting plenty of factual information about the options open to them helps couples to feel confident about the forthcoming experience and to feel more in control. Factors to consider include: whether the couple would like the baby to be born at home or in hospital, whether the mother wants pain relief during labour and whether the baby will be breast-fed.

It is important for couples to be prepared in advance for the fact that unexpected interventions may be necessary.

### LEARNING BABY-CARE

Women can become so involved with reading about pregnancy and birth that they overlook learning how to care for a new baby. Unfortunately, when they actually have the baby there is little time for this. The last trimester can be a time to gain experience in the care of babies with friends' children.

### GOING INTO LABOUR

Women can be disappointed when the expected date of their confinement passes and there is still no sign of labour. Only about five per cent of babies arrive on the actual expected day. Depression in women may result if pregnancy continues for a long time after the due date.

An obvious sign that labour is imminent is the appearance of a 'show', when the plug of mucus that seals the cervix during pregnancy becomes dislodged. The show is translucent, and may be bloodstained; its appearance signifies that the birth is likely to happen within the next 12 days.

*With the onset of labour, the mother will be admitted to the labour ward. Very few births actually occur on the predicted due date.*

*Before the birth, mothers will discuss a birth plan with their midwife. Considering all the options available helps to prepare for the onset of labour.*

# The first month

Once the blastocyst is firmly implanted in the uterine wall, the pre-embryonic
stage starts and all the major systems of the human body begin
to develop. In the fourth week, rapid changes produce a recognizable embryo.

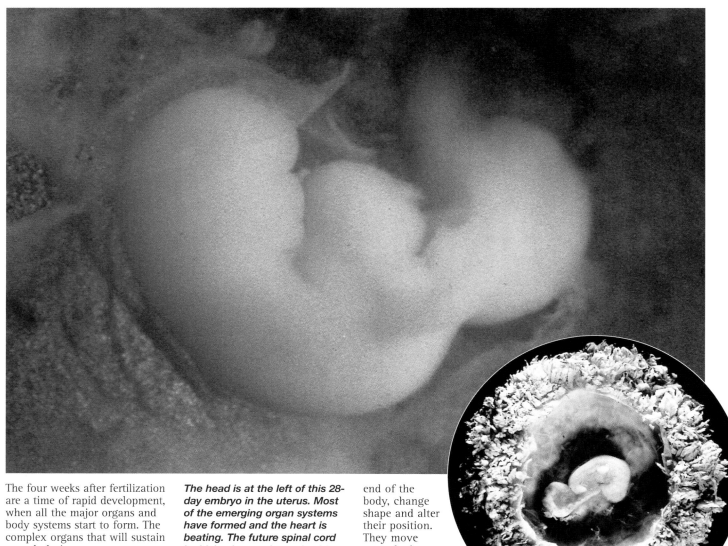

The four weeks after fertilization are a time of rapid development, when all the major organs and body systems start to form. The complex organs that will sustain growth during pregnancy – including the placenta, the umbilical cord and the amniotic sac – are also being formed.

### THE GERM CELLS
During the early stages of implantation, three different types of cells (germ cells) develop. They will eventually form the complete embryo:
■ The **ectoderm** will become the tissues and organs of the nervous system, including the brain, as well as the tissues of the outer surface of the body such as the skin and the hair.
■ The **endoderm** develops into the lining of the gastrointestinal tract, plus the liver, the pancreas and the thyroid gland, as well as the tissue lining the

*The head is at the left of this 28-day embryo in the uterus. Most of the emerging organ systems have formed and the heart is beating. The future spinal cord is thickening on the underside.*

respiratory system, the bladder and the urethra.
■ The **mesoderm** will develop into the skeleton, the connective tissues, the circulatory system, the urogenital system and most skeletal and smooth muscles.

The ectoderm and endoderm develop while the blastocyst is burrowing into the wall of the uterus. The mesoderm appears later, during the third week.

Initially, the germ cells have no form to indicate which end of the mass will be the head.

### THE THIRD WEEK
During the third week (days 15-21), some of the ectoderm cells, at what will become the rear

end of the body, change shape and alter their position. They move towards the centre of the cluster of cells. As they multiply, they stack up, forming a structure called the primitive streak.

Once ectoderm cells are in the primitive streak, they lose their characteristic shape, becoming more rounded and spreading forward to become mesoderm cells.

Some of these cells will eventually develop into vital internal body systems such as the muscles and the blood. Others become the notochord, a group of cells which develops along the back of the embryo as a supportive central rod. In due course, this will form the foundation of the spinal cord.

*This cross-sectional view shows a 28-day embryo inside the chorion – the membrane that surrounds it from implantation and later forms the placenta. The projecting villi, which anchor the chorion to the uterine wall, are visible around the outside.*

Also during this third week, the rounded mass of cells becomes more pear-shaped. The head of the embryo will form at the broad end, while the lower spine forms at the pointed end.

## Week 4: development of the embryo

*The cells undergo very rapid change in the fourth week after fertilization. This is the start of the embryonic period. By the end of the week, there is a recognizable embryo.*

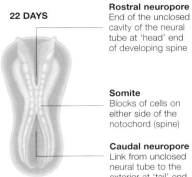

**22 DAYS**

**Rostral neuropore**
End of the unclosed cavity of the neural tube at 'head' end of developing spine

**Somite**
Blocks of cells on either side of the notochord (spine)

**Caudal neuropore**
Link from unclosed neural tube to the exterior at 'tail' end of embryo

**25 DAYS**

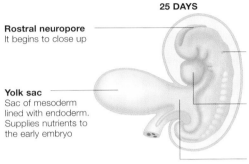

**Rostral neuropore**
It begins to close up

**Yolk sac**
Sac of mesoderm lined with endoderm. Supplies nutrients to the early embryo

**Otic placode**
Area of ectoderm which will become an

**Heart prominence**
Site of simple, tube-like heart

**Midgut**
Middle part of the gut; develops into the intestines

**27 DAYS**

**Umbilical cord**
Carries umbilical vein and artery for food and oxygen to the embryo

**Otic pit**
Otic placode develops and becomes indented

**Branchial arches**
Tissue here will form head and neck structures

**Yolk stalk**
Becomes gradually incorporated into the embryo's body

**Placenta**
Attaches to the wall of the uterus, and links to the embryo via the umbilical cord

### DEVELOPMENT OF SUPPORT STRUCTURES

The amniotic sac, the protective membrane around the developing embryo, is starting to form. Although extremely small at this stage, it will later fill with amniotic fluid and accommodate the baby and its placenta.

The tissue that will become the placenta – the chorion– is also developing. The chorion is the outermost layer of cells that develops from the blastocyst. It becomes firmly attached to the lining of the uterus by villi, tiny projections that secure themselves in the tissue of the uterine wall. The villi are surrounded by maternal blood, and help to exchange oxygen, nutrients and waste products.

The tissue of the connecting stalk, later to become the umbilical cord, is also developing at this stage.

### THE FOURTH WEEK

During the fourth week (days 22-28), the embryo develops segmented blocks of mesodermal cells called somites. These blocks are formed in pairs, on either side of the notochord – the rod of cells that will become the spinal cord. The somites will eventually become cartilage, nerve cells, bone and muscles.

### CHANGES IN THE NOTOCHORD

The notochord alters, causing certain areas of ectodermal cells to change in ways that will eventually form the nervous system. The ectodermal cells in this area begin to form a valley, called the neural groove. The edges of this valley, the neural folds, grow towards each other, fusing to form the neural tube. The neural tube extends towards the head of the embryo, where a broad fold becomes visible that will grow into the brain. It also grows towards the back, where it will form the spinal cord.

### THE BEATING HEART

As a result of the folding that takes place to make a distinct head and tail, a rudimentary heart – in the form of a straight tube – develops during the fourth week. This folding brings clusters of mesodermal cells, originally at the front of the embryo, to a position on the underside that corresponds roughly with the embryo's chest. During the fourth week, these cells meet in the middle of the developing gut. They form a single, central space that becomes a tube.

As the branchial arches – folds of tissue that will become the jaws and other structures of the head and neck – develop, the tube is forced down into the chest. This forms an obvious bulge in the underside of the embryo: the primitive heart. It begins pumping almost immediately, pushing newly formed blood cells around the tiny embryo still buried in the wall of the uterus.

### OTHER DEVELOPMENTS

Important blood vessels are being produced outside the embryo. Some develop into an extensive network in the wall of the yolk sac that provides nourishment for the early embryo. Others form an umbilical vein and artery through the connecting stalk – the umbilical cord – that links the embryo to the developing placenta. Both sets of blood vessels are vital routes for food and oxygen for the rapidly enlarging embryo.

### How big is it?

From the fourth week, the developing embryo is usually described in terms of its length. It is measured from the crown of the head to the rump.

- **First week after fertilization:** pre-embryo is 0.15 mm (0.006 in) long.
- **Second week:** pre-embryo is about 0.36–1 mm (0.02–0.04 in) long.
- **Third week:** pre-embryo is about 1.25–1.50 (0.05–0.07 in) mm long.
- **End of the fourth week:** the embryo is now about 4–5 (0.15–0.2 in) mm long.

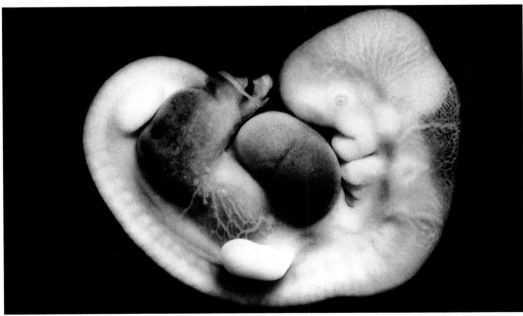

*On this light microgram of an embryo at 31 days, the eye is taking shape, and the limb buds are beginning to form.*

# The second month

During weeks five to eight, the embryo becomes much more recognizably human in form. Facial features will develop, the limbs will grow, the torso straightens and internal organs will start to function.

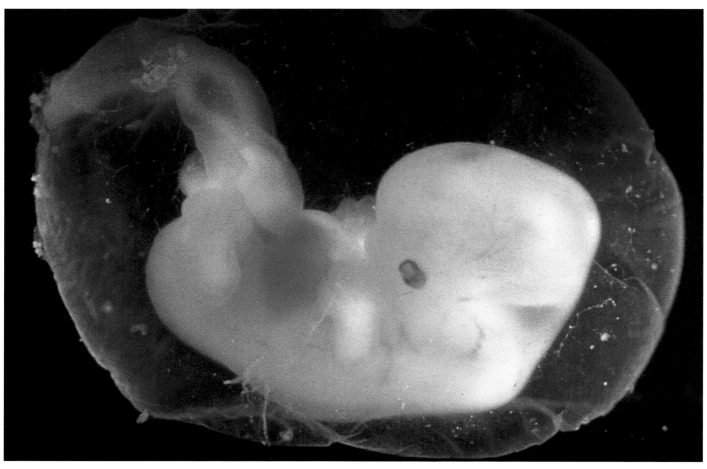

By the end of the second month the embryo is much more recognizable as a human being, especially with regard to facial features such as the eyes, tip of the nose, jaws and mouth. The tail between the buttocks has disappeared, and the trunk is now less curved and C-shaped.

The limbs have become jointed at the elbows, and distinct fingers and toes have begun to appear. Most of the internal organs have formed, and some will be beginning to function quite well.

### WEEK FIVE

During the fifth week, the leg buds are beginning to appear. The arm buds, which developed in the fourth week, have grown longer and have divided into a hand segment and an arm and shoulder segment. The hand and foot buds have a flattened plate at the end where the fingers and toes will develop.

In addition, the external ears will begin to become visible, and pits mark the position of the developing nose. The upper and lower jaws, formed from the branchial arches, are beginning to develop.

The heart now bulges from its position in the front of the chest. By this time, it has divided into separate right and left heart chambers. The primary bronchi – the air passages – in the lungs are already present. The cerebral hemispheres, which make up the two sides of the brain, are also growing, while the eyes and nostrils are developing and the tongue is recognizable.

By the end of the fifth week, all the other internal organs, such as the liver, pancreas, stomach, gall bladder, kidneys and sex organs have begun to form, although they are barely recognizable except as tiny buds of tissue.

### ALIMENTARY TRACT

Although a five-week-old embryo does not have a fully formed alimentary (digestive) tract, the folding of the cell layers that produced the heart, tail and head also initiate the early construction of the gut.

The alimentary tube, which is initially closed at both ends, opens at the mouth during the fifth week. However, the end that will eventually become the anus does not open until much later in the baby's development.

### WEEK SIX

During the sixth week, the embryo is continuing to grow and change rapidly. By the end of the week, the embryo will measure about 20–25 mm (0.8–1 in) from crown to rump. The main internal organs have finished forming, although they are still at a rudimentary stage.

At this time, the embryo's head is still large in relation to

*At five to six weeks, the embryo's umbilical cord can be clearly seen, as can the retina of the eye. The heart bulges up, and the arms and legs*

the rest of the body, and the facial features are becoming much more distinguishable. The eyes and the nostrils, which were originally at the side of the head, have now moved to the front with the growth and development of the face.

Pigment is beginning to appear in the retina of the eye, but the eyes are covered by the skin that will eventually form the eyelids. They will remain closed until weeks 24 or 25.

The inner and middle ear, which are responsible for balance and hearing, are growing fast but the external ear has not yet formed, though it will shortly. The tip of the nose is also present.

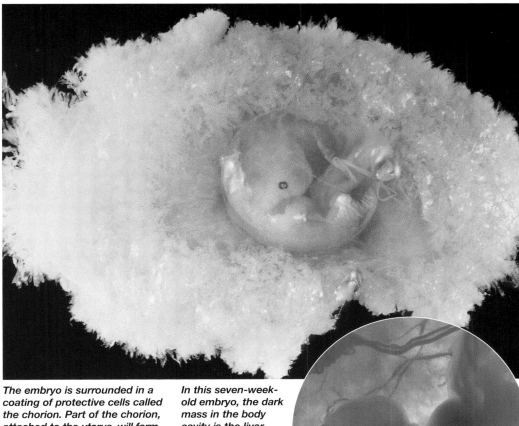

*The embryo is surrounded in a coating of protective cells called the chorion. Part of the chorion, attached to the uterus, will form the placenta.*

The embryo's limbs are growing and its hands are beginning to take shape. The feet will not clearly form for another week. The embryo's trunk is getting longer and beginning to straighten out.

The arms and legs extend forward and the arms have grown longer. They bend at the elbows and curve slightly over the heart. At this point the fingers are becoming separated but the toes are still outlines.

The heart, which is already present and beating strongly, will develop the aortic and pulmonary valves. The tubes leading from the trachea (windpipe) to the bronchi (the functioning part of the lungs) are becoming branched.

### WEEK SEVEN
During the seventh week, the embryo will be forming many of the internal organ systems, a process called organogenesis, and they will begin to function. For example, the stomach will start to make digestive fluids, and the liver and kidneys will begin to work. The crown to rump length is 22–30 mm (1–1.2 in), close to the size of a large green olive.

The torso of the embryo begins to elongate, and the body will become more square in shape. The embryo's arms and

*In this seven-week-old embryo, the dark mass in the body cavity is the liver, which makes red blood cells until the bone marrow takes over.*

legs continue to grow longer and extend in front of the body. The tips of the fingers are slightly swollen, where the fingertips are developing, and the thumbs begin to differentiate from the other fingers. The toes start to be visible, and the legs and feet may now be long enough to meet in front of the torso.

In addition, some of the neck and trunk muscles will begin to move spontaneously, and the arms and legs will move. Although these movements can be detected on an ultrasound scan, they will not be felt by the mother for another few weeks.

The head, face and neck are also developing. The head is becoming more erect, the skin that will become the eyelids almost covers the eyes, and the external ears are evident. The tip of the nose is also now distinct. The inner ear is almost complete, while the jaw, lips and mouth are becoming clearly formed. And at this time the tiny teeth buds are beginning to develop.

*This eight-week-old embryo is surrounded by its amnion membrane (the amniotic sac), which is a fluid-filled membrane formed within the chorion.*

the external genitalia of the male and female initially appear very similar. It will be another few weeks before the sex can be clearly determined on an ultrasound scan.

### WEEK EIGHT
The development of the organ systems and the body is well underway, and the embryo is looking much more human. At this point the head is still large compared with the rest of the body, but the face and features are even more recognizable. The eyes can clearly be seen beneath the eyelid skin, and the tear ducts have formed. The ears, which began on the neck, are moving up towards the head.

The ankles and wrists are forming and the fingers and toes are now clearly visible, although they are still covered by thin webbing. During this time, the upper limbs begin to bend at the elbows, and the fingers will curve slightly over the chest region. The arms and legs increase in length.

By the end of the eighth week, the embryonic period is over, and the embryo becomes a fetus. It is during these first two months that the embryo has been most vulnerable to factors that could interfere with healthy development and growth. Most congenital (present at birth) malformations occur before the end of week eight. Although problems with the fetus can still occur during the remainder of the pregnancy, the most critical period has now passed. The crown to rump length of the embryo is now about 25–35 mm (1–1.5 in). The fetus will continue to grow extremely rapidly until about the 20th week after fertilization, and then will begin to slow down.

As a result of all these rapid changes, the embryo can now be seen to be a human being, although it is still extremely small. However, it is probably still impossible to distinguish whether it is male or female.

Although the sex of the baby was determined at conception, in the early stages of development

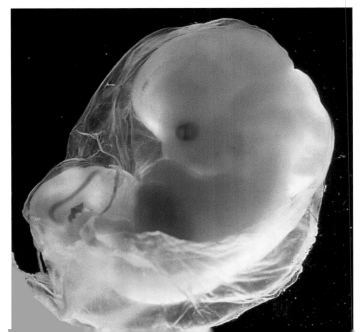

# The third month

In weeks nine to twelve, which bring the first trimester of pregnancy to a close, the fetus almost doubles in length. It begins to resemble a baby, as the eyes move to the front of the face and the ears to the side of the head.

The start of the third month is the beginning of the fetal period. From this time onwards what was known as the embryo is now called the fetus. The end of the third month marks the end of the first trimester, or first third, of pregnancy.

The term trimester is used to define periods of embryonic and fetal development. The period of pregnancy, as dated from fertilization, is divided into three trimesters, each about 13 weeks long. During the third month, fetal growth is rapid, and will continue to be so until around the 20th to 22nd week. However, during the third month the head, which initially was large in

*This coloured ultrasound scan is a side-view of a healthy nine-week-old fetus in the womb. The head is yellowish, the umbilical cord is at top centre, and above that is the mauve-pink placenta.*

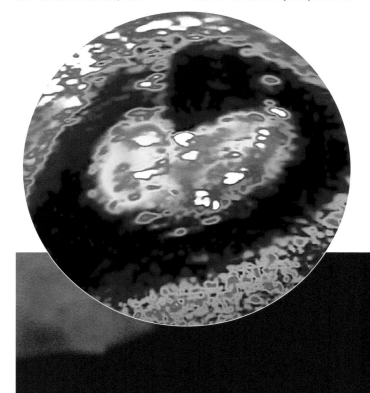

comparison with the body, will begin to grow more slowly while the body will grow more rapidly.

By the end of the month the fetus is very well formed, and many of the internal organs and body systems will actually be functioning normally.

### WEEK NINE
By the ninth week, the head makes up almost half of the entire length of the fetus. The crown to rump length is about 44 mm (1.8 in). The head begins to extend and incline towards the spine so that the chin raises up and is no longer resting on the chest. The neck is beginning to develop and lengthen, which helps make this process easier.

Other changes are also taking place. The nails on the fingers and toes begin to appear, with the fingernails appearing first, but they are covered by a thin

*In this close-up of the fetus at 10 weeks, the forearm, wrist, hand and fingers are all visible. The eye is on its way to the front of the face and the forehead is high and bulging.*

layer of skin. The eyelids are fused and the eyes remain closed until much later in pregnancy. The external genitalia become much more distinguishable during this week, though the sex of the baby is still not evident visually if examined on an ultrasound scan.

### WEEK 10
With the growth of the fetus continuing at a rapid pace, the crown to rump length is about 60 mm (2.3 in). The fetus has almost doubled in size since week seven. The weight of the baby is also increasing rapidly.

Few organs or structures still remain to be formed. Instead, the remainder of the pregnancy is taken up with encouraging growth and further development, and the body systems will start to function.

The bones of the skeleton, which started to develop early on, are now beginning to go through a process called ossification, in which bone begins to replace cartilage. The fingers and the toes have all separated and the nails on both continue to grow. Scattered

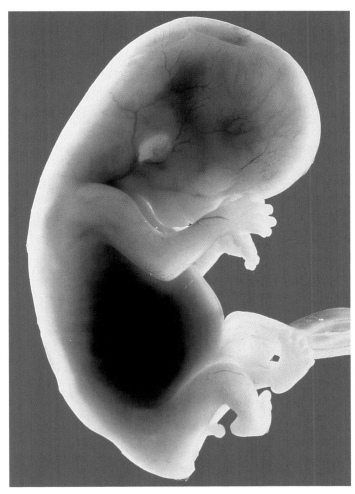

*By week 11, lips and eyelids have formed and the ears are on the side of the head. Fingers and toes are visible, as is the penis. The head is almost half the*

areas of fine hair will begin to appear on the body, and the external genitalia continue to develop.

The small intestine of the digestive system is now beginning to be capable of producing the contractions, called peristalsis, that push food through the gut. The pituitary gland, which is located at the base of the brain, is beginning to manufacture a number of hormones, including growth hormone.

The nervous system has developed further and the fetus is

*A coloured ultrasound scan of a 12-week-old fetus. The large, rounded head is on the right and the nose can be seen in profile. At this stage the fetus will weigh between 20 and 30 grams.*

continuing to move around inside the uterus, although as yet this movement will not be felt by the mother.

### WEEK 11

It is around this time that the head begins to grow more slowly, while the body growth rate speeds up. This reduces the ratio of head-to-body size. The crown to rump length is around 65–75 mm (2.5–3 in, and the fetus is now about the size of a peach. The face of the baby is beginning to look much more human. The ears are moving up the neck, which is where they

were initially, and they will soon come to lie in their final position at the side of the head. The eyes, which started out on the side of the head, are moving closer to the front of the face, which will be their ultimate position.

In the mouth, the two halves of the palate begin to fuse. If this does not occur, a condition known as cleft palate may be present at birth, which usually requires surgical treatment so that the baby can feed properly.

### WEEK 12

By the end of week 12, the fetus has grown tremendously in size. The crown to rump length is now around 85 mm (3.5 in). The face is much more recognizable because the eyes have moved to the front and the ears are situated at the side of the head. The neck has continued to get longer and the chin no longer rests on the chest.

The fetus is able to swallow and also to move its upper lip. If the lips were touched or stroked they would move. This ability is probably the initial stage in the development of the rooting reflex, which is an instinct that enables a newborn baby to find the nipple and feed after birth.

During this time, the fetus becomes able to produce urine. When amniotic fluid is swallowed and utilized by the fetus, sterile waste urine is excreted back into the amniotic fluid. The urine is removed as

the amniotic fluid is exchanged and refreshed.

Also at this point, the fetus will begin to receive all its nutrition through the placenta, which has also been growing and developing during the third month. The amount of amniotic fluid has increased considerably, and the fetus has plenty of room to move around.

The fetal movements, which began a few weeks ago, are continuing. However, these are still undetectable to the mother. By this point the external genitalia are sufficiently well developed to be seen under ultrasound examination. At this point it would usually be possible for an obstetrician to determine whether the fetus is male or female by examining the ultrasound scan.

The majority of the organs and body systems have now developed, even though some are still rudimentary, and the fetus is considered to be fully formed from this point onwards. The remaining months of the pregnancy are primarily concerned with further growth and the maturing of existing organs, rather than with the development of new ones.

*To show the bone development of this 12-week-old fetus, an orange-red dye has been used. It can be seen that all the major bones of the skeleton have already formed. At this point, the fetus measures 80 mm (3.2 in) from crown to rump.*

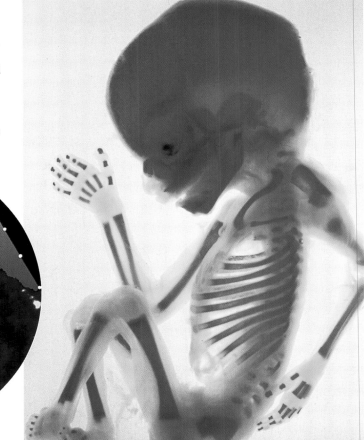

# The fourth month

Weeks 13 to 16 of pregnancy see the fetus increasing rapidly in size and weight. For the first time, the mother will become aware of the movements of her growing child as it starts to respond to outside stimuli.

The fourth month marks the beginning of the second trimester (three-month period) of pregnancy. During this time, the fetus continues to grow fairly rapidly. More subtle changes, such as the development and positioning of the eyes and ears, will take place, making the fetus look much more human. It is usual during this period for the mother to become aware of the baby's movements. Although the fetus will have been moving for some weeks, it is not usually detectable by the mother before now. Movement would have been observable, however, on an ultrasound scan performed earlier in the pregnancy.

### WEEK 13

By the 13th week, the crown to rump length is about 95–105 mm (3.7–4.1 in). The skin is very thin, and the blood vessels underneath can be seen clearly at this stage of development. Very fine downy hair, known as lanugo hair, begins to develop all over the fetus. This growth will continue during the pregnancy until it

covers most of the baby's body. In most instances, it disappears before the baby is born.

The skeleton continues the process of ossification; the bones are hardening and retaining more calcium. If an X-ray were done at this time the skeleton would be visible.

The eyes continue to move to the front of the head, but they are still widely separated. The external structure of the ears continues to develop and look more human. The fetus is now able to suck its thumb, and this can also be seen on an ultrasound examination.

### WEEK 14

The fetus is still growing rapidly, and by this time the crown to rump length will be around 105–115 mm (4.1–4.6 in). The fetal circulation is now well established, and blood is being pumped around the body effectively.

The fine lanugo hair has grown on the head of the fetus, and the fingernails are well developed and formed. The umbilical cord, which is

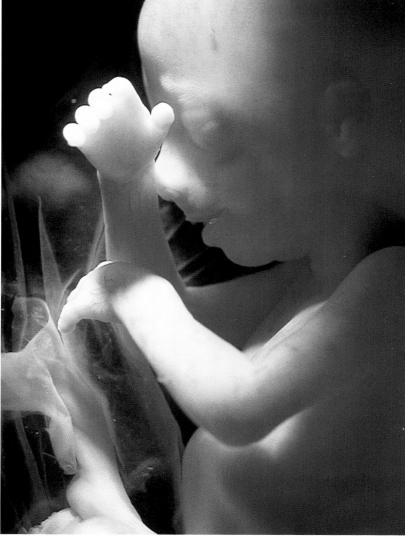

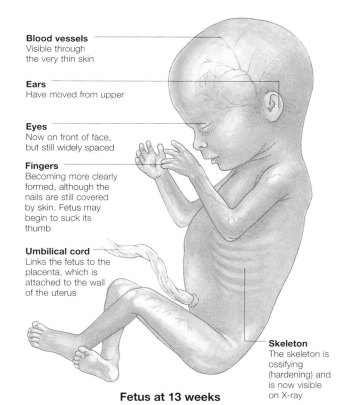

**Blood vessels**
Visible through the very thin skin

**Ears**
Have moved from upper

**Eyes**
Now on front of face, but still widely spaced

**Fingers**
Becoming more clearly formed, although the nails are still covered by skin. Fetus may begin to suck its thumb

**Umbilical cord**
Links the fetus to the placenta, which is attached to the wall of the uterus

**Skeleton**
The skeleton is ossifying (hardening) and is now visible on X-ray

**Fetus at 13 weeks**

attached to the abdomen, has moved relatively lower down the body than it was before. Although both sets of limbs have been extending, the legs are now longer than the arms.

Both sets of limbs move frequently, and these limb movements begin to become co-ordinated. This movement is called 'quickening', and is easily seen during an ultrasound examination. Movement may become more apparent to the mother during this period, but it may take a few more weeks before it is obvious.

The time quickening begins varies from pregnancy to pregnancy. If the movement is not felt during this week, it

*By now recognizably human, a fetus of 15 weeks still has much developing to do. The ears, for example, are rather rudimentary, although they have now reached their final position, and the eyelids have not fully formed.*

is certainly no cause for concern. Some babies are simply more active than others, moving more often and with greater vigour. Mothers may not be aware that the movements or sensations they are experiencing are caused by the fetus, and instead may assume they are caused by something else, such as digestive action.

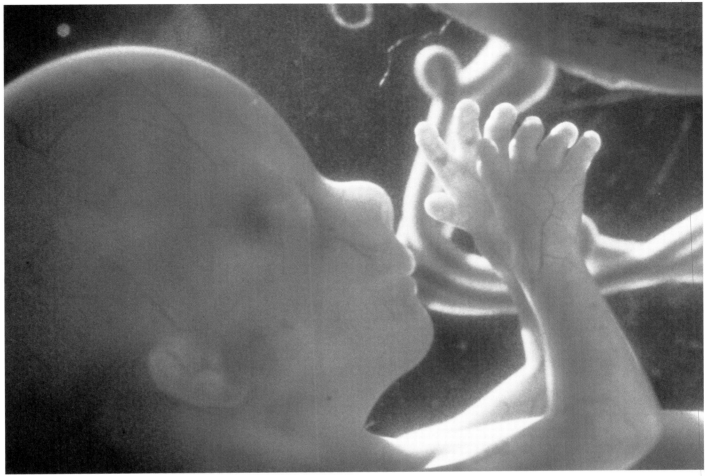

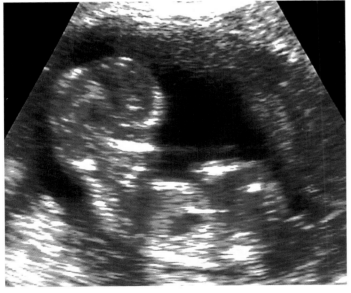

*A fetus of four months has well-formed fingers, which are more advanced than the toes. The umbilical cord, carrying nourishment to and waste from the fetus, can be seen in the*

follicles in the skin around the time of birth.

A greasy white substance called vernix caseosa has begun to form on the skin. It is composed primarily of a combination of dead skin cells and oily secretions from the skin's sebaceous glands. Vernix caseosa is thought to provide a protective coating for the skin, which is still very thin and transparent. It also protects the fetus against heat loss and helps to ease the passage of the baby through the birth canal during delivery. By now, the fetus looks very human. The eyes and ears are close to their final position, the nipples are visible in both sexes and tiny ridges are forming on the soles of the feet, the toes and the fingertips.

Many women will have an ultrasound examination at this point in their pregnancy as part of their antenatal care. This can detect various abnormalities of the heart, for example.

Another test that may be carried out is amniocentesis. This involves taking a sample of the amniotic fluid surrounding the fetus, and analysing it to determine whether the fetus is suffering from certain conditions, such as Down's syndrome.

## WEEK 15

The fetus is now growing dramatically in weight and length, and the crown to rump measurement is about 115–130 mm (4.5–5.1 in). One of the major changes occurring during this week is that so-called brown fat, or adipose tissue, begins to form around the lower back and buttocks. This fat is important both for heat production and effective metabolism. At this stage, water

*A 15-week-old fetus is shown here in side view on an ultrasound scan, with the head at upper left. Its head-rump length is 130–140 mm (5–5.3 in), and weight is around 180–200 g (5.7–6.4 oz).*

makes up the majority of the volume of the fetus, and fat is only a small proportion. However, this ratio will be reversed by the time the baby is born. The mother may

now be feeling the quickening much more definitely. The fetal movements have usually become sustained, stronger and more frequent if she has already felt them. It is thought that from this point the fetus will be aware of loud noises from outside the womb, such as raised voices or loud music. If so, the fetus may react by kicking or moving more often or more strongly. Hair on the crown of the head, as well as the eyebrows and eyelashes, may be present.

## WEEK 16

The very rapid growth that has characterized the preceding weeks will begin to slow during this week. The crown to rump length will be around 140–150 mm (5.5–6 in). The lanugo hair that has been developing now covers most of the body. Exactly why lanugo hair develops is not known; it will later be shed and replaced by hair from secondary hair

# The fifth month

The fetus is very active by this time, and ultrasound scans reveal recognizably human features. Basic physiological functions, such as digestion, are also evident, and they put an additional strain on the mother's body.

The middle of the fifth month of gestation marks the halfway point in the development of the unborn baby. The rapid growth that has been taking place over the past few weeks begins to slow down, and the overall proportions of the fetus begin to change. This means that the arms and legs become in proportion with the length of the body. The body begins to fill out with muscle and fat so that it no longer looks small in comparison with the head.

The fetus will usually be moving vigorously and regularly within the uterus. The mother will definitely be feeling the 'quickening' that might have been apparent during the fourth month.

During this month, the skeleton becomes even more ossified, developing more hard cells, and the digestive system is functioning in a basic manner. The skin, too, has become more mature and is developing a basic network of blood capillaries and nerve endings. Even the tiny fingerprints are beginning to develop.

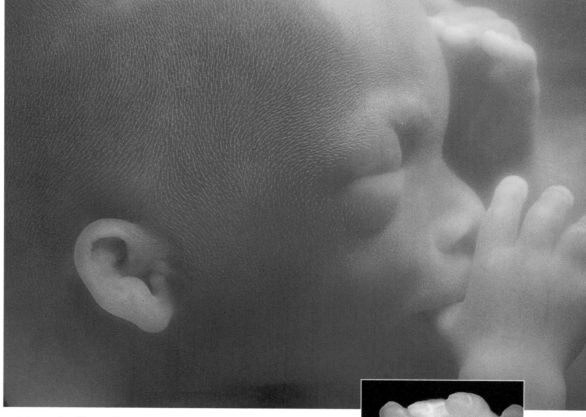

### WEEK 17
The fetus will now be growing at a slower rate than it has been for the past few weeks. By the end of this week, the crown to rump length will be around 140–150 mm (5.5–6 in). The baby is continuing to gain

*This coloured ultrasound image clearly shows the profile at 20 weeks. The head is still large in relation to the body at this stage, but the fetus is looking extremely human and is becoming very active.*

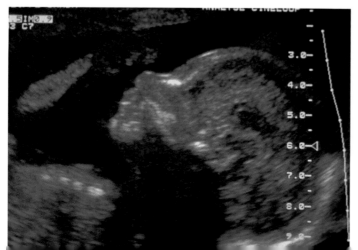

weight, and will usually increase its weight more than 15 times between now and delivery.

The proportions of the baby are beginning to change, although it still looks thin for its length at this stage. Certain parts of the leg will reach their relative proportions, and the head and face are continuing to develop. The neck muscles are growing stronger, which makes it possible for the fetus to move its head back and forth. If 'quickening' – fetal movements

*At 19 weeks, the fetus has fully developed nose, lips and chin. Co-ordinated activity – such as thumb-sucking – will be visible on ultrasound scans.*

– has not been felt by the mother before this stage, this will normally become apparent at 17 weeks. The fetus can move around vigorously in the amniotic fluid, kicking, touching its toes and moving the hands near its face and head. Tiny milk teeth are being formed in the jaws, although these will not break through the gums until well after birth, when the baby is four to six months old.

### WEEK 18
This is the halfway mark in the pregnancy, which is around 20 weeks of pregnancy when dated from the last menstrual cycle before conception. The crown to rump length of the fetus is around 160 mm (6.3 in). The skin of the fetus is developing rapidly and

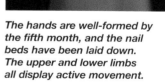

*The hands are well-formed by the fifth month, and the nail beds have been laid down. The upper and lower limbs all display active movement.*

changing. Initially, the embryo is covered by a single fragile layer just one cell thick, but by now the skin is separating into two layers, the epidermis (outer layer) and the dermis (deeper layer), each of which performs different functions. The epidermis is the layer which protects the body from external substances and elements; it also contains epidermal ridges, which constitute the unique genetically determined patterns on the surface of the fingertips, palms and soles of the feet. The dermis begins to develop a tiny network of blood vessels and nerve endings which make the skin more sensitive to touch. It also begins to contain larger amounts of fat, which help in controlling body temperature.

The sebaceous or oil-producing glands of the skin are also beginning to develop and function, and by now the fetus may be well covered with vernix caseosa, the greasy white substance that forms a barrier and helps to protect the fragile skin from the harsh amniotic fluid. The fetus is also well covered with fine, downy lanugo hair and may have some hair growth on the head, upper lip and eyebrows.

The proportions of the head

*The facial features are well developed, and lanugo hair is growing on the head and body. The eyelids have formed but are still joined together – they will separate during the sixth month.*

and body are beginning to change. Until now the head has been large for the size of the body, but during this period the body begins to grow more quickly and catches up with the head, making the fetus look more 'balanced'.

### WEEK 19

By now the rapid growth rate has slowed, and the crown to rump length of the fetus is around 175-180 mm (6.8–7 in). As fat is being laid down under the epidermis, the body and limbs of the fetus are beginning to fill out, and the muscles are beginning to develop. This makes the fetus appear stronger and sturdier and the skin to look less wrinkled.

Rather than growing larger, the various organs and systems of the body begin to mature and function, even if only in a rudimentary fashion. The digestive system can now not only absorb water, but also some enzymes and nutrients from the amniotic fluid. The small intestine will already have some movement, which pushes substances through it. The small intestine is already

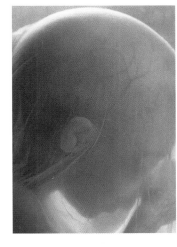

*The maturation of the nervous and muscular systems enables the fetus to perform simple reflex actions. It begins to suck in amniotic fluid, which is absorbed in the digestive system; waste is drained back into the amniotic fluid.*

capable of removing sugar from amniotic fluid and passing it into the baby's body.

The fetus can also swallow, and this is easily observable during an ultrasound examination. It is not certain exactly why babies begin to swallow amniotic fluid this early in pregnancy, although there are various theories. It is thought that it helps to stimulate muscles developing along the digestive tract so that they expand and contract regularly. Although the swallowed amniotic fluid provides few calories to be used as energy, it may be that the fluid helps to provide essential nutrients to the growing baby. The baby may develop hiccups

when swallowing amniotic fluid, but they will probably not be felt by the mother.

### WEEK 20

By the end of this week, the crown to rump length will be around 185-190 mm (7.3–7.5 in), about half the size of a full-term baby. During this time, the hands and feet have been developing and maturing. The nails, which appeared a few weeks earlier, are now clearly visible, and have grown so that they almost reach the end of the fingers and toes. The muscles in the digits are becoming stronger, and the fetus may be able to wriggle its toes and grip with its hands. The eyelids and eyebrows are quite well developed, too.

The arms and legs have grown longer and achieved the proportions that they will be at birth. The various organs and systems of the fetus are becoming more specialized and the baby may begin to develop a pattern of activity and sleep that will be noticeable to the mother.

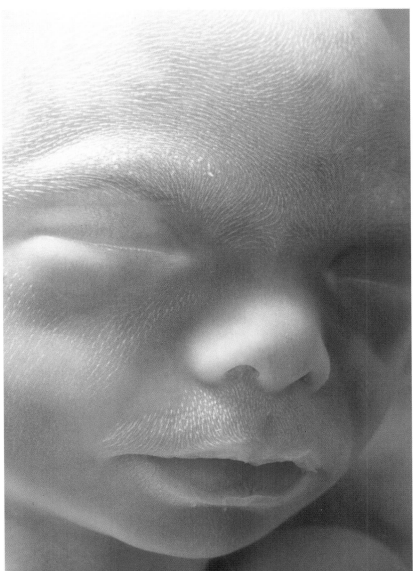

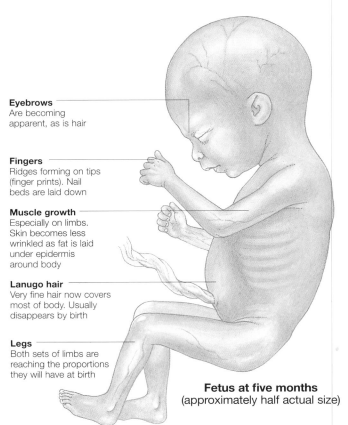

**Eyebrows**
Are becoming apparent, as is hair

**Fingers**
Ridges forming on tips (finger prints). Nail beds are laid down

**Muscle growth**
Especially on limbs. Skin becomes less wrinkled as fat is laid under epidermis around body

**Lanugo hair**
Very fine hair now covers most of body. Usually disappears by birth

**Legs**
Both sets of limbs are reaching the proportions they will have at birth

**Fetus at five months**
(approximately half actual size)

# The sixth month

The sixth month – the end of the second trimester of pregnancy – may mark the fetus' first blink. The fetus may also start to distinguish any light that penetrates the womb. It will grow another 5 cm (2 in) in length this month.

By the end of this period, the mother is entering the third and final trimester (three-month period) of pregnancy. The size of the fetus' head and the length of the limbs in comparison to the body will have evened out to appear much more balanced.

The lanugo hair, the downy hair that covers the body, may have darkened by this point, and the eyelids and eyebrows are fairly well developed. There may

also be more vernix caseosa, the greasy substance that protects the skin from the amniotic fluid, covering the body. Initially the skin may be somewhat wrinkled, but it smoothes out as more subcutaneous fat is laid down.

The face and the body of the fetus are beginning to resemble those of a baby at birth. The eyelids, which have been fused together, may open at this time so that the fetus can open and

close its eyes. Also, the retina may now be able to distinguish light from dark.

### WEEK 21
The growth rate is still slow compared to the previous weeks, although this will change again shortly. The crown to rump length of the fetus is about 195–200 mm. Although it is not growing in length as much as before, it is putting on weight quickly. The body of the fetus is continuing to become larger and fill out as fat is laid down under the dermis, the deeper layer of the skin. It is usually around this time that the lanugo hair begins to darken.

By this point in pregnancy the face of the fetus is much more defined. There are well-formed features, with an obvious browline and eyebrows,

although the eyelids are still fused shut. It is thought that the fetus can hear sounds at this point, and may even have some ability to taste and smell.

### WEEK 22
The fetus is continuing to fill out. The crown to rump length is around 210 mm. This is only an average, of course, as the size of the fetus will vary from woman to woman and even from pregnancy to pregnancy.

The proportions of the fetus are continuing to change, and

*The profile of a 21-week-old fetus is clearly defined on this false-colour ultrasound scan. The rounded cranium (left) and facial features are well developed and will change little before birth.*

*By the 21st week of pregnancy, the hands and fingers of the fetus are almost fully formed. The fingernails are visible here, as is the structure of the left ear. In the background, the membrane around the amniotic sac is visible.*

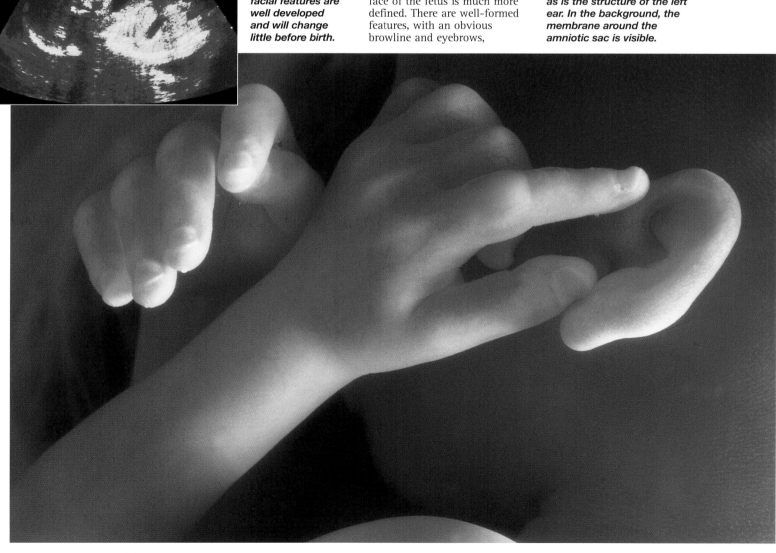

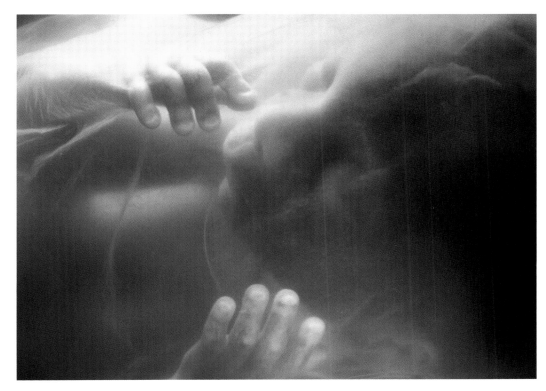

*The amnion, the membrane surrounding the fetus, is clearly shown enveloping this 22-week fetus.*

One of the major changes by this time is in the development of the eyes. These have been developing throughout early pregnancy, and were initially located on the side of the head.

Over the succeeding weeks, they gradually moved closer to the front of the face into their final position. During this early period, the blood vessels that lead to the eye began to form and the pupil developed during the eighth or ninth week of pregnancy. At the same time, the nerve connection from the eyes to the brain – the optic nerve – was forming.

The eyelids, consisting of a very thin layer of skin, have been present, but fused together, since around the 10th week of pregnancy. At this stage, they begin to separate, so that the fetus will be able to open and close its eyes. The muscles around the eyes that control the eyelids also begin to develop rapidly at this stage.

The iris – the coloured part of the eye – is usually blue in all fetuses at this point, regardless of their ethnic background. The final colour of the eyes will depend, however, on the baby's ethnic origin. For example, most Caucasian babies have blue eyes at birth, although this can subsequently change.

The retina at the back of the eye is responsible for receiving and transmitting images of light to the brain. By this point in the pregnancy, the retina has developed to receive and process information about light and to pass these sensations to the brain. The fetus can now probably differentiate between lightness and darkness through the mother's abdominal wall.

the head is now much more in keeping with the size of the body. The fetus is well covered by a layer of vernix to protect its delicate skin from the surrounding amniotic fluid. The skin itself is becoming less wrinkled as fat stores are gradually being laid down.

It is possible that a fetus born at this point would survive, although it would be very small and would need much medical attention and intensive care. Its survival would depend very much on how well developed the internal organs and body systems were.

## WEEKS 23–24

The 23rd week of the pregnancy constitutes the end of the second trimester. The crown to rump length is around 220 mm (8.6 in). The fat stores are continuing to be deposited as the fetus puts on weight fairly rapidly. It is looking more and more like a miniature newborn baby. The space available inside the uterus is becoming more cramped as the fetus grows larger, and it may change position to adapt to this shortage of space. During the 24th week, the fetus starts to grow rapidly again, in both size and weight. The crown to rump length is around 225–230 mm (8.7–9 in), and it is increasing at about 10 mm per week. The fetus is also putting on weight at an increasing rate, and now weighs around 0.75 kg (24 oz). This additional weight causes the limbs of the fetus to appear fuller.

## WEEK 25

This week marks the beginning of the third trimester of pregnancy. The crown to rump length of the fetus is around 240 mm (9.5 in), and if it were measured from head to toe it would probably be around 340 mm (13.4 in) in total length.

*The head of a 25-week fetus (on the right, facing the top left-hand corner of the picture) can be seen on this false-colour ultrasound womb scan.*

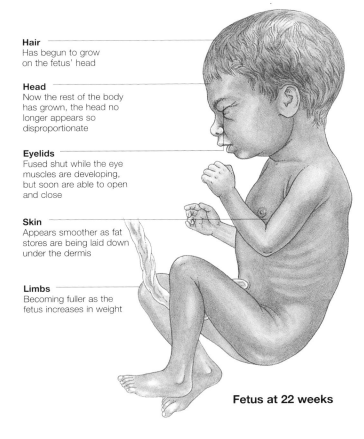

**Hair**
Has begun to grow on the fetus' head

**Head**
Now the rest of the body has grown, the head no longer appears so disproportionate

**Eyelids**
Fused shut while the eye muscles are developing, but soon are able to open and close

**Skin**
Appears smoother as fat stores are being laid down under the dermis

**Limbs**
Becoming fuller as the fetus increases in weight

**Fetus at 22 weeks**

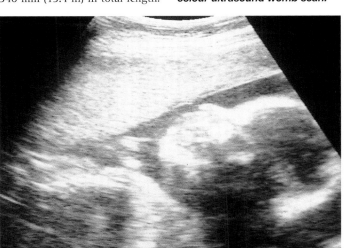

# Antenatal care

Antenatal clinics provide a number of services for pregnant women,
from the first weeks to the final stages of pregnancy. This
care ensures that mother and fetus are in the best possible health.

Antenatal care dates from the turn of the century, although it was not until the 1930s that such services became more widespread. Today, the majority of pregnant women have a very low risk of complications, but some women with complicated medical or obstetric histories will require more intensive monitoring.

Antenatal care aims to provide the appropriate level of care to each individual. In addition to the midwifery and medical input during the antenatal period, antenatal care also aims to help women prepare for their delivery and the care of their babies in the postnatal (six weeks following birth) period.

### PRE-PREGNANCY COUNSELLING

In an ideal world, every woman would have the opportunity to plan her pregnancy; this would enable her to begin pregnancy in the best possible health. At the moment, however, advisory services are currently targeted at women who have medical disorders, such as diabetes or high blood pressure, or those who have had previous unfortunate pregnancy outcomes.

*There is a wide variety of health products available for pregnant women. These include folic acid supplements to reduce the risk of defects such as spina bifida.*

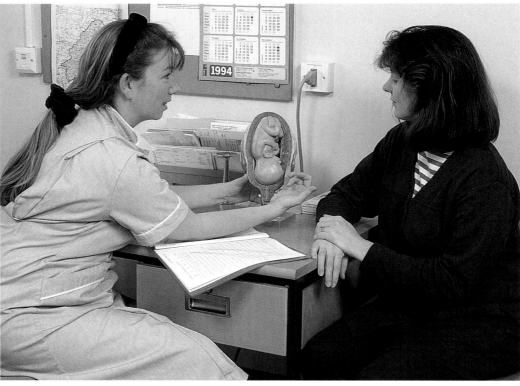

Pre-pregnancy counselling reviews the individual's dietary, smoking and drinking habits. All regular drug usage would also be reviewed. Some women would benefit pre-conceptually by consulting with specialists if they have existing health problems such as heart disease, hypertension, kidney disease, diabetes, epilepsy or mental

health disorders. Women are currently advised to use folic acid in the pre-conceptual period and the first trimester (three-month period) of the pregnancy to reduce the incidence of spina bifida and other disorders of neural (nerve tissue) development.

In some families, there is a possibility of inherited disorders,

*A pregnant woman's first visit to the antenatal clinic is very important. She will be examined by a doctor or midwife and receive important information.*

such as haemophilia or sickle-cell disease. These families should be informed about the possible tests available to them before and after the pregnancy.

## Types of antenatal care

Women are able to choose different types of antenatal care, in conjunction with their general practitioner or midwife. These choices may be determined by a number of factors, such as local facilities and transport arrangements.

At present, the majority of women opt to deliver in a

hospital environment. Less then one per cent of women initially choose home delivery, although some home deliveries are unplanned.

Once the women has chosen where she wishes to deliver and the sort of antenatal care that is appropriate, the plan of visits can be established.

| Type of care | Carers | Setting |
| --- | --- | --- |
| Shared care | GP, midwife and hospital doctors | GP surgery/hospital |
| Full care | Hospital doctors and midwives | Hospital |
| Midwifery | Midwife | Community/hospital |

# The booking visit

The preliminary consultation, or 'booking visit', with the midwife is possibly the most important, and takes place in the first three months of the pregnancy

The first meeting during the pregnancy with a doctor or a midwife should, if possible, be made in the first 12 weeks. This is usually the longest consultation and a detailed medical, family and obstetric history is taken. This should include all previous serious medical and surgical conditions. Details about previous infections, including hepatitis, HIV or rubella should be noted and alcohol and cigarette consumption discussed.

### PAST OBSTETRIC HISTORY

The outcome of any previous pregnancy should be discussed. Although sometimes difficult, it is important to mention any previous miscarriages or terminations of pregnancy, as these may be of relevance in a current pregnancy.

Complications arising from previous pregnancies may have a bearing on future obstetric care. In women who have had previous miscarriages, sometimes it is appropriate to consider additional investigations or the recommendation to insert a cervical suture, depending on the circumstances of the loss. Some pregnancy-related complications are more likely to

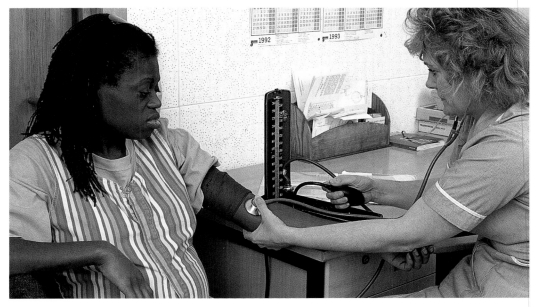

recur in subsequent pregnancies, for example postpartum haemorrhage, premature labour or thrombosis.

### PRESENT PREGNANCY

Important information concerning the present pregnancy includes the first date of the last menstrual period (MP). Dating of the pregnancy will also depend on whether the

menstrual cycle had been regular and of normal length, the prior use of contraception, (particularly oral contraception) and details on when and if it was stopped. Vaginal bleeding in pregnancy is surprisingly common, although abnormal, and will usually be an indication for an ultrasound scan to ensure that a normal pregnancy is continuing.

*Blood pressure is always measured at the booking visit. This is an important indicator of the woman's general health.*

An early ultrasound scan is especially important in women with a previous ectopic pregnancy (when the embryo implants outside the uterus), as they are more likely to have a subsequent ectopic gestation.

## Early pregnancy checks

During the course of the booking visit, a number of checks will be carried out by the doctor or midwife. The woman's weight and height will be recorded; her chest and heart will be listened to and, most importantly, blood pressure will be measured. Further detailed medical examination will be determined by the woman's medical history.

The abdomen will be examined and, from 14 weeks' gestation, the fetal heart can be heard using a hand-held Doppler probe. However, a vaginal examination will be performed only if there is a specific reason to do so.

It is completely safe to have a smear test in pregnancy and this may be particularly important in women who have had previously abnormal smears or irregular bleeding. Women who have had treatment or surgical operations on their cervix will also be carefully examined.

**1** *All of the woman's details will be recorded during the examination. Height and weight are measured, providing a reference for comparison as the pregnancy progresses.*

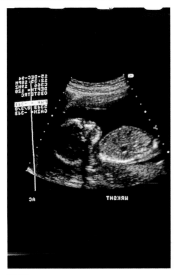

**2** *Depending on the patient's medical history, a cervical smear may be performed. This is a routine procedure in many pregnancies and is not harmful to the developing fetus.*

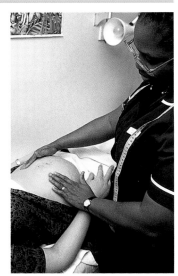

**3** *After the woman's first visit, she will return for monthly appointments up until the 36th week of pregnancy, when she will attend weekly. Her abdomen will be palpated on every visit.*

# Assessing body changes in pregnancy

When a woman is pregnant, she experiences changes to her anatomy, metabolism and cardiovascular and respiratory systems. Most of these changes are temporary, but require careful monitoring to confirm normal progress

Antenatal care in pregnancy is vital to ensure the health and well-being of both mother-to-be and fetus. Most women will see their GP or midwife every month for routine tests up to the eighth month of pregnancy. After this point, visits will be more regular at two-week intervals. During the final month, visits may be made every week.

### PHYSICAL CHANGES
The changes that occur in pregnancy minimize stress on the woman and provide the fetus with the optimal environment for growth and development. For example, the loosening of the pelvic girdle is required to enable the baby to exit through the birth canal.

The principal changes affect the uterus, the cervix and the breasts. Less obvious changes are seen in the vagina, vulva, the abdominal wall and in the joints of the bones. Some changes are barely noticeable and cause little discomfort. The woman also experiences changes to her skin, most of which disappear after the birth.

The midwife or doctor will assess and record these changes throughout the pregnancy at each antenatal visit.

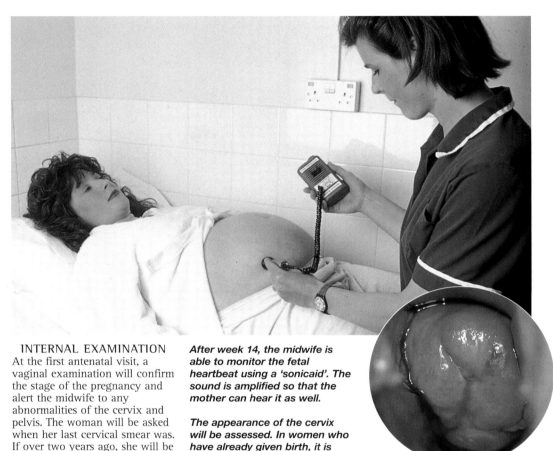

### INTERNAL EXAMINATION
At the first antenatal visit, a vaginal examination will confirm the stage of the pregnancy and alert the midwife to any abnormalities of the cervix and pelvis. The woman will be asked when her last cervical smear was. If over two years ago, she will be offered another one.

*After week 14, the midwife is able to monitor the fetal heartbeat using a 'sonicaid'. The sound is amplified so that the mother can hear it as well.*

*The appearance of the cervix will be assessed. In women who have already given birth, it is usually 'clover-shaped', as here.*

## Cervical changes

The cervix is the muscular neck of the uterus, at the top of the vagina. Its function is to retain the fetus in the uterus during pregnancy. Towards full term, it dilates to allow the passage of the fully grown baby.

During routine examination, the midwife will confirm that the cervix is closed, and it should remain this way until the onset of labour. If the cervix is weak, and this is not detected, a miscarriage may result, especially after the third month.

Just before labour, the cervix will become softer, enabling the birth canal to dilate (become wider) ready for delivery. This is called the ripening of the cervix.

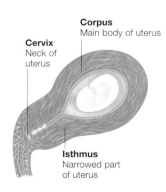

**Cervix** Neck of uterus

**Corpus** Main body of uterus

**Isthmus** Narrowed part of uterus

*Eight weeks into the pregnancy, the shape of the uterus has just begun to change. The cervix is tightly closed.*

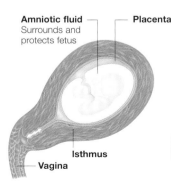

**Amniotic fluid** Surrounds and protects fetus

**Placenta**

**Isthmus**

**Vagina**

*At 12 weeks, the uterus is expanding. As the fetus grows, the isthmus is incorporated into the body of the uterus.*

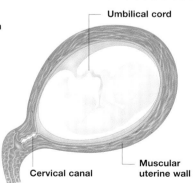

**Umbilical cord**

**Cervical canal**

**Muscular uterine wall**

*At full term, the uterine wall has thinned, so that three distinct layers of muscular tissue are identifiable.*

# Observing uterine development

The most obvious change to a woman's body during pregnancy is her swollen abdomen. She will not begin to 'show' until week 14, but as the pregnancy continues the effect of the growing fetus on a woman's anatomy is striking.

### ULTRASOUND

Whilst the progressive growth of the woman's uterus will be visible externally, ultrasound scanning is used to give a picture of the growing fetus. Most women are offered a scan after 16 weeks, although one may be suggested at any stage of the pregnancy. The great advantage of ultrasound is that, unlike X-ray, it does not expose the fetus to potentially harmful radiation.

The position of the placenta will also be noted on ultrasound. If the placenta is close to the cervical opening, there may be a risk of bleeding, although the placenta normally moves up and away from the opening.

### CONTRACTIONS

From week 14, the uterus is able to contract and this may be stimulated by physical activity. To begin with, the contractions are weak and irregular, and the woman may not even be aware of them, although she will have been told what to expect.

From week 30, the contractions become stronger and more frequent, and they are termed Braxton-Hicks contractions. They are not a sign of impending labour, however, until much closer to full term.

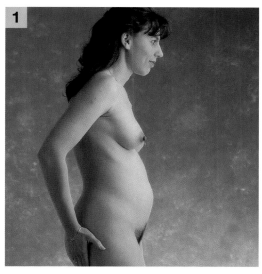

*At week 14, the abdomen begins to protrude, and the uterus extends above the joint between the pubic bones of the pelvis (level with the hips).*

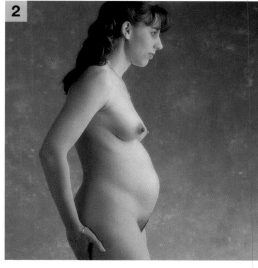

*The top of the uterus reaches the level of the umbilicus (navel) by week 20. It is now beginning to exert pressure underneath the lungs*

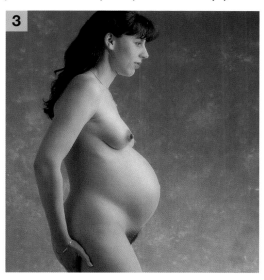

*By week 30 the uterus has reached the ribcage. This restricts the diaphragm, often causing the mother breathlessness.*

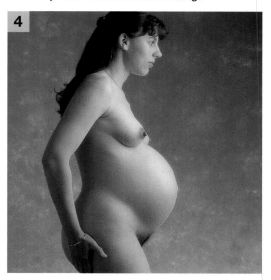

*At 34 weeks, the woman stands with an exaggerated curvature of her lower back, owing to the weight of the uterus.*

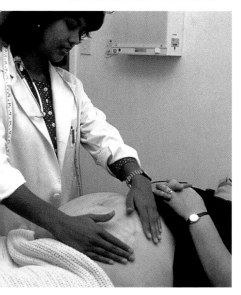

*The doctor or midwife uses the technique of 'fundal palpation' to locate the fetus. This involves palpating (or feeling) the uterus through the abdominal wall.*

## Breast examination

At the first antenatal visit, the woman's breasts will be examined, to check for any abnormalities. The shape of the nipples will also be checked; if they are inverted, for example, the midwife may advise the use of a nipple shield if the woman intends to breast-feed.

Breast changes occur in the first weeks of pregnancy. Women with small breasts will notice an increase in size early on. The breasts often become slightly uncomfortable with a tingling sensation. The brownish circles around the nipples (the areolae) enlarge and become darker and the network of veins in the breast becomes prominent.

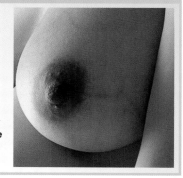

*The breasts increase in size due to enlargement of the mammary glands and deposition of fat. The veins near the surface of the skin may become more visible.*

# Tests during pregnancy

During the course of pregnancy, women are offered various types of routine screening. These include blood tests for specific conditions, ultrasound scanning and amniocentesis.

## Blood tests

A range of tests will be performed on a pregnant woman's blood. These include:

■ Full blood count: will detect anaemia. In the majority of cases the result will be normal, but if the result is abnormal, but if the result is abnormal, further blood tests will be recommended to find the cause. If the woman is anaemic, iron tablets are usually prescribed.

■ Electrophoresis: will determine whether an individual has a hereditary form of anaemia, in particular sickle-cell disease or thalassaemia. These conditions are rare, but if a woman is found to be a carrier it will be recommended that the father be tested to find out if he is also a carrier. If both parents are

carriers, there is a chance that the disease may affect the baby, and further tests will be offered.

■ Blood group: about 85 per cent of women are blood group rhesus positive, and are unlikely to have any complications. Women with the rarer rhesus negative blood group will be recommended to have two injections (called Anti-D) during the antenatal period to prevent their blood reacting against the baby's. The baby's blood group is tested after delivery to see if any further injections of Anti-D are necessary.

*Blood tests are performed at an early stage of pregnancy. They will reveal medical conditions that require special care.*

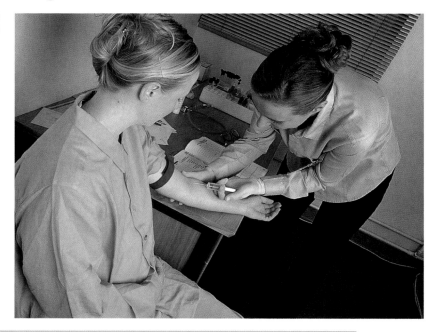

## STD tests

Blood will be examined for evidence of sexually transmitted diseases (STDs). Some women may have an STD without realizing it, and this can affect the health of the baby. The doctor or midwife will check for:

■ Syphilis: a rare sexually transmitted disease which may be passed to the baby. A woman can have this disease without feeling unwell. If this infection is

*Urine and blood tests, combined with consultations, can be used to check for sexually transmitted diseases in the mother-to-be.*

transmitted to the baby, it can affect its development, however, treatment with antibiotics, if begun early, prevents any ill-effects to the fetus.

■ HIV: the human immunodeficiency virus infects and damages the immune system and can be passed from mother to baby during pregnancy, labour or breast-feeding. Rapid advances have been made in the treatment of HIV and AIDS. Without proper advice and treatment, the risk of a baby being infected is up to 30 per cent. However, if appropriate

precautions are taken the risk of the mother passing HIV to her baby is less than two per cent.

■ Hepatitis B: a viral illness that affects the liver and may lead to liver failure. A small proportion of the population carry the hepatitis B virus and most of these will not know about it. It can be transmitted sexually or via contact with infected blood or other body fluids. It is possible for a mother to pass this infection onto her baby, but the baby can be protected from the infection by a course of vaccinations soon after birth.

## Other tests

Rubella and diabetes are two conditions that can be passed across the placenta, greatly affecting the health of the unborn child.

■ Rubella (German measles) Most people will have been vaccinated against this condition in childhood and will be immune. However, sometimes the level of immunity may fall, and it is important for vaccination to be offered following delivery in such cases.

Those who are not immune

should avoid contact with potentially infected individuals during the course of the pregnancy. Rubella, passed on to the unborn child, can result in blindness, deafness, heart problems and learning difficulties.

■ Diabetes
Two per cent of women will develop diabetes during pregnancy. Diabetes is the condition whereby insulin is not converting sugar into energy, and this has major implications

for the well being of both mother and baby. Too much sugar in the mother's body means that the baby could be born extremely large.

Some units will screen for diabetes by regular urine tests, while others use blood tests.

*There a number of conditions that a pregnant woman may have – or develop – that can greatly affect the health of her unborn child. Analysis of blood and urine will reveal the presence of these conditions.*

## Ultrasound examination

The ultrasound examinations offered to women in pregnancy will vary between hospitals. Most will offer a booking scan at the time of the booking visit, which helps in dating the pregnancy.

A more detailed scan is often performed at 20 weeks' gestation to check the development of the fetus. If the doctor or midwife has any concerns regarding the welfare either of the fetus or of the mother, further scans may be organized.

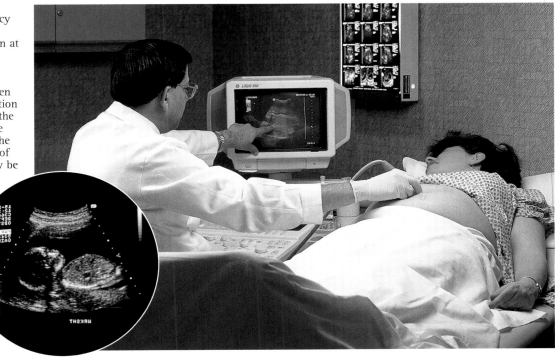

*The ultrasound probe is moved over the abdomen to create a two-dimensional image of the fetus on a monitor.*

*Ultrasound is important for monitoring the fetus' size. This helps to indicate the expected delivery date (EDD).*

## Amniocentesis

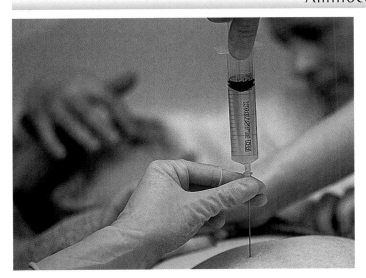

Amniocentesis (taking a sample of the amniotic fluid which surrounds the fetus in the uterus) may be offered in three different ways, depending on local facilities. Amniotic fluid contains cells from the fetus which can be analysed to monitor how the unborn baby is progressing. Chromosomal abnormalities (such as Down's syndrome) can be diagnosed using the test.

In some hospitals, all pregnant women over a certain age (which may vary between 35

*The procedure of amniocentesis is used to detect serious genetic abnormalities in the fetus. Not all pregnant women will need to undergo this test, however.*

and 38) will be offered an amniocentesis.

However, the majority of hospitals now offer some sort of universal testing, usually a blood test at approximately 16 weeks into the pregnancy. The blood test measures different proteins and hormones related to chromosomal abnormalities, and enables pregnant women to learn what risk their pregnancy is at from such conditions. In 95 per cent of cases, the risk will be low – typically less than one in 250.

In the remaining five per cent, the risk may be greater than this, and it is these women who will be offered a routine amniocentesis.

## Regular checkups

The frequency of subsequent visits will vary depending on the local arrangements, whether this is a first or subsequent pregnancy and other relevant medical and obstetric factors. Typically, a woman might be seen every four weeks up to the last month of pregnancy when the visits become more frequent.

At these visits, the blood pressure will be checked and a urine sample analysed for protein content. In addition, the abdomen will be examined to clinically estimate the baby's growth and to hear the baby's heartbeat. It is also an opportunity for mothers to

inquire as to how the pregnancy is progressing, and if they have any questions relating to the pregnancy or the delivery, these can be addressed.

From 32 weeks of pregnancy, much more emphasis is concentrated on the delivery itself, and mothers will often attend antenatal classes. These classes are designed to inform mothers about the mechanism of labour, methods of pain relief and care of the newborn.

*In addition to the healthcare available in pregnancy, antenatal classes are important for the woman to prepare for the birth.*

# Monitoring a healthy pregnancy

Ultrasound scanning is a widely used imaging technique for looking at structures inside the body, including the uterus and fetus. The high-frequency sound waves used are safe for the developing baby.

From a transducer held by a sonographer, high-frequency sound is sent in short pulses through the fluid surrounding the fetus; these are bounced back from various body structures and displayed as a moving picture on a monitor. As the amniotic fluid surrounding the baby transmits ultrasound very well, high quality images can be produced safely. In this way, it is possible to see evidence of pregnancy just a few days after the missed menstrual period, and to monitor the fetus throughout pregnancy.

### PERFORMING A SCAN

The 40 weeks of pregnancy are divided into three 'trimesters'. In the first trimester the fetus is either scanned through the mother's lower abdomen when her bladder is full, or by a vaginal scan. The latter involves the introduction of a transducer, or probe, into the vagina when the bladder is empty; because the probe is very close to the uterus, high quality images are produced.

*From about eight weeks, the fetus may be scanned through the abdomen. A contact jelly is smeared on the mother's abdomen to aid transmission of the sound waves.*

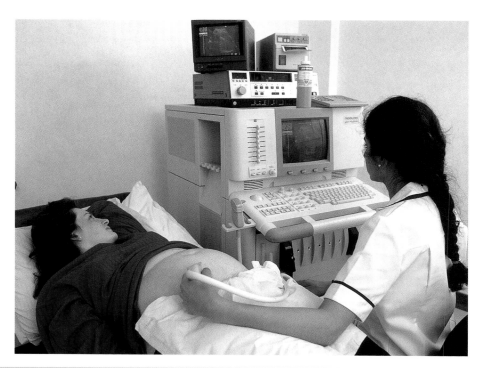

## First trimester

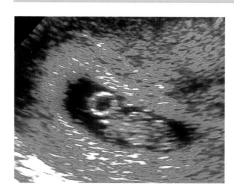

*This is a scan of a five-week embryo. The gestation sac (central black shape) contains the embryo (right) and yolk sac (left).*

### Early transvaginal scan

Scanning the uterus through the vaginal wall is useful for determining the size of an early pregnancy (structures as small as a few millimetres may be seen), for checking the embryo when there has been vaginal bleeding and for the early detection of some developmental problems.

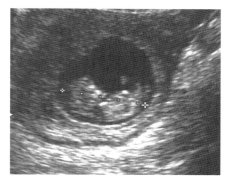

*This scan shows an eight-week fetus. The crosses delineate the crown-to-rump length of the fetus.*

### Monitoring development

The measurement of the crown–rump length from a transabdominal scan of a fetus within the first trimester is usually a more accurate prediction of fetal age than the dating from the mother's last period. It is useful as a baseline for monitoring fetal development later in pregnancy.

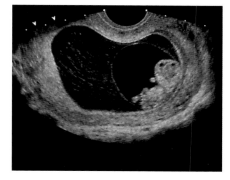

*This detailed transvaginal scan of a nine-week fetus shows the developing limbs, as well as the early placenta membrane (P).*

### Late first trimester scan

Transvaginal scanning provides very detailed images of first-trimester fetuses. From about eight weeks, the fetus is usually also visible on transabdominal scans, but this requires the woman to have a full bladder in order to lift the uterus into the lower abdomen.

## Second trimester

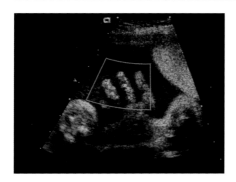

*This image shows the fingers (within the box) and palm of a hand of a fetus in the second trimester. A colour flow scan has been used to show blood flow in the digits.*

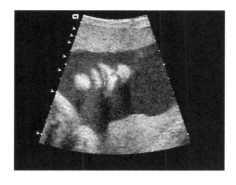

*From the left of this image, the fetal chin, lips, nostrils and nose are visible. Such scans give a clear impression of the baby's developing facial characteristics.*

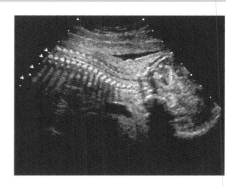

*With the baby's head to the right of the picture, the bones of the spine in the neck and chest can be seen as the row of white dots.*

# Hands and fingers

After about the 16th week of pregnancy, the fetus has grown beyond the reach of vaginal probes and an abdominal scan with a full bladder is required. A routine scan is offered to all pregnant women in the UK and is performed early in the second trimester at around 18 to 20 weeks' gestation. This is the occasion when parents can best recognize many parts of their baby and see its movements. Several measurements of the baby are made – for example, of the head, abdomen and limbs – to check growth or size.

# Facial detail

The detailed scan at 18 to 20 weeks' gestation is also known as 'the anomaly scan' because the anatomy of the fetus is examined for any structural abnormality, such as may occur with the lips or palate. The size of the fetus at this stage of its development means that only one part of it can be seen at any one time by the transducer. However, the sonographers are skilled at orientating the transducer to visualize individual structures, and they can then explain to the parents what can be seen.

# Spinal column

As the pregnancy enters the second trimester more detailed scans can be obtained, so that any abnormalities of development can be detected and treated appropriately. The structures examined in detail include the heart, diaphragm, stomach, spine and kidneys. Scans of the spine are used to assess spinal formation and structure, looking in particular for evidence of problems such as spina bifida (failure of closure of the spinal column in the midline), and spinal masses, such as meningoceles.

## Third trimester

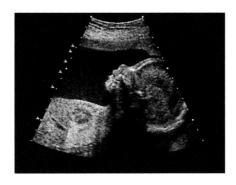

*This is an ultrasound scan of a third-trimester fetus showing a clear profile of the baby's face. The brain within the skull and the heart and spine can also be seen.*

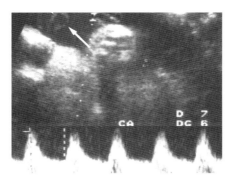

*This Doppler scan shows the rate of blood flow through an umbilical artery. The umbilical cord contains the umbilical vein and two smaller umbilical arteries.*

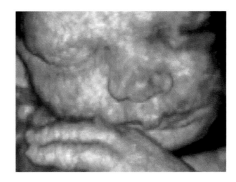

*This is a three-dimensional image of a fetus' face and hands. Such images are created by computer composition from sequential ultrasound sections.*

# Growth and weight

In the third trimester, ultrasound is used to check the placental position and to assess fetal growth and weight. By taking measurements of the head, abdominal girth and length of the thigh bone, and adding these to a formula, the weight of the fetus can be predicted. The baby's weight may be less than the calculated value, but this may simply be because the mother and/or father are of short stature. However, it may mean that the baby is is not growing as it should, and action can be taken.

# Doppler ultrasound

The technique of Doppler ultrasound can show the distribution of blood and oxygen to the fetus. Certain fetal blood vessels, such as the umbilical artery in the cord, the internal cerebral arteries in the head, and veins within the fetal liver, are highlighted in colour and examined. Often the blood flow within vessels is transmitted audibly as pulses of sound. Doppler ultrasound is also routinely used to detect the fetal heartbeat throughout pregnancy and during labour to monitor fetal health.

# 3D ultrasound imaging

This technique is not yet routine and its value is still being studied. However, as seen from the above image, the face, hands and feet can be studied in detail and any abnormalities identified; decisions can thus be made as to the management of the pregnancy at an early stage. Another study performed in the third trimester is known as a biophysical profile, which examines fetal activity such as breathing and various movements. As a result of these scans, decisions may be made as to where, when and how a baby is delivered.

# Monitoring the metabolism in pregnancy

In order to provide for a developing baby, a woman's body must increase its metabolic rate. This produces noticeable changes in weight, respiratory rate and cardiac output, all of which are routinely monitored.

The average weight gain in pregnancy is 12.5 kg (27 lb). However, there is a wide variation and women may gain between 5 kg (11 lb) and 17 kg (37 lb). The average weight gain for a woman after the twelfth week of pregnancy is about 0.4 kg (14 oz) per week.

Women are advised to keep weight gain to a minimum, whilst ensuring fetal growth, in order to reduce stress on their joints and cardiovascular system. The metabolic rate of the body increases by up to 25 per cent during the pregnancy. Most of this increase is to ensure the normal metabolism of the fetus and its supporting tissues. The demand for calories increases and therefore the appetite is stimulated.

*Folic acid, one of the B vitamins, helps fetal development. It can be taken as a dietary supplement.*

*Swollen ankles are common in pregnancy. The swelling is caused by water retention and is eased by raising the legs.*

## Weight gain in pregnancy

The average increase is made up as follows:

| | |
|---|---|
| **Fetus** | 3.4 kg (9.1 lb) |
| **Placenta** | 0.65 kg (1.8 lb) |
| **Amniotic fluid** | 0.8 kg (2.1 lb) |
| **Uterus** | 1.0 kg (2.2 lb) |
| **Breasts** | 0.8 kg (2.1 lb) |
| **Body fat, protein and fluid retention** | 6 kg (13 lb) |

*Women are weighed regularly during pregnancy. This checks that the baby is growing well.*

### FOLIC ACID
Often deficient in pregnant women, folic acid is necessary for the activities of the enzymes involved in the manufacture of nucleic acids (cell genetic material). Supplements are advised in the first three months, because they can help to prevent congenital malformations, such as spina bifida, in the fetus.

### WATER RETENTION
Oedema, or water retention, is often exhibited in pregnant women. It is commonly due to distended veins in the legs that leak fluid into the surrounding tissues. In some women, it may be a sign that the kidneys are malfunctioning. These women will be tested for the presence of protein in their urine.

## Cardiovascular changes

At the first antenatal examination, the mother's heart will be checked, together with that of the fetus.

A woman's cardiac output typically increases by up to 40 per cent during pregnancy. This is a result of an increased pulse and a small increase in the volume of the blood pumped with each heart contraction. This change occurs early in the first half of the pregnancy and tends to level out during the second.

### OXYGEN DEMANDS
The increased cardiac output is designed to cope with the greater demands placed on the heart as more oxygen is required by the developing tissues. The baby's rapid growth demands and the significant changes in the maternal anatomy require a considerable oxygen supply. The vaginal walls become softer and more relaxed. In addition a mother's muscles use more oxygen to cope with the increased workload in pregnancy. The extra cardiac output is achieved by the increase in the amount of blood pumped, and by an increased rate of heart contraction.

Some women develop high blood pressure (hypertension) in pregnancy. Although minor fluctuations are normal, variations will be carefully monitored and, if necessary, treated with medication.

*Later in the pregnancy, the doctor or midwife can use a stethoscope for a fetal heartbeat examination. The woman's own heartbeat will also be measured.*

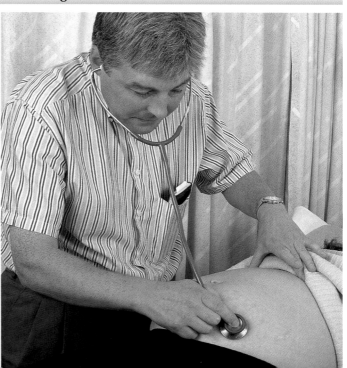

# Effects of increased hormones

Many of the anatomical and physical changes of pregnancy are hormonally induced. Some of them have unwanted side effects that require treatment.

### BREATHLESSNESS
Many women experience a feeling of shortness of breath during pregnancy – this is probably an effect of the hormone progesterone. The hormone increases the sensitivity of the brain to changes in the blood carbon dioxide levels leading to stimulation of respiratory centres.

The principal anatomical change is the elevation of the diaphragm, particularly in late pregnancy. This is caused by an upward flaring of the rib cage. These sensations are tolerated to different degrees but may also give rise to the sensation of marked shortness of breath.

### RISK OF URINARY INFECTION
Blood flow to the kidneys rises by 40 per cent during pregnancy, increasing the ability of the kidney to filter waste products. Again, the hormone progesterone is implicated in the muscular changes that give rise to a relaxation of the blood vessels and muscle. The marked increase in the frequency of micturition (urination) is due to increased urine production, which is more noticeable in early pregnancy.

In late pregnancy, the enlarging uterus compressing the bladder also raises the frequency of micturition. Progesterone also

## Changes to the urinary tract

**Before pregnancy**

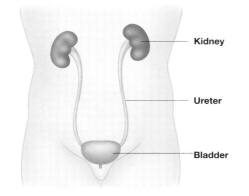

Kidney

Ureter

Bladder

**During pregnancy**

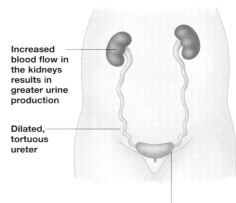

Increased blood flow in the kidneys results in greater urine production

Dilated, tortuous ureter

Bladder compressed by growing uterus

*During pregnancy, the ureters lengthen and become more tortuous and dilated. The expanding uterus puts pressure on the bladder below.*

has an effect on the muscle walls of the ureters, causing them to dilate. One possible detrimental effect of this change is an increased risk of urinary tract infection. For this reason, routine screening for bacteria in the urine is often carried out

### BACKACHE
It is quite common for a pregnant woman to suffer from backache. The body releases hormones that soften the

ligaments and muscles supporting the pelvic girdle. Joints in which the bones are separated by cartilage are particularly affected, such as the back vertebrae and the sacroiliac joints in the pelvis. Without the loosening of the joint between the pelvic bones (symphysis pubica), a newborn could not fit through the birth canal.

If a woman is suffering from joint pain the best remedy is rest. Paracetamol is preferred by many women to relieve the pain, but non-steroidal anti-inflammatory drugs, such as ibuprofen, may be used with the GP's consent, if necessary up to

the last four weeks of the pregnancy. If the pain persists, a woman may need treatment from an obstetric physiotherapist, who can take her through a series of pelvic and back exercises to improve her posture and ease the discomfort.

If a pregnant woman is experiencing pain in her legs, she may require further examination. Investigation by radiography (X-ray) may become necessary to eliminate conditions, such as congenital bony anomalies, a prolapsed intervertebral disc or osteoporosis of pregnancy.

*Backache in pregnant women is very common. Antenatal classes can give advice on good posture to ease the pain.*

*Regular rest is needed to take the pressure off the lower back. Straining the spine should be avoided.*

# Detecting chromosome abnormalities

Pregnant women may be offered screening and testing for certain chromosome abnormalities that can affect the fetus. A range of tests are available to identify conditions such as Down's syndrome.

Any pregnancy, irrespective of maternal age, may be complicated by a chromosome abnormality, such as Down's syndrome, which is the commonest live-born chromosome anomaly. There are many other potential chromosome abnormalities, some of which are fatal and will result in the early loss of a pregnancy. Other chromosome abnormalities may result in the pregnancy continuing initially but ending in either a late intra-uterine death or death of the newborn.

## FETAL CELLS
In pregnancy, the definitive investigations to detect chromosome abnormalities rely on obtaining fetal cells so that the chromosome makeup of the fetus can be determined.

Ideally, fetal cells would be obtained without having to put the pregnancy at risk. Research has been undertaken to attempt to isolate fetal cells from the mother's blood, and this might lead to the ability to determine the fetal karyotype without having to place the pregnancy at risk.

Ultimately, the determination of fetal chromosomes relies on invasive tests: chorion villus sampling, amniocentesis and cordocentesis. These tests are undertaken from 11–14 weeks of gestation, at 15-19 weeks and after 20 weeks respectively.

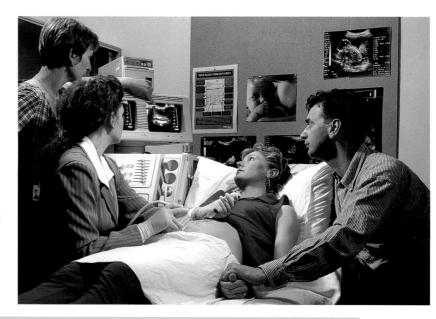

*Ultrasound scanning is used in conjunction with invasive tests: this imaging technique can be used to guide a needle to a site where tissue can be sampled.*

## Tests at 11–14 weeks

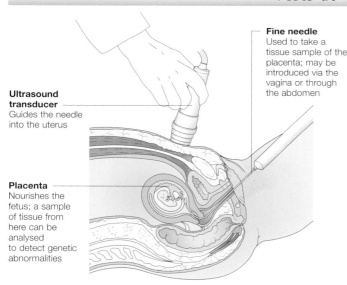

**Fine needle**
Used to take a tissue sample of the placenta; may be introduced via the vagina or through the abdomen

**Ultrasound transducer**
Guides the needle into the uterus

**Placenta**
Nourishes the fetus; a sample of tissue from here can be analysed to detect genetic abnormalities

From 11 to 14 weeks of gestation, women may be offered a nuchal translucency scan; if warranted, chorion villus sampling may then be undertaken.

### ■ Nuchal translucency
Ultrasound observations in the late 1980s and early 1990s suggested that a small space at the back of the baby's neck may increase in size in babies with chromosome abnormalities. The dimensions of this space, the mother's age and the size of the baby allow a calculation of risk. In addition, measurements of proteins and hormones in early pregnancy, combined with information from an ultrasound scan, provides a more accurate risk estimate.

*Chorion villus sampling is an invasive procedure whereby a needle is passed through the vagina or the abdominal wall to take a sample of placental tissue.*

Evidence suggests that nuchal translucency screening detects 85–90 per cent of chromosome defects. The scan is performed at 11–14 weeks' gestation. Women with a positive screen may be offered chorion villus sampling, amniocentesis or a detailed anomaly ultrasound scan.

### ■ Chorion villus sampling
This is an invasive procedure in which a small piece of placental tissue is removed. Because the placenta originates from the fertilized egg it will normally contain the same cells as the fetus.

Two techniques are used: in the transcervical approach a fine needle is guided by ultrasound through the cervix into the placental tissue; in the abdominal approach a needle is inserted into the placenta through the mother's abdomen. Local anaesthetic is usually given prior to insertion of the needle, and about 30 mg of placental tissue is aspirated for examination. There is a 1–2 per cent risk of miscarriage.

Chorion villus sampling before nine weeks has been associated with abnormal limb formation in some babies, so early tests are no longer undertaken. The test has the advantage of early diagnosis of potential abnormalities.

*Once a sample of placental tissue has been taken it can be analysed for genetic abnormalities. This tissue has the same genotype as the fetus.*

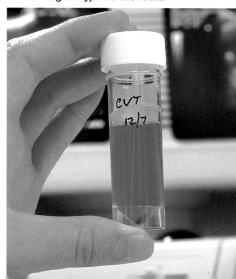

## Tests at 15–19 weeks

Later in the pregnancy, further testing and screening to look for abnormalities may be undertaken.

### ■ Amniocentesis

Amniocentesis is performed under ultrasound guidance and involves guiding a fine needle through the abdomen into the amniotic sac. This test is usually performed at 16 weeks' gestation and is routinely offered to women over 35.

Approximately 15-20 ml of amniotic fluid is aspirated and sent for analysis. In some

centres a provisional result can now be obtained for common chromosome abnormalities within three days; however, the final culture result takes between two and three weeks.

Unfortunately the test has a risk of miscarriage of approximately one per cent. There is also a small risk of the cells failing to grow and therefore giving no result, or the cells growing in a confusing manner, resulting in a mixture of cells (a 'mosaic'), necessitating another test.

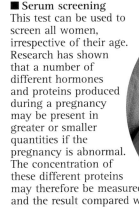

### ■ Serum screening

This test can be used to screen all women, irrespective of their age. Research has shown that a number of different hormones and proteins produced during a pregnancy may be present in greater or smaller quantities if the pregnancy is abnormal. The concentration of these different proteins may therefore be measured and the result compared with the expected level.

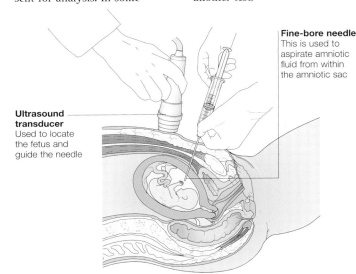

**Fine-bore needle**
This is used to aspirate amniotic fluid from within the amniotic sac

**Ultrasound transducer**
Used to locate the fetus and guide the needle

### ASSESSING RISK

Combining the results of the test with the mother's age and the gestation of the pregnancy allows each pregnancy to be given an individual assessment of the likelihood of being affected by Down's syndrome. This risk may vary from as much as one in two to – more commonly – one in several hundreds or thousands.

An amniocentesis would normally be offered to a woman if the risk of her child being

*Amniotic fluid is sampled through a fine needle, which is guided into the uterus via ultrasound. This test involves a small risk of miscarriage.*

*Amniotic fluid withdrawn from the amniotic sac contains fetal cells. These can be cultured in order to look for common chromosome abnormalities.*

affected proved to be one in 250 or less.

It is important to stress that serum testing is a screening test and is not diagnostic. It is able to pick up approximately 60-70 per cent of pregnancies affected by Down's syndrome, assuming that the majority of women who are given a high-risk score will elect for the option of invasive testing. This test is offered in the majority of maternity centres.

## Tests after 20 weeks

At 20 weeks' gestation many fetuses with chromosome abnormalities will have structural defects. For example, around one-third of fetuses with Down's syndrome will have a cardiac defect. Many babies with trisomy 13 or 18 (additional chromosomes) will have abnormal finger, toe, kidney, lip or brain formation.

### ■ Anomaly scanning

Structural abnormalities can be identified on an anomaly ultrasound scan. Babies in whom

*Ultrasound testing is carried out again at about 20 weeks into a pregnancy. By this time it is often able to detect physical abnormalities of the fetus.*

more than one of these abnormalities are detected will be considerably more at risk of potential problems. Depending on the nature of the abnormality it may be appropriate to offer invasive testing to determine whether or not the abnormality observed is caused by a chromosome defect.

The ultrasound scan is not a diagnostic test, and without invasive testing it will detect approximately 50 per cent of babies with Down's syndrome.

### ■ Cordocentesis

This is the least common type of invasive test, performed only in specialist centres from 20 weeks. The procedure involves inserting

*If an anomaly scan has detected physical abnormalities, the woman will be offered invasive tests in order to give a more accurate diagnosis.*

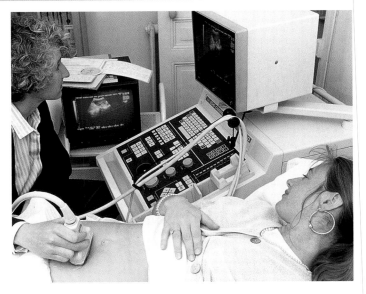

a fine needle into the umbilical cord and taking fetal blood for examination. In specialist hands the risk of miscarriage is around one per cent; the risk of culture failure or confusing results is much smaller.

The test will more often be offered if there are abnormalities detected during scanning which

are associated with chromosome abnormalities. For example, heart defects are known to be associated with Down's syndrome, and therefore the detection of these at the anomaly scan at 20 weeks would normally be an indication to offer the option of invasive testing.

# Multiple pregnancy

A multiple pregnancy is often diagnosed by ultrasound scanning early in the pregnancy. Multiple pregnancies are demanding on the mother's body and are almost always delivered pre-term.

Throughout history, multiple births have always been considered a fascinating phenomenon, bringing about a wide variety of emotional responses in their parents, ranging from delight to fear. More multiple pregnancies occur today than has ever been the case, yet they remain high risk and care during pregnancy and labour should be provided by experienced doctors and midwives.

### EARLY SIGNS AND DIAGNOSIS

Multiple pregnancy may be suspected when the patient has a strong family history multiple births, or when the following indicators are present:
■ Larger uterus than would be expected for a woman's dates
■ Heightened symptoms of pregnancy, in particular nausea and vomiting.

Definitive diagnosis is made by ultrasound scan, which can take place as early as six weeks of pregnancy when, with twins, two separate heartbeats may be seen. It is now known that many more pregnancies start out as twins than are born, with up to 20 per cent of early twin pregnancies resulting in miscarriage of one embryo before the end of the first trimester.

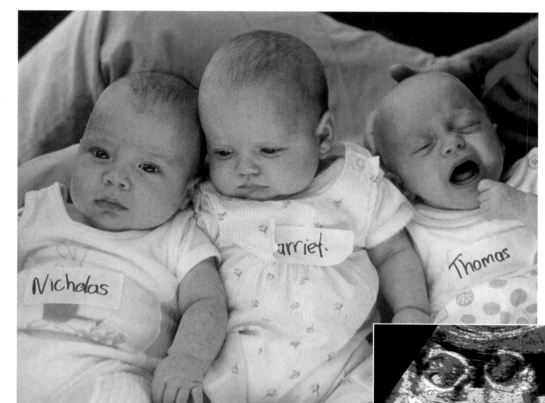

**With the development and increasing use of assisted reproductive technology, the incidence of multiple pregnancies has increased.**

**Multiple pregnancies are usually confirmed on routine ultrasound scans. This coloured scan shows twins – their heads are seen in the upper part of the image.**

## Embryonic development of twins

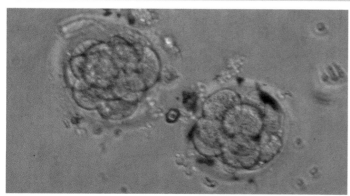

**Two fertilized embryos consisting of eight cells can be seen in this micrograph. Fertility treatments often result in multiple pregnancies.**

*It is recommended that expectant mothers carrying a multiple pregnancy take extra care to reduce the risk of high blood pressure.*

### INCIDENCE

The rate of identical twin births is fairly constant throughout the world at about four per 1,000, but the chance of non-identical twins is dependent upon factors such as race, age and number of previous children.

A 37-year-old woman is four times more likely to have twins than a 20-year-old woman. Overall, around 1 in 80 natural births are twins and 1 in 6400 are triplets – the true birth rates are higher than this because of the widespread use of fertility drugs.

Twins can arise in two ways:
■ One egg is released and fertilized, and divides very early during development
■ Two eggs are released, each being separately fertilized by an individual spermatozoon.

The first case results in identical twins (known as monozygotic), who have the same genetic make-up; the second explains the more common finding of non-identical twins (dizygotic).

# Monitoring a multiple pregnancy

Once a multiple pregnancy has been confirmed,
a woman will undergo regular scans to monitor the
growth of the fetuses and to watch for complications.

Most pregnant women are
referred to hospital between 14
and 20 weeks' gestation; this is
when a multiple pregnancy is
usually confirmed.

## POSSIBLE COMPLICATIONS
Most complications of pregnancy
are more common with multiples,
and therefore additional antenatal
care is required. Some of the
complications relate to the extra
load on the maternal metabolism
of a twin pregnancy, including:
■ Production of an extra half-
litre of blood
■ Faster and stronger heartbeat
■ Extra nutritional requirement.
   High blood pressure is two to
three times more common in
twin pregnancies and is more
likely to begin earlier.
   Fetal growth is usually the
same as single development
until about 32 weeks; after this
time, the chance of growth
problems increases.

## SPECIFIC TESTS
A blood test to screen for
Down's syndrome is much less
accurate for twin pregnancies,
but the risk can be assessed by
using an ultrasound scan to look
for a thickened neck fold or
nuchal translucency. These
issues will be discussed at the
first visit, and a scan at 18–20
weeks is usually offered to check
everything else appears normal.
   Where babies share a placenta
and membranes (monochorionic)
there is a risk of a rare condition
where connecting blood vessels
can lead to one baby growing at
the expense of the other (twin-
to-twin transfusion syndrome).
Scans for this problem usually
begin at 24–26 weeks.

## DELIVERY
Around one-third of twins are
delivered before 37 weeks and
prematurity is one of the greatest
risks with multiple pregnancy.

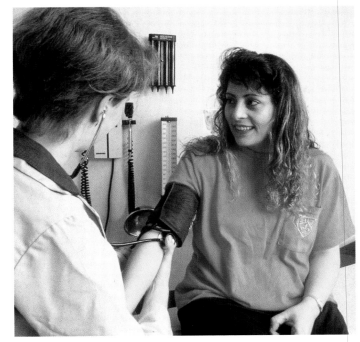

The average length of pregnancy
for twins is 37 weeks, whereas
triplets are delivered 35 weeks,
and quadruplets 28 weeks after
conception. Multiple births are
more likely to be delivered by
Caesarean section.

*Twins are almost always
delivered before their due
date. This is because an over-
distended uterus can lead to
premature labour.*

*It is routine for a paediatrician
to be present at a twin delivery
as there is an increased risk of
complications. The mother also
requires careful assessment.*

*Raised blood pressure is a
common complication of
multiple pregnancies. Regular
monitoring of the mother's blood
pressure will therefore be needed.*

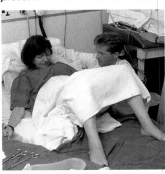

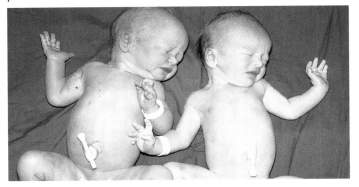

## Fetal presentations

### Head/head

*At the end of pregnancy, 80 per cent of
twins present with the first baby head-
down, and in just over half of these both
babies deliver head-first. It is quite safe to
have an epidural for twin labour, and many
obstetricians actively encourage this as it
provides very good analgesia in case any
assistance is required.*

### Head/breech

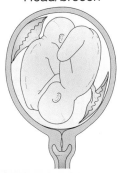

*In general, the important factor is the
presentation of the first baby – even if the
second twin is breech, it is usually safe to
have a routine delivery. Head/breech
presentations account for approximately
25 per cent of deliveries. Sometimes the
second twin will require assisted delivery
or possibly a Caesarean section.*

### Breech/breech

*Sometimes it is safe to deliver
breech/breech twins vaginally, but for the
breech/head combination Caesarean
section is usually advised. Triplets and
higher multiples are usually delivered by
Caesarean section. The risk of post-partum
(post-birth) haemorrhage is increased in
multiple deliveries.*

# Common problems during pregnancy

Pregnancy involves a large number of physical changes for women. These in turn may give rise to certain awkward problems, such as varicose veins, stress incontinence and carpal tunnel syndrome.

The many physical changes which can affect women during pregnancy include:

■ Softening and stretching of ligaments and muscles – due to the increase in the levels of progesterone and relaxin. These 'pregnancy hormones' help the body to prepare for the birth of the baby. However, the changes they bring about are thought to contribute to musculoskeletal problems, such as back pain, sacro-iliac pain and pubic symphysis pain. The muscles of the pelvic floor can become less efficient, resulting in stress incontinence.

■ Pressure on structures of the body – caused by the growing fetus. Pressure is exerted downwards on the pelvic veins and pelvic floor muscles and is a contributing factor in varicose veins and stress incontinence. The fetus can also press upwards on the diaphragm and ribcage.

■ Water retention – can cause carpal tunnel syndrome.

*Physical changes occur during pregnancy to accommodate the baby. These changes can have unpleasant symptoms, and may cause the mother discomfort.*

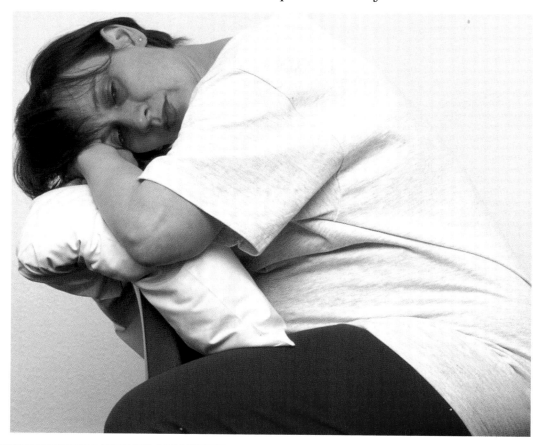

## Varicose veins

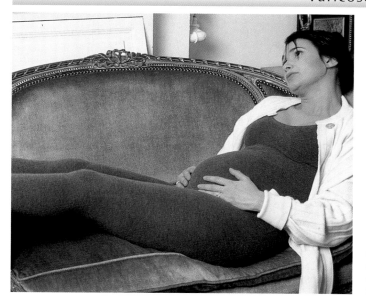

*Varicose veins are common during pregnancy. To minimize discomfort pregnant women can elevate their feet, helping blood to flow to the heart.*

Varicose (distended) veins can be aggravated or appear for the first time during pregnancy.

### CAUSES
Varicose veins can be caused by the growing fetus putting pressure on the pelvic veins and on the inferior (lower) vena cava, which takes blood from the lower body back up to the heart. Progesterone causes the walls of the blood vessels to relax, making them less efficient. Pregnant women may in addition suffer from haemorrhoids and varicose veins around the vulva.

### REDUCING PROBLEMS
Several measures can help to alleviate varicose veins:

■ Moving up and down on tiptoe – helps to activate the calf muscles when standing for long periods of time

■ Resting on the left side – this decreases the pressure on the vena cava, which is on the right

■ Elevating feet when resting – helps blood flow to the heart

■ Not crossing legs

■ Not wearing short, tight-fitting socks

■ Wearing maternity support tights – if doing a job that involves much standing

■ Doing pelvic floor exercises – improves the blood flow in women suffering from haemorrhoids or vulval varicose veins.

# Stress incontinence

Stress incontinence is the involuntary loss of urine due to an increase in intra-abdominal pressure, such as when coughing, sneezing or laughing or in physical activity. It often occurs after childbirth, although many women suffer while pregnant.

Women who have already had children are most likely to suffer from stress incontinence, as the muscles that close off the bladder and prevent leakage of urine have already been stretched and weakened. These muscles are called the pelvic floor muscles. It is thought that the increased levels of the hormones relaxin and progesterone during pregnancy are responsible for softening and relaxing them.

## MANAGING STRESS INCONTINENCE

It is important that women start doing pelvic floor exercises during pregnancy. Not only will this strengthen the muscles during pregnancy, but it will make it more likely that the muscles continue to strengthen after the baby is born.

Research has shown that women who do pelvic floor exercises while pregnant suffer from less stress incontinence than those who wait until after the birth of their baby.

## CONTRACTING PELVIC FLOOR MUSCLES

The pelvic floor muscles are used when attempting to stop the flow of urine while on the toilet. A woman can feel these muscles contract if she puts a finger inside her vagina and tightens the muscles.

It is a good idea for women to practise contracting and relaxing these muscles several times every day during pregnancy.

## STRENGTHENING EXERCISES

There are a number of exercises for pregnant women which can help to strengthen the pelvic floor muscles; these include the following:

■ When sitting or standing –

placing hands on the stomach below the navel with the fingers pointing down towards the pubic bone. The pelvic floor muscles are then contracted as if wanting to pull them up towards the hands. This involves squeezing as hard as possible, and then relaxing.

■ When sitting or standing – imagining the pelvic floor as a lift. It is then contracted for a

*Pelvic floor muscle exercises can be done lying down, sitting or standing. Contracting and relaxing these muscles helps women to strengthen them and gain muscle control.*

count of five, and tightened hard; then counting from five down to one, the pelvic floor should be lowered, relaxing the muscle. This is a good exercise for gaining muscle control.

## Carpal tunnel syndrome

At the base of the palm is a tight area (the carpal tunnel), through which tendons from the arm and the median nerve have to pass to enter the hand.

### Compressed nerve

If fluid retention during pregnancy reduces the space in the carpal tunnel sufficiently, the nerve can become compressed. This results in a tingling sensation and numbness in the thumb and index, middle and ring fingers.

Pain and discomfort can be worse at night when the hand 'wakes up' after being compressed during the day.

*Carpal tunnel syndrome is caused by fluid retention during pregnancy. The reduced space in the tunnel compresses the median nerve, causing tingling.*

### Splinting

A physiotherapist will assess the condition and may prescribe a splint to keep the hand in a neutral position. This is the position which maximizes the amount of space for the passage of the nerve through the tunnel.

### Alleviating pain

Keeping the arms hanging down by the side for long periods of time will encourage fluid build-up and so this should be avoided as much as possible.

If tingling at night is a problem, sitting in an armchair with the arms on the armrests before going to bed may reduce the swelling sufficiently for the tingling sensation to die down before bedtime. The problem usually disappears shortly after childbirth.

# Treating musculoskeletal disorders in pregnancy

Musculoskeletal disorders, such as back and rib pain, are a common problem during pregnancy. Almost 50 per cent of pregnant women are thought to suffer from them.

Back pain in pregnancy is caused by an increased laxity of the ligaments of the spine due to high levels of the hormones relaxin and progesterone. This makes the spine more vulnerable during strenuous exercise and lifting. The sacro-iliac joint (in the pelvis) is particularly vulnerable owing to an increase in shear forces between the sacrum and the ilium.

As the fetus grows, changes in posture and weight-bearing lead to stress on different areas of the spine. This can be aggravated by poor posture.

### AREAS OF PAIN

The pain may be localized to the low back or radiate into the groin, buttock or leg. Pain down the back of the leg may be due to irritation of the sciatic nerve. Pain from the sacro-iliac joint is usually localized to one side of the sacrum, although it can also be felt in the groin.

### AVOIDING BACK PAIN

Pregnant women should take particular care when lifting (such as taking shopping out of the car). Although exercise is beneficial, certain activities (weight-lifting, for example) can provoke back pain, as certain movements can put a strain on the pelvis. Simple activities such as breaststroke when swimming can aggravate sacro-iliac joint

pain. While special antenatal yoga classes can help improve posture and breathing, over-stretching should be avoided.

When sitting for long periods in a chair there should be lumbar support. Putting one foot on a low stool when standing will reduce the lumbar lordosis (the arch in the lower back). Wearing low-heeled shoes and practising pelvic tilting to straighten the back will help.

### MANAGING BACK PAIN

The transversus abdominis is part of the deep abdominal group of muscles which act like a corset and support the spine. Women with a history of low back pain may benefit from improving the postural tone of this muscle early in pregnancy.

If the pain is severe or lasts for more than a few days a referral to a physiotherapist or osteopath for an assessment may be needed. He or she will be able to mobilize the spine gently to relieve the pain and prescribe remedial exercises.

A maternity support belt can relieve the pain from sacro-iliac joint problems, as it maintains the stability of the pelvis.

*Back pain affects around half of all pregnant women. Those who have suffered previously from back pain are more likely to have a recurrence during pregnancy.*

## Rib pain

Pain in the ribs may be experienced in the third trimester of pregnancy. This may be due to the fetus in the uterus pushing up inside the ribcage or to a strain of the muscles and ligaments around the ribcage. It is often worse on one side and can be very sore, especially when the baby kicks. Women usually experience relief once

*Rib pain during the late stages of pregnancy is caused by the baby pushing upwards into the ribcage. Stretching the arms above the head relieves this.*

the fetus has moved down into the pelvis in late pregnancy.

### MANAGING RIB PAIN

When sitting down, the small of the back should be supported. Particular care should be taken when sitting in a car; a small cushion or rolled-up towel placed in the small of the back may help. Stretching the arms above the head may relieve rib pain. A physiotherapist or osteopath can perform gentle mobilization techniques and give advice on pain-relieving positions.

# Pubic dysfunction

The two main bones of the pelvis join at the front to form the pubic symphysis. During pregnancy, the hormones relaxin and progesterone soften the ligament in this joint, which can result in excessive movement and severe pain.

The softening of the pubic symphysis in pregnancy, thanks to increased hormone levels, can lead to pubic dysfunction. While it is important for the pelvis to be flexible enough to allow the baby to pass through it during childbirth, excess movement at the pubic symphysis can cause severe and debilitating pain.

Although this is not a common complication of pregnancy, the symptoms should be recognized so that remedial action can be taken.

### SYMPTOMS
Pain is usually felt in the pubic region but can also radiate into the groin, abdomen and legs. If the problem is severe the joint may 'click' when one leg is moved up and down.

Going up and down stairs, standing on one leg, walking and even rolling over in bed may be painful. The pubic symphysis may be extremely tender to the touch.

### RELIEVING PUBIC DYSFUNCTION
A physiotherapist or osteopath experienced in obstetric problems will be able to offer advice to pregnant women with pubic dysfunction. A maternity support belt will be useful to help limit movement between the two pubic bones.

Women will be taught how to do certain activities such as getting out of bed and the car without placing stress on the pubic symphysis.

It is important that everyone involved in the labour is made aware of the problem, as stretching the legs wide apart to deliver the baby may aggravate the condition.

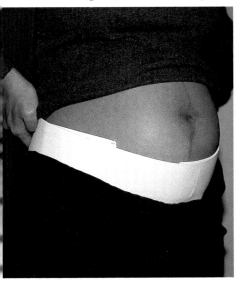

*Women with pubic dysfunction may find certain movements painful. Learning how to move without straining the pubic symphysis, for example when getting out of a car, can help.*

*A maternity support belt will help reduce lower back pain during pregnancy by supporting some of the weight of the baby.*

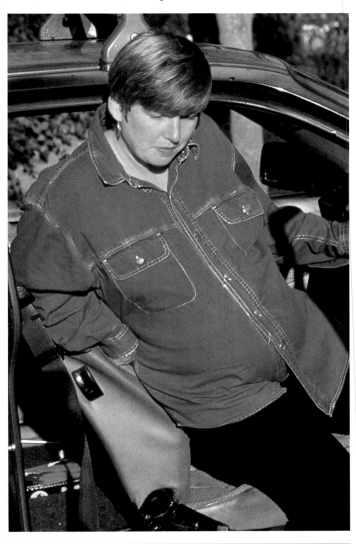

---

## Prenatal exercises

There are a number of exercises that may help reduce some of the discomfort experienced during pregnancy. It is important that pregnant women perform these exercises in moderation.

*Gently arching the back while positioned on all fours helps to stretch the spine. By strengthening the muscles in the back and pelvis this exercise also helps to reduce backache.*

*Doing sit-ups with the legs raised on a chair will help to ease leg cramps and reduce varicose veins in the leg. This exercise will also strengthen the abdominal muscles.*

*Drawing the leg up and across the body while lying on one side, stretches the spine and pelvis. This exercise helps to reduce the pressure of the fetus on the spine, relieving backache.*

# Bleeding during pregnancy

Bleeding during pregnancy can, if serious, threaten the lives of both mother and baby. There are a number of possible causes, and treatment involves close monitoring and, sometimes, Caesarean section.

Bleeding during pregnancy, or antepartum haemorrhage, is defined as significant bleeding from the birth canal after the 24th week of pregnancy. This may lead to an inadequate blood supply to the baby, and therefore poses a risk to the well-being of both mother and baby.

## CAUSES

There are several causes for bleeding; the likely diagnosis depends on the exact symptoms and degree of bleeding. Most bleeding is minor, and settles spontaneously, but all bleeding in pregnancy should be reported.

*A cardiotocograph is used to detect uterine contractions and monitor fetal heartbeat. The first signs of premature contractions may be detected this way.*

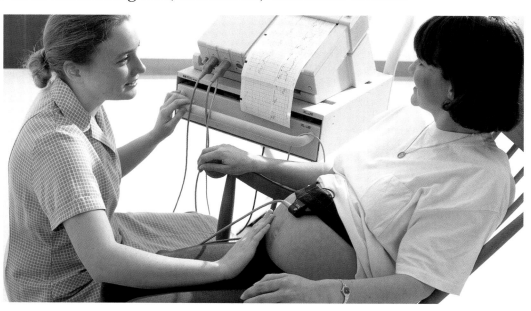

## Possible causes of bleeding

The bleeding comes from either the placenta or the cervix. A vital distinction is whether the placenta is located low in the uterus (placenta praevia) or not.

■ **Bleeding from the cervix**
During pregnancy the lining of the cervical canal may become everted, a condition called cervical erosion or ectropion. The canal lining is delicate and may bleed. Bleeding is usually minor and often occurs after sexual intercourse. Sometimes infection can cause an ectropion along with an offensive vaginal discharge.

■ **Placenta praevia**
This is defined as a low-lying placenta after 28 weeks' gestation. At 18 weeks one in six women has a low-lying placenta, but as the uterus grows, the relative positions change and most placentas are found at the top of the uterus by 28 weeks. It is more common in smokers, women who have had a previous Caesarean section, and older mothers.

■ **Placental abruption**
If the placenta separates from the uterus, it is called an abruption. This is a serious condition, particularly when the abruption affects a large area of placenta. The bleeding may lead to premature labour. Major placental abruption requires immediate Caesarean delivery as the blood supply to the baby is cut off. Minor degrees of suspected abruption can be managed without delivery, but both mother and baby must be monitored closely.

■ **Marginal bleed**
Marginal bleeding arises from a small area at the edge of the placenta, and does not harm mother or fetus. When the cervix appears normal and there is no placenta praevia or suggestion of abruption, the final diagnosis – a marginal bleed – is made by exclusion. Typically, the bleeding settles within 24 hours.

## Common causes of bleeding

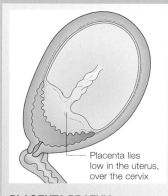

Placenta lies low in the uterus, over the cervix

**PLACENTA PRAEVIA**
*Bleeding may be profuse with circulatory collapse – this is life-threatening for mother and baby. Caesarean section will be necessary.*

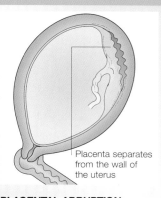

Placenta separates from the wall of the uterus

**PLACENTAL ABRUPTION**
*This is potentially life-threatening to mother and baby, and gives rise to acute abdominal pain and maternal collapse. Immediate delivery is often necessary.*

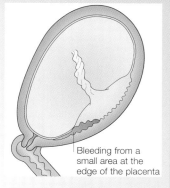

Bleeding from a small area at the edge of the placenta

**MARGINAL BLEED**
*A tablespoon of blood may be lost without compromising fetal or maternal circulation. Recovery usually takes place within 24 hours.*

# Assessing mother and fetus

A medical assessment is essential if bleeding occurs during pregnancy to enable diagnosis and to minimize the risk of further bleeding. There are several methods doctors can use to assess and manage the condition of the mother and baby.

Any woman with bleeding during pregnancy should be seen urgently, either in the antenatal day ward or in the delivery suite. Examination of the abdomen may suggest a cause: in an abruption, the uterus is firm and tender, while placenta praevia is associated with a breech lie, as the fetus' head cannot engage with the pelvis.

### INTERNAL EXAMINATION

An internal examination may reveal an ectropion, but it is only done once a placenta praevia has been ruled out by ultrasound scan. In this situation, an internal examination may precipitate more blood loss and should be avoided.

Blood tests are taken to check the mother's blood count and to ensure that cross-matched blood is available for transfusion in case of emergency. An intravenous drip is usually sited as a precaution.

### ASSESSING THE BABY

The baby is assessed by monitoring the cardiotocograph (CTG), or fetal heart rate pattern. Placental bleeding can lead to irregular contractions, or even premature labour and the first signs may be detected on the CTG monitor. An ultrasound scan is done to rule out placenta praevia and to assess the growth and well-being of the fetus.

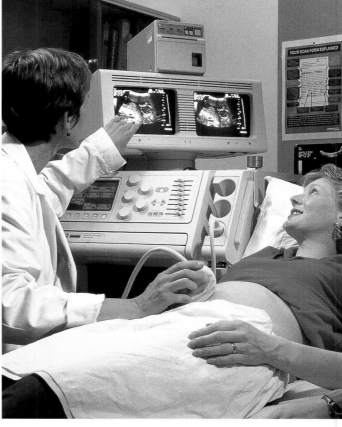

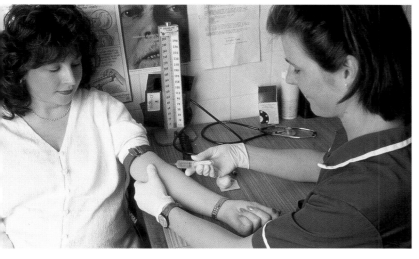

*Most bleeding in pregnancy is minor, and settles spontaneously. However, it is important that blood pressure is taken and blood count checked.*

*Diagnosis of placenta praevia may be made during ultrasound scanning of the uterus. Ultrasound can also be used to assess the condition of the fetus.*

## Further management

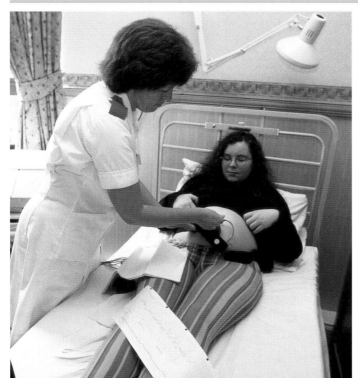

*Moderate bleeding in a pregnant woman raises the risk of premature delivery. The fetus' heartbeat is closely monitored to detect any signs of fetal distress.*

A pregnant woman who has vaginal bleeding is usually admitted to hospital for observation. In most cases the bleeding is minor and settles spontaneously, only requiring admission for 24 hours.

However, bleeding from a placenta praevia is unpredictable and many patients will need to be admitted to hospital for long periods of time. The risk of a large haemorrhage is greatest when the placenta is completely covering the cervix, which may make a normal delivery impossible, and facilities for emergency Caesarean section must be close at hand.

### PREMATURE DELIVERY

Moderate bleeding of any cause raises the possibility of premature delivery - either spontaneously or electively by Caesarean section.

The most significant difficulties faced by a premature baby are related to immaturity of the lungs. Mothers at risk of early delivery are given a low-dose steroid injection to accelerate maturation of the fetus' lungs; this causes no harm if the baby is born later, at term.

### BLOOD GROUP

Around one in 15 women is known to have a Rhesus-negative blood group. In order to prevent problems for future pregnancies it is vital that they receive an Anti-D injection within 72 hours of any antepartum haemorrhage.

97

# Miscarriage

## Miscarriage is the most common complication of early pregnancy, affecting hundreds of thousands of women each year. There are several causes of a miscarriage, not all of which are fully understood.

The medical definition of miscarriage is the spontaneous loss of a pregnancy before 24 weeks' gestation. In most cases there is no way of preventing it and it is nature's way of making sure that only a healthy pregnancy will continue throughout gestation.

Most miscarriages happen early in the pregnancy; they are much less common after three months. Studies suggest that as many as one quarter of pregnancies miscarry, the most risky time being from before the

*A sperm is seen on the surface of an egg in this micrograph. Problems may occur during the exchange of chromosomes, leading to a miscarriage.*

first period is missed until around eight weeks (as dated from the last menstrual period).

The most common symptom is bleeding, which can range from light spotting to discharge heavier than a period. There may be cramps or period-type pains. Some women experience cessation of the usual symptoms of pregnancy, such as breast tenderness.

### CAUSES OF MISCARRIAGE
In over 60 per cent of miscarriages there is a problem with the exchange of chromosomes when the egg is fertilized. This is due to nothing more than bad luck. Another cause is failure of implantation of the embryo into the lining of the uterus. A weak cervix is uncommon and typically leads to late miscarriage (after three months). Miscarriage is more common as a woman gets older due to the ageing of her eggs. Miscarriage is not due to stress or a lack of rest.

*Early miscarriage is a very common occurrence. The causes are not entirely known but in most cases a miscarriage cannot be prevented.*

## Types of miscarriage

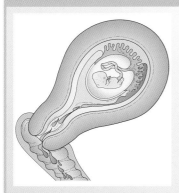

**1 Threatened miscarriage**
This is diagnosed when a woman bleeds in early pregnancy (she may or may not experience pain). Vaginal examination reveals that the cervix is closed and ultrasound scanning shows a normal amniotic sac and fetal heartbeat. Almost all pregnancies will continue to term normally.

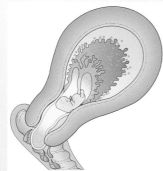

**2 Inevitable miscarriage**
Bleeding in early pregnancy with strong, painful uterine contractions. On examination, the cervix is dilated and part of the amniotic sac may have been pushed through the opening of the cervix. As the miscarriage continues, the uterine contents are often incompletely expelled.

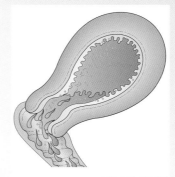

**3 Incomplete miscarriage**
After a miscarriage has started, the products of pregnancy will be expelled. Incomplete miscarriage occurs when some tissue remains in the uterus. Ultrasound scanning will reveal the amount of tissue remaining in the uterus which will need to be removed.

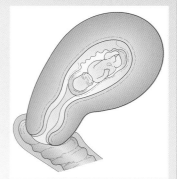

**4 Missed miscarriage**
The pregnancy stopped growing some weeks earlier but there is no bleeding at this time. There is usually a slight dark brown blood loss and absence of pregnancy symptoms. This is also called a 'blighted ovum' and has the same causes as a normal miscarriage.

# Investigating miscarriage

Many women with bleeding in early pregnancy are referred to the Early Pregnancy Assessment Unit at their local hospital for testing and assessment.

A nurse and doctor will see the woman and arrange some tests after taking a history and an examination. These tests include:

■ **Blood count**
This is performed to ensure that bleeding hasn't caused anaemia
■ **Blood group**
Women who are a negative blood group (for example, O negative) need to have an injection to prevent problems with subsequent pregnancies
■ **Pregnancy test**
A blood test for the pregnancy hormone, human chorionic gonadotrophin (hCG), is taken
■ **Ultrasound scan**
This will show the uterus and developing embryo. If all is well and the pregnancy is developed far enough, a heartbeat can be seen. The most accurate scan is an internal, or transvaginal one, which gives high quality pictures.

### FINDINGS
By comparing the results of the hCG test and the scan, it is often possible to discover what is happening. For example, the scan may confirm a heartbeat, which is reassuring for the pregnancy. If it does not show much in the uterus, but the hCG level is very low, the pregnancy may not be as advanced as expected. If the embryo is larger than 10 mm (0.4 in), but no heartbeat is heard, then a missed miscarriage is certain. The scan may be repeated after 7–10 days to monitor the fetus.

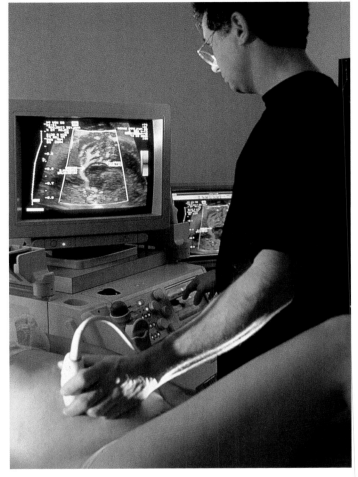

*Right: Ultrasound scanning allows the doctor to visualize the fetus and detect a heartbeat. It is important for assessing bleeding in pregnancy.*

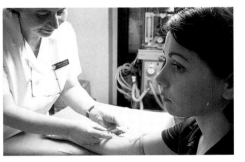

*Left: A blood sample will be taken to check that the woman is not anaemic, to determine her blood type and to test for the pregnancy hormone hCG.*

## Treatment options

If the miscarriage was complete, no further treatment is needed. Inevitable, incomplete and missed miscarriages often require further treatment. In some cases it is appropriate to await events and let nature take care of things. For missed miscarriage, when the pregnancy is further on than six to eight weeks or when there is heavy bleeding, women will be offered medical or surgical treatment:
■ **Medical treatment**
This involves using a drug called misoprostol to make the uterus contract and expel the remainder of the pregnancy. Although this avoids an operation, bleeding is more prolonged and there is only a 50 per cent success rate.
■ **Surgical treatment**
This is a short operation to empty the uterus, known as an evacuation of retained products of conception (ERPOC), but is sometimes called a dilatation and curettage (D and C). The procedure takes about five minutes and involves passing a soft plastic tube through the cervix into the uterus and removing the tissue by suction.

*Further treatment may be necessary after a miscarriage and may either be surgical or medical in nature. Counselling may also be offered.*

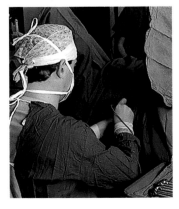

*Some women will need to undergo a short surgical procedure to clear the uterus of any remaining tissue. This is called dilatation and curettage.*

## After a miscarriage

Following a miscarriage, the bleeding will settle down in about 10 days and the next period will return in around six weeks' time. Infection can make the bleeding last longer or cause an offensive discharge; this is treated with a course of antibiotics.

Grief is a very normal reaction to miscarriage and it may be as intense as that after any other loss. Many women describe a feeling of numbness and emptiness following a miscarriage. Some couples withdraw, feeling alone and isolated; others may wish to talk about it. Most hospitals provide a contact number for someone to talk to for advice and support.

### Recurrent miscarriage
Around one in 30 couples has a second miscarriage. Once a couple has had three miscarriages it is important to investigate for an underlying cause and referral to a specialist is advisable.

# High blood pressure in pregnancy

Pre-eclampsia is the medical term for high blood pressure during pregnancy. It affects 1 in 10 pregnancies and if untreated may lead to eclampsia, which is dangerous both for mother and baby.

High blood pressure is one of the most common problems in pregnancy, and it is also remains one of the most dangerous. Pre-eclampsia, when severe, is one of the leading causes of maternal death and can also result in fetal growth problems and early delivery. Recognizing the early signs of pre-eclampsia can be life-saving.

## TYPES OF HYPERTENSION DURING PREGNANCY

Pre-eclampsia and other hypertensive diseases affect around 1 in 10 first-time mothers. However, for most women they are a minor inconvenience, meaning little more than a few extra midwife checks towards the end of pregnancy. There are three main types of hypertension that affect women during pregnancy:

■ Pre-existing hypertension – this complicates an otherwise normal pregnancy; sometimes it is first diagnosed during pregnancy

■ Pregnancy-induced hypertension (PIH) – this develops during pregnancy. There is no protein in the urine and it completely resolves by six weeks after delivery

■ Pre-eclampsia – high blood pressure with a range of effects on other body systems, the most common being leakage of protein in the urine.

*Pre-eclampsia is a serious complication of pregnancy, and can even lead to maternal and fetal death. However, most cases are managed successfully.*

## Risk factors

When high blood pressure is detected it is important to determine which type of problem is present and assess the severity. Often this can be done without hospital admission, but sometimes this is necessary to carry out further investigations.

There are several risk factors that can contribute to pre-eclampsia:

■ First pregnancy
■ Pre-eclampsia in a previous pregnancy
■ Age under 20 or over 35 years
■ Short stature
■ Migraine
■ Family history of pre-eclampsia or eclampsia
■ Pre-existing hypertension
■ Being underweight
■ Multiple pregnancy
■ Other diseases, such as lupus, diabetes and Raynaud's disease.

*Pregnant women who are believed to be at risk of pre-eclampsia will be carefully assessed and monitored throughout the pregnancy.*

## Symptoms of pre-eclampsia

Pre-eclampsia may have serious implications, affecting maternal as well as fetal well-being. Hypertensive disorders in pregnancy must receive treatment in order to prevent eclampsia, a condition which is characterized by convulsions and coma.

Early recognition and treatment of symptoms will prevent the development of eclampsia. Symptoms include:

■ Flashing lights, stripes before the eyes, floaters or black-outs
■ Light hurting the eyes (photophobia)
■ Headache
■ Pain at the top of the abdomen, or on the right side under the ribs
■ Vomiting
■ Malaise (general feeling of being unwell).

*Often, the main symptom of pre-eclampsia is high blood pressure. This is often detected during routine antenatal checks in the course of pregnancy.*

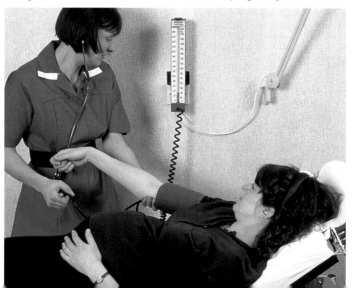

# Managing herpes infection

During the first trimester of pregnancy (0–12 weeks) there is a small chance that a primary attack of genital herpes will cause a miscarriage. If this does not happen, the pregnancy will usually continue with no abnormalities occurring in the baby. There is no evidence to suggest that women who have a primary attack of genital herpes in the first trimester should have the pregnancy terminated.

### MEDICATION
Many pregnant women choose or are advised not to use any medication during pregnancy.

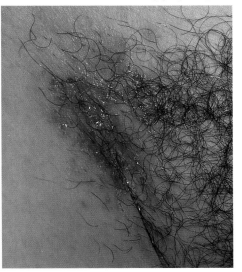

*Herpes can result in sores developing on the skin around the genital area. Medication can reduce symptoms and may benefit pregnant women.*

*If a woman has a primary attack of herpes at the time of labour there is a risk the virus will be transmitted to the baby. Thus, a Caesarean may be required.*

There is, however, no evidence that the treatment for herpes, involving administration of a drug called aciclovir, has any harmful effects on unborn babies. If it reduces the symptoms in the mother it will have proved its value.

An expert opinion should be sought to determine whether treatment should be considered.

The same information holds true for primary attacks in the second trimester (12–24 weeks) of pregnancy.

### THIRD TRIMESTER
Women who have a primary attack of genital herpes during the third trimester (24–36 weeks) are at risk of pre-term delivery. They are also at risk of transmitting the virus to their babies during vaginal delivery, particularly if the attack occurs at around the same time as labour begins.

For this reason, the current UK guidelines on the management of genital herpes during pregnancy recommend that a Caesarean section should be considered for all women developing primary herpes in the last trimester. This particularly affects women with symptoms that occur up to six weeks pre-delivery.

Sometimes it is not possible to perform a Caesarean section.

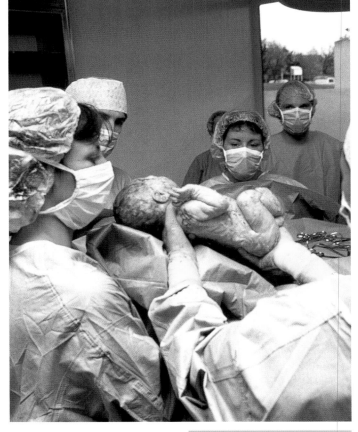

This may be because the mother is admitted to the hospital too late and is about to deliver the baby, or there are medical reasons why a Caesarean section would be dangerous or impossible to perform. In this case the obstetrician may recommend treating the mother and baby with aciclovir.

# Recurrent herpes

In women who have a history of genital herpes, subsequent attacks during pregnancy are unlikely to affect the outcome of that pregnancy. There is a small risk of transmission to the baby if a herpes attack occurs at the time of delivery. If there are no visible sores at the time of delivery, many obstetricians will allow the baby to be delivered through the vagina.

### CAESAREAN SECTION
If herpetic sores are visible at the onset of labour, the baby should be delivered by Caesarean section. However, because the risks to the baby are small, the risk of a Caesarean section needs to be weighed against this.

*In women with recurrent herpes there is less risk of transfer to babies during birth. Therefore, vaginal deliveries are possible.*

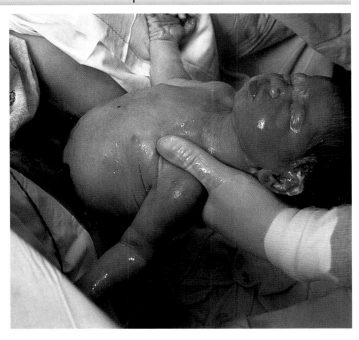

## Advice

To limit the risks of herpes, pregnant women should:
■ Inform their doctor at the pregnancy booking visit if they have had genital herpes before
■ Avoid sexual intercourse with their male partner, if he has herpes, at the time of his attacks. Women may need to consider using condoms throughout their pregnancy and especially in the last trimester. They might consider not having sexual intercourse in the last trimester or after 36 weeks' pregnancy
■ Request a blood test if their male partner has genital herpes and they do not think they have ever had it. This may help them to know whether they have been exposed to herpes previously or not. However, this test is not yet widely available and its interpretation has not yet been perfected
■ Discuss herpes at their local genitourinary medicine clinic where there is good advice and leaflets
■ Remember that the herpes virus from cold sores can be transmitted to the genitals through oral sex.

# Countdown to birth

The final weeks of pregnancy see the fetus completing its incredible development in preparation for its entry into the world. After birth, it will have to breathe independently for the first time in order to survive.

These are the final few weeks of fetal development. By the end of this period, the fetus will be full-term. All of its uterine development will be completed, and it will have laid down enough subcutaneous fat to enable it to regulate its own temperature.

Although there is much variation in what constitutes a normal birth weight, the average weight of a healthy full-term baby is about 3.4 kg (7 lb 7 oz). Male infants tend to weigh more than female infants, and very young women, such as teenage mothers, tend to have smaller babies. Few full-term babies weigh over 4.5 kg (10 lb).

By the end of fetal development, the fingernails and toenails have reached the ends of the digits. The majority of lanugo hair has disappeared. If any does remain, it will disappear soon after birth. The body usually still has a covering of vernix caseosa, primarily in the folds of the skin, where it may be very thick.

The average pregnancy lasts 38 weeks from fertilization, or

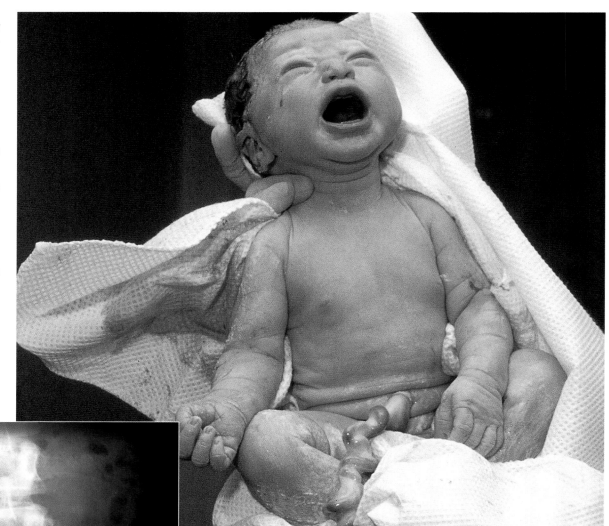

40 weeks when calculated from the first day of the last menstrual cycle. It is not unusual, however, for pregnancies to last longer than this.

However, there can be complications with an overdue pregnancy, and steps may be taken to induce labour.

### WEEK 36

The fetus is continuing to grow fairly steadily, though the weight gain has slowed down compared

*Most fetuses are positioned ready for birth by the ninth month. As this false-coloured X-ray shows, the baby's head (green) engages in the mother's pelvic cavity.*

*Seconds after birth, this baby girl has air in her lungs for the first time. There is still some of the white vernix on her skin.*

with previous weeks. The crown to rump length is around 360 mm (14 in) and the overall length is around 480 mm (18 in). The fetus now weighs around 3.15 kg (8.5 lb).

The nails on the fingers and toes have reached the end, or almost to the end, of the digits. They may be quite sharp and can scratch the baby's face or the birth canal during delivery.

### WEEK 37

The fetus will continue to put on weight right up to the last week of pregnancy, but will not grow much more in length. It is close to full-term size, with the crown to rump length being around 370 mm (14.5 in) and the overall head to foot length about 490 mm (19.3 in). It weighs around 3.3 kg (8.8 lb).

The size of the fetus is now such that there is little room for it to move around in the uterus, and there is less amniotic fluid than there was even a few weeks ago. Fetal movements will be less free than they were, although the fetus may still make 'jabbing' movements with its arms and legs. These can easily be felt by the mother.

### WEEK 38
This is usually considered to be the final week of pregnancy, although many pregnancies, especially in first-time mothers, continue after this point with few or no problems. By this time, the average crown to rump length is about 380 mm (14.8 in), and the head to foot measurement is around 500 mm (20 in). The final birth weight is around 3.4 kg (8.9 lb).

In most first pregnancies the fetus' head has engaged – dropped down into the mother's pelvic girdle – in preparation for delivery. However, in subsequent pregnancies, this shift may not occur until after labour has commenced.

The baby is plump and generally unwrinkled because of the deposition of subcutaneous fat. During the final weeks, 10–15 g (0.3–0.5 oz) of fat is laid down every day.

The hair on the head is about 2–4 cm (0.8–1.6 in) long, and the lanugo hair has mostly disappeared from the rest of the body. There may be a covering of vernix caseosa still remaining. This greasy substance often collects in the creases of the body, especially the groin, armpits and inside the elbows. The eyes are usually a bluish colour at this stage, and will not take on their permanent colouring until a few weeks after birth.

Having spent the last nine

*This chart shows the average increase in size of a fetus throughout the 38 weeks of pregnancy. Weeks one to four comprise the pre-embryo period, during which the total size of the embryonic fetus is measured. From week five onwards, the crown to rump length is the reference point for assessing fetal growth.*

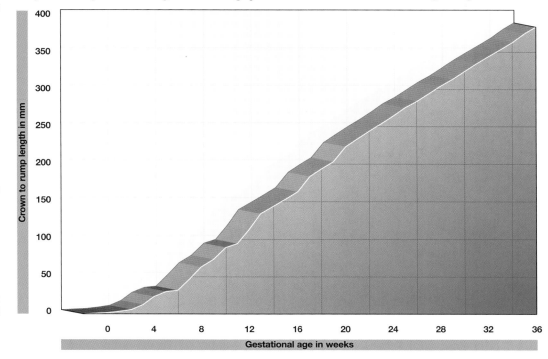

Crown to rump length in mm / Gestational age in weeks

## When a baby is overdue

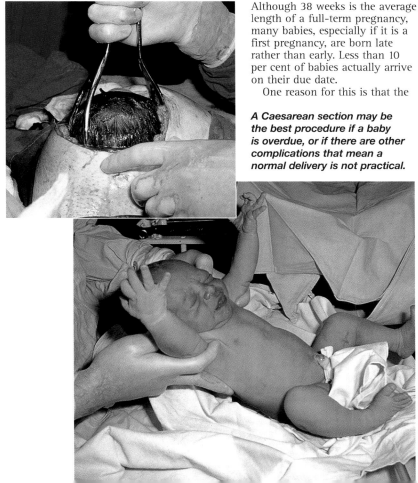

*A Caesarean section may be the best procedure if a baby is overdue, or if there are other complications that mean a normal delivery is not practical.*

*After a Caesarean birth, the umbilical cord will be clamped and cut as usual. The baby then undergoes the standard checks to ensure it is healthy.*

Although 38 weeks is the average length of a full-term pregnancy, many babies, especially if it is a first pregnancy, are born late rather than early. Less than 10 per cent of babies actually arrive on their due date.

One reason for this is that the date was miscalculated or inaccurate, based upon the time of the last menstrual period. If the due date is incorrect, the baby still grows normally to reach the size and appearance of a full-term baby. However, if the baby is actually overdue, known as post-term, a number of changes can take place that may be harmful and cause problems during delivery.

Much of the vernix coating has disappeared or thinned out, so the baby's skin is vulnerable to the harsh effects of the amniotic fluid. The skin may begin to absorb the fluid, and become puffy and bloated. This is noticeable at the joints, such as those of the fingers. The skin can also become dry, cracked or begin to peel.

A post-term baby may continue to grow in weight in the uterus. If it becomes very large, especially if it is bloated due to retention of amniotic

fluid, there may be problems during delivery. The baby's head may grow too large to allow a normal vaginal delivery, and the use of forceps or delivery by Caesarean section is common with post-term babies.

The opposite can also occur – the baby may begin to lose weight. This is because the placenta begins to deteriorate from the 30th week of pregnancy onwards. If labour begins too long after the estimated due date, the placenta becomes less efficient at providing nourishment and assisting in respiration for the fetus, and may no longer be able to sustain the baby properly. Some overdue babies appear long and thin, and their skin may be very wrinkled. This is because they have lost some of their fat stores, having used them for nourishment.

For these reasons, an overdue or post-term pregnancy will be closely monitored. If the natural process of labour does not begin within two weeks of the calculated due date, the pregnancy may be induced artificially using drugs, or a Caesarean section performed.

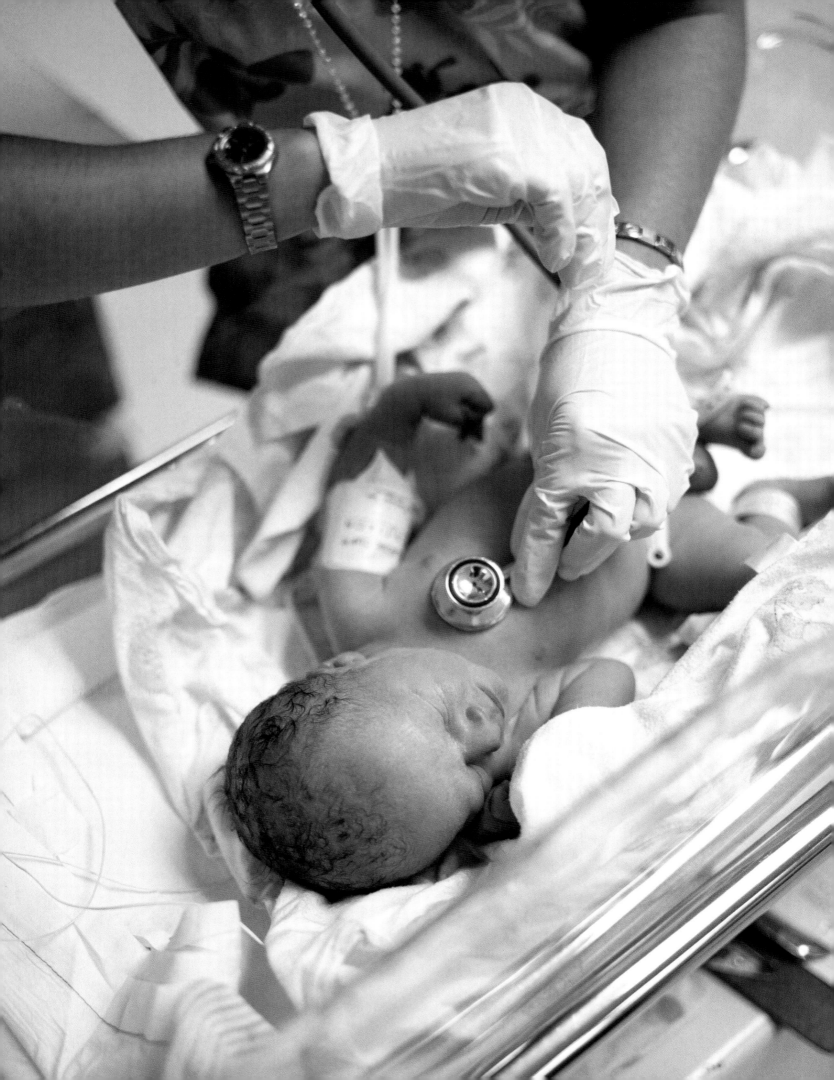

# Birth

As well as being the most natural process of life,
childbirth has the support of highly sophisticated
health services, so little is likely to go wrong.

However, giving birth can be a difficult experience and
no one can fully prepare a woman for the undertaking.
For this reason, the presence and support of a birthing
partner is vital and should be given priority
at this challenging time.

Today, birth can take place either at hospital or
at home; the location will depend on the parents'
preference and whether there are any
predicted problems.

Given the nature of labour, it is important to be
flexible and to be prepared to abandon preconceived
ideas if circumstances change.

Left: A nurse examines a
newborn baby in a hospital crib.
Newborn checks ensure that the
baby is healthy and provide the
first of many records of the
baby's post-natal progress.

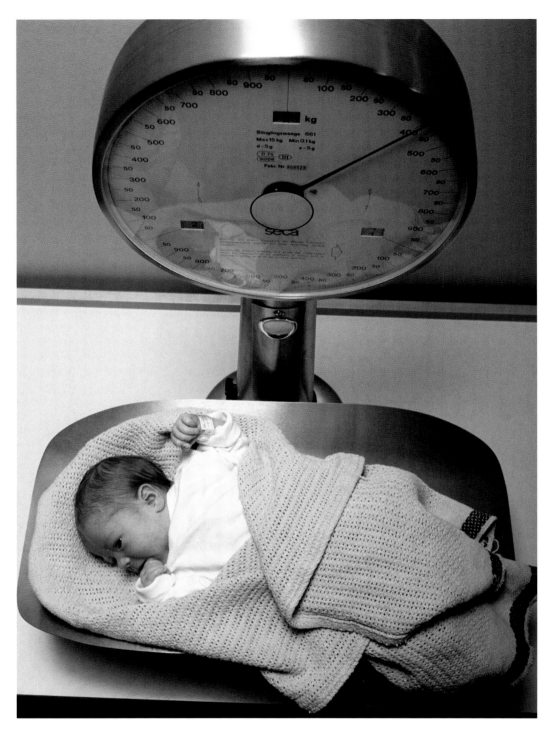

Newborn babies are weighed shortly after the delivery to establish their birth weight for medical records.

when the protective amniotic sac around the baby ruptures so that the fluid leaks out - this is known as the 'waters breaking'.

So that the baby can pass from the uterus, the cervix gradually shortens and opens (dilates) to an eventual width of 10 cm (4 in), when it effectively becomes one with the uterus and temporarily forms the birth canal. The initial contractions serve to dilate the cervix, a process which can take up to 12 hours or more, and tend to be longer for a first delivery. During this first stage, the baby's heartbeat will be regularly monitored, along with other signs that might indicate fetal distress.

Pain is a key feature of labour, although every woman will describe a different experience. Some women prefer to experience childbirth without painkillers while others find the pain intolerable. Various forms of pain relief are available to ease the process, including drugs such as breathable Entonox ('gas and air') and injectable pethidine, or the highly effective epidural anaesthesia. A water birth can be of benefit, as can massage, aromatherapy and transcutaneous nerve stimulation (TENS).

## THE STAGES OF LABOUR
A few weeks before delivery, the baby will usually move further down into the pelvis in readiness for birth. The mother will already have started to experience Braxton Hicks contractions – mild, painless tightenings of the abdomen that occur as the uterus prepares itself. However, true labour is heralded by the onset of more powerful and painful contractions of the uterine muscle. During labour, there are three distinct stages: the cervix (which has softened over the course of the pregnancy) dilates; the baby passes down the birth canal and is born; and the placenta and membranes that surrounded the baby during its uterine life are delivered.

## LABOUR BEGINS
The first sign of labour is often a 'show' – the release of the mucus plug that has sealed the cervical opening during pregnancy. The second common sign occurs

## THE BABY IS BORN
Once the cervix is fully dilated, the second stage

A few hours after giving birth, a mother cradles her newborn baby in her arms.

of labour begins. Over the next 20 minutes to two hours, the baby moves down and out of the birth canal. The contractions now fulfill the purpose of expelling the baby, and begin to occur more frequently. Pushing becomes an uncontrollable urge and a woman will feel an overwhelming need to give birth – reactions can be intense at this time and expressions of anger are common. Strong physical reactions, such as nausea and an urge to defecate are also frequent. As the baby moves and rotates through the birth canal, deep pressure in the rectum and an increased desire to push are experienced, then a stinging or burning sensation as the head passes through and out of the vagina (this is often called 'crowning'). If the crowning process is difficult, an episiotomy may be necessary to avoid tearing. Throughout the process, an experienced midwife or doctor is present to support and guide a woman and her partner through this tempestuous time.

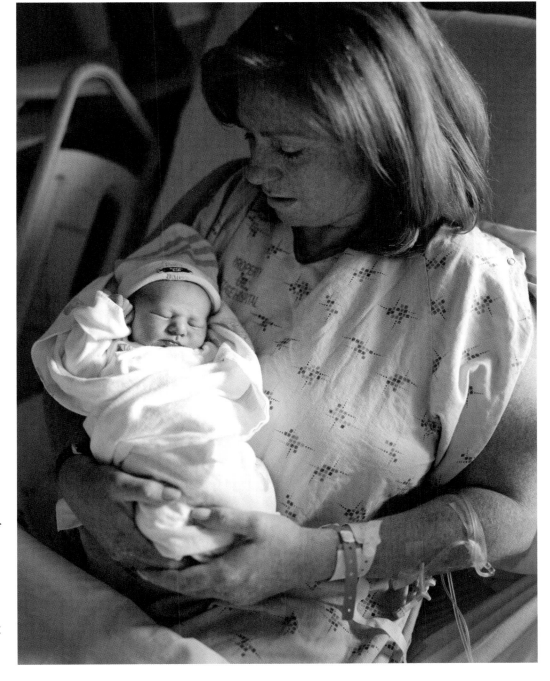

### DELIVERING THE PLACENTA
During the third stage, the uterus continues to contract to expel the placenta and membranes. The midwife often helps the process along by the injection of a specialized drug and by gentle manipulations of the uterus. As the placenta peels away from the lining, the blood vessels are sealed by the powerful contractions of the uterus, which shrinks to become a hard ball-shaped organ. If uneventful, much of this final stage may go unnoticed by the mother, who may be too excited or too exhausted by the birth of her baby.

### WHEN HELP IS NEEDED
There are occasions when it is necessary for the midwife or doctor to intervene, for example if the labour is not progressing as it should, or if the baby is in distress. Some interventions can be anticipated before labour – for example if the baby is in an abnormal position – and home birth is often still possible with foresight and careful planning. However, circumstances may dictate that the birth should occur in hospital and in some cases a caesarian section may be necessary. It is important to note that interventions are carried out to ensure the safety of both mother and child. No woman should consider it a failure if she requires an interventional delivery.

# Giving birth

During childbirth, women will go through many physical
and emotional changes. Labour starts with the dilatation of the
cervix and is complete after the expulsion of the placenta.

Labour is divided into three
distinct stages. Every woman's
experience is unique and the
timing of each of the stages
varies enormously between
women and between different
labours. An average labour lasts
about 12 to 14 hours for first-
time mothers, and about seven
hours for subsequent labours.

### CONTRACTIONS
In the first stage of labour the
cervix opens fully to allow the
baby to pass through.
Throughout the pregnancy the
cervix has served the important
function of keeping the baby in
place. Now in the first few hours
of labour, cervical function
changes completely and it is
transformed into a wide, open,
smooth passage for the baby to
move down.

The transition period marks
the time when the uterus
changes its way of contracting
from spasms that dilate the
cervix to spasms that can push
the baby out into the world.
During this period women often
experience dramatic physical
and emotional changes.

The contractions become more
intense and closer together, with
women sometimes experiencing
two or three contractions
together with hardly a breathing
space between. This can be
accompanied by physical
symptoms such as shaking,
diarrhoea or even vomiting.

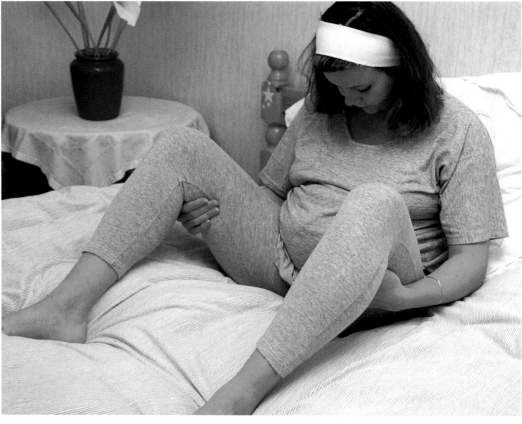

### EMOTIONAL CHANGES
At this time the emotional
changes can manifest themselves
in uncharacteristic behaviour.
Women may become extremely
irritable and upset. It is common
for a woman in labour to
become angry with her partner,
blaming him for the pain she is
in. Some women say that at this
stage they felt they had had
enough and did not want the
baby any more. Others can be
surprised by the way they start
to moan.

### BIRTH OF THE BABY
The second stage begins when
the cervix is fully dilated and
lasts until the birth of the baby.
This is the expulsive stage,
when the mother pushes the
baby out. Many women find the
idea of pushing impossible to
imagine, and are surprised by
the fact that it is instinctive and
caused by the involuntary
action of the uterus. They are
powerless to resist. As the baby
passes through the outlet of the
vagina women experience a
stinging or burning sensation,
which some have described as

*Holding her child for the first
time, a mother experiences
many emotions. The overriding
emotion will be that of relief.*

*The onset of labour begins when
the cervix is at least 2 cm (0.8 in)
dilated. Contractions then
become painful and regular with
diminishing intervals.*

feeling like a 'Chinese burn'.
Some will reach down and
touch the baby's head to
welcome the child into the
world as it emerges.

### THE AFTERBIRTH
For women who have already
been handed their newborn baby
by the medical staff, the delivery
of the afterbirth (the final stage
of labour) is barely noticed and
passes in the general blur of
excitement and euphoria.

Once the child is safely in
their arms mothers generally feel
an overwhelming sense of relief.
The nine months of their
pregnancy have finally come to
an end, the pain of delivery has
passed, and their baby is
healthy.

It is important that parents are
given time alone at this stage to
bond with their baby.

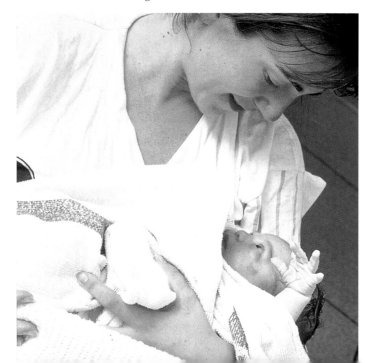

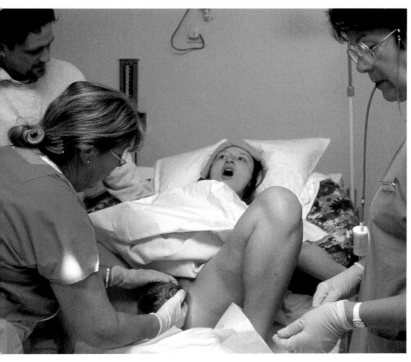

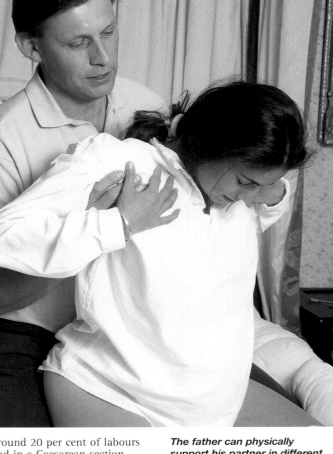

## DEALING WITH PAIN

Most women experience considerable pain during contractions, and anticipation of this pain is one of the greatest anxieties they have about childbirth. Much of the pain experienced during childbirth is due to a woman's cultural expectation of birth being a painful event.

The result is a vicious cycle of fear producing tension and pain, which results in more fear and stress, and more pain. It is important for women to realize that the pains of contractions do not indicate that something is wrong, but that these pains are normal and even functional.

Pain does not emanate directly from the uterus itself, but results from the lack of

*After the birth the mother and father are able to hold and admire the baby. The arrival of a baby marks a new stage in their lives together.*

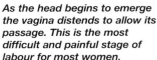

*As the head begins to emerge the vagina distends to allow its passage. This is the most difficult and painful stage of labour for most women.*

blood in the abdominal tissues caused by the uterus squeezing and contracting. There is even evidence to suggest that pain is an important cue to the brain, prompting women to move in ways appropriate to the process of labour.

While many women recall childbirth as being an extremely painful experience, they say that they were able to endure the process because of the joyful purpose of the event – the birth of the baby.

Since no one can tell a first-time mother what labour will feel like in advance, it is important that she keeps an open mind about using pain relief and does not dismiss it out of hand. Couples also need to be prepared for the fact that

around 20 per cent of labours end in a Caesarean section. After a Caesarean, women may feel cheated that they did not have a vaginal delivery.

## ROLE OF THE FATHER

If they are present at the birth, fathers often have an important role to play in helping their partner to feel comfortable, supporting them in different positions, providing drinks and helping them to feel emotionally secure. They may be allowed to catch the emerging baby and cut the umbilical cord.

Despite the efforts of the mother and hospital staff to help fathers feel involved, many recall feeling they have no real

*The father can physically support his partner in different positions during labour. He can also provide important emotional support if needed.*

role to play at a time when something very important that they contributed to is reaching its climax. Some feel ignored or shut out because all attention is focused on the mother. They may feel rejected if their partner behaves uncharacteristically when she is in pain.

## REACTIONS TO THE BABY

Parents' reactions to the birth of their baby can be anything from tears, and whoops of joy to awed silence and exhaustion.

Some couples feel an instant rush of love for their baby. Others feel relieved that the birth is over, proud of their achievements, but strangely uninterested in the child.

It may take time to adjust to the reality of a newborn baby. Babies can be smaller than expected, with misshapen heads and a covering of a white, greasy substance called vernix. Once parents start to care for their baby, they will find that the baby will respond to their voice and that love will grow naturally. For first time parents the arrival of a baby is the start of a new phase in their lives.

# Normal hospital birth

Labour is the process by which the fetus is delivered into the outside world through the birth canal. Most women will experience this in a hospital environment, under the supervision of a midwife and other professionals.

Labour can be divided into three distinct stages. The first stage is from the onset of regular contractions to full dilatation (widening) of the cervix and descent of the baby's head. The second stage is from full dilatation to delivery of the baby; the third is the delivery of the placenta.

The first stage is considered to have begun when the woman has experienced regular contractions for a period of two hours or more. Most of the first stage consists of further painful contractions and can last up to 12 hours. The cervix will dilate up to 10 cm (4 in).

The onset of labour is also marked by a 'show' – a mucous plug that comes away from the neck of the cervix and indicates that it is widening. Part of the amniotic sac and fluid surrounding the fetus is forced into the opening and may also rupture under the pressure. The rupture is apparent in an obvious flow of fluid coming away from the vagina ('waters breaking').

As the contractions continue, the uterus begins to change shape in preparation for delivery, and undergoes the process of retraction. The upper part becomes shorter and thicker, and the cervix is 'taken up' into the lower section of the uterus to form a continuous birth canal.

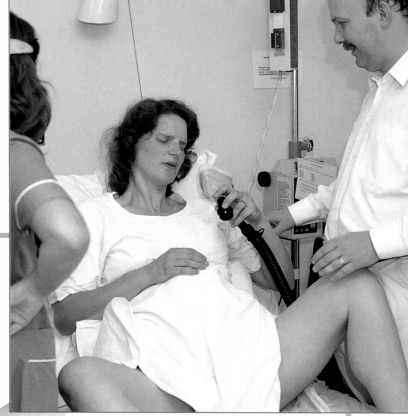

## First stage of labour

During the first stage of labour, the length of the cervix is shortened and effectively becomes a continuation of the uterus. This causes the fetus to be pushed downward and forward as the head and the amniotic fluid press on the cervix, forcing it to open.

The contractions come in waves, starting strongly, reaching a peak and then tailing off. They can be 15–20 minutes apart in the early stages of labour, and occur more frequently as labour progresses.

*The illustration shows the fetus at the onset of the first stage of labour, with the head engaged at the start of the birth canal and the cervix beginning to dilate. The management of the labour is seen in the photograph: the midwife is undertaking observations of the baby and the mother. The mother is taking pain relief in the form of oxygen and nitrous oxide ('gas and air').*

*The cervix continues to dilate and the baby's head descends in a downward and backward movement. The woman is attached to a cardiotocograph (CTG) machine which monitors the frequency and length of contractions. The baby's heart rate may also be monitored by this machine.*

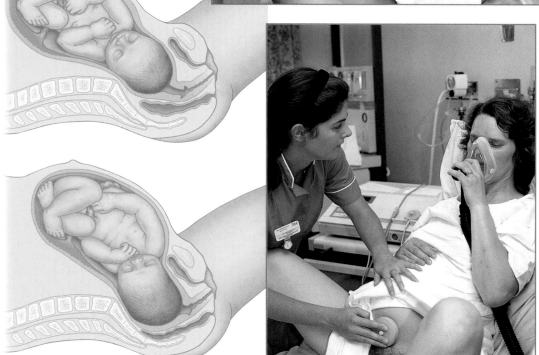

## Second stage of labour

The second stage of labour begins with full dilatation of the cervix and can last from 20 minutes to two hours, depending on whether the woman has given birth before. The midwife is able to confirm that there is full dilatation of the cervix on vaginal examination, or the baby's head may become visible. The head needs to descend as far down the birth canal as possible.

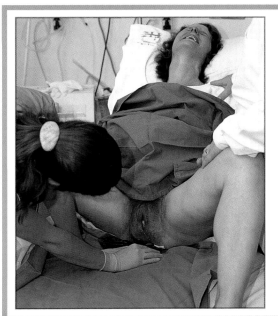

*The head has descended further still and is now pressing on the rectum and the lower spine. The woman feels a strong urge to push with the strengthening contractions.*

*The perineum – the muscles between the anus and the vagina – is visibly bulging and there are changes in the surrounding structures as the muscles 'fan out'.*

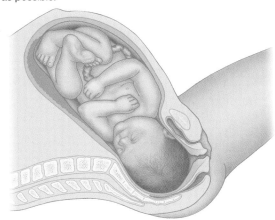

## Emergence of the head

As the top of the head begins to emerge, the vagina distends to allow its passage. The bladder has temporarily become an abdominal organ, and the perineum flattens. These structures adapt to allow the optimum amount of space for the expansion of the birth canal.

*Once the head has descended fully, the occiput (back of the skull) meets the resistance of the pelvic floor. It then flexes and rotates in a spiral movement to pass beneath the pubic arch of the mother's pelvis.*

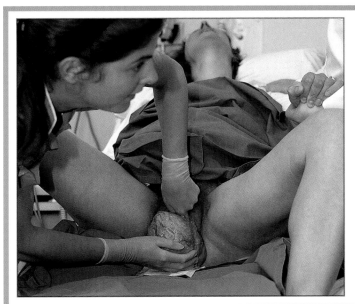

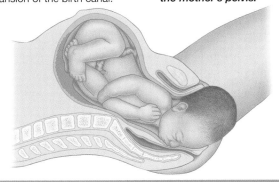

## Baby's body descends

While the head is being born, the body of the fetus descends with the continuing muscular contractions of labour. The trunk is now engaged in the pelvis and the shoulders rotate. The rest of the body will follow shortly.

*Once under the pubic arch, the head rotates externally to allow the release of the posterior shoulder (the one which is further behind as the baby emerges).*

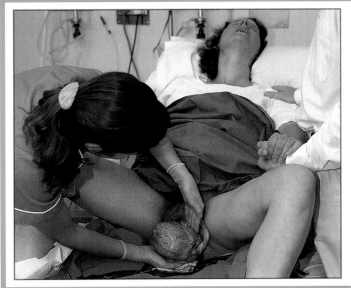

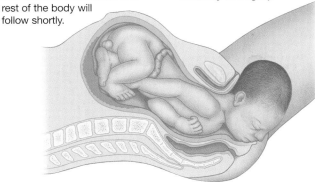

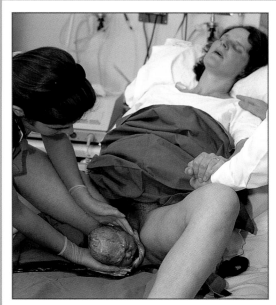

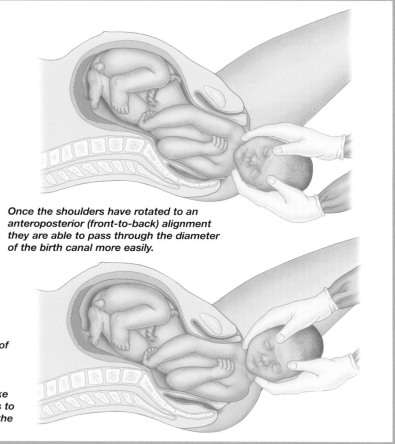

*Once the shoulders have rotated to an anteroposterior (front-to-back) alignment they are able to pass through the diameter of the birth canal more easily.*

## Delivery of the baby

The head flexes after the face and chin pass the perineum, allowing the anterior (forward-facing) shoulder to meet the pelvic floor and rotate forward under the pubic arch. The posterior shoulder follows, and the trunk and legs are born immediately afterwards.

*With the head and shoulders born, the rest of the baby's body follows. The midwife will support the baby's head on both sides and then gently take hold under the shoulders to assist in carefully lifting the newborn out.*

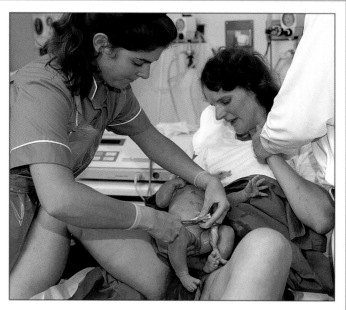

## Third stage of labour

The third and final stage of labour is the delivery of the placenta and membranes that surrounded the fetus during pregnancy. This stage generally lasts from five to 25 minutes.

On delivery of the shoulders, the mother will have been injected with a uterotropic, a drug that helps the uterus contract and reduces bleeding during the third stage.

*The baby is delivered bodily in a downward and forward movement and is lifted up to be shown to the mother. The midwife clamps the umbilical cord, wraps the baby in a sterile cloth and hands her to the mother.*

*The delivered baby: the umbilical cord has been clamped and cut and an identification band placed on the baby's right ankle. Often the baby is handed straight to the mother before the cord is cut. This helps to establish the strong physical and emotional bond between them.*

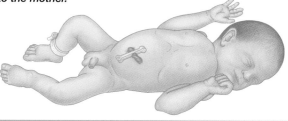

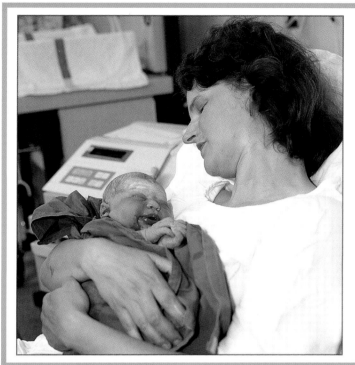

## Uterus contracts

The contractions of the uterus put pressure on the inelastic placenta, and it begins to tear away from the uterine wall. At this stage, the midwife or doctor will assist by supporting the uterus through the abdomen and taking hold of the umbilical cord to release the placenta in a controlled manner.

*The cord is pulled gently to release the placenta. Haemorrhage is arrested by the contraction of the uterine muscles that help to close off the blood vessels and sets up the clotting mechanism for the uterus. Extensive bleeding from the placental site is therefore restricted.*

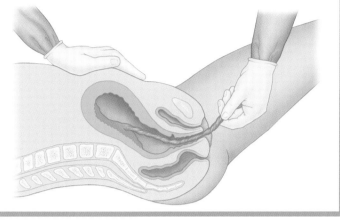

## Post-birth checks

Following the birth, the baby is kept warm and dry to maintain its temperature. The midwife's examination of the newborn is intended to identify any physical abnormalities or conditions that may be present at birth, such as missing digits, an imperforate (obstructed) anus, dislocated hip joints or skin defects. If medical or surgical treatment is required, it will be given immediately.

*The baby is cleaned, assessed and fully examined by the midwife for any congenital problems. She is then returned to her mother.*

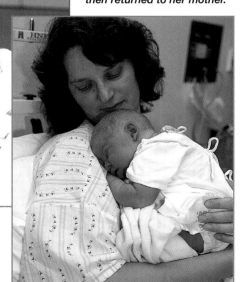

*It is normal practice for the baby to stay with the mother at all times. She is handed to the mother immediately after birth and may be put to the breast. This promotes bonding between mother and child and allows them to become used to each other. Regular contact with her baby encourages the woman's mothering skills.*

### AFTER THE BIRTH

The midwife ensures that the mother is not bleeding excessively after delivery by checking the uterus is firm and well contracted. If the perineum was cut to assist delivery, this episiotomy is carefully repaired by suturing (stitching), performed by the midwife. The local anaesthetic given before the incision is usually sufficient to numb the area, or another injection may be given.

Observations are done by the midwife to ensure that the mother's temperature, blood pressure, pulse and blood loss are all normal. After a period of rest, the mother will have a bath and a light meal, allowing her to recover after the hours of exertion during labour.

### THE NEWBORN

Following delivery, an identification band is placed on the baby's wrist or ankle. The baby is weighed by the midwife and its length and head circumference are measured and recorded. Its temperature is checked, and it is further examined in detail for any physical abnormalities or signs of infection.

The baby is encouraged to feed from the breast or by bottle and the midwife will check when the baby has passed urine or a stool for the first time.

The key principle of neonatal practice is to allow the mother and baby to spend as much time as possible together in the hours after birth.

# Home birth

The majority of births take place in a hospital environment.
However, an increasing number of women are now choosing to give
birth at home, wishing labour to be more of a personal experience.

In the past, giving birth at home was the sole option available to pregnant women. It is only in the past century that hospitals have become the routine venue in which to give birth.

### PREFERENCE
While many women feel safer in the medical surroundings of a hospital, some may feel intimidated by the machinery and bright lights that are inevitably found in such institutions, and may opt to give birth at home. Some mothers choose to have a home birth since it seems to offer a more natural environment for birth.

Another reason some women choose to give birth at home is that it allows their partner and perhaps, according to the circumstances, other members of the family, to become more involved in the birth.

### INCREASING POPULARITY
Home births are becoming more popular as an increasing number of women prefer to take more control over their pregnancies, wishing the birth

to be a more personal experience rather than a medical event.

Research has suggested that mothers who give birth at home are generally more relaxed during the birth, and as a result will be less likely to require pain relief.

### PREPARATION
When a woman first visits her GP to confirm her pregnancy she will be asked about her preferences for the birth. This gives her the opportunity to discuss her wishes.

### RISKS
In most instances having a child at home is as safe as giving birth in hospital. However, if a woman has a complicated medical history (such as a previous difficult delivery) or is likely to experience complications during birth (such as breech presentation) which could require medical assistance, then her GP will advise against a home birth.

Having decided upon a home birth, the mother will be assigned a midwife who is well

practised in home deliveries. The midwife will support the mother throughout her pregnancy and attend the birth. In a few cases two midwives may need to be present for the delivery.

*Home births are generally safe for mother and baby. If, however, the midwife or doctor suspects that there might be complications, a hospital birth will be recommended.*

## Preparing for the birth

*A home birth requires planning and preparation. Everything necessary to make the birth as comfortable as possible should be readily available.*

Before the due date the midwife will visit the home to ensure that it is a suitable environment for the birth. Good access to the home (in case the need arises for urgent transfer to hospital), good ventilation, and adequate heating, lighting and running water are all essential.

The midwife will usually give the mother a list of useful items to obtain, including:
■ Buckets – useful for the mother to squat on, depositing the placenta, and for clearing up
■ Clean towels and a flannel
■ An anglepoise lamp or torch
■ A thermometer
■ Disinfectant and kitchen roll
■ Plastic bin bags and sheeting
■ Personal touches, such as soothing music and candles to help relaxation during the birth.

### MIDWIFE'S EQUIPMENT
The midwife will bring most of her equipment with her at the time of the birth, but at around 36 weeks she will leave a delivery pack containing instruments to clamp and cut the umbilical cord as well as sterile pads and dressings.

On the day of the birth the midwife will carry an ultrasound fetal heart monitor for checking the baby's heart rate and a sphygmomanometer for measuring the mother's blood pressure.

For pain relief during the labour the midwife will provide a cylinder of Entonox (gas and air) and, if necessary, pethidine.

In case of an emergency the midwife will carry all the resuscitation equipment necessary for the baby, including: oxygen, intubation equipment (to maintain an open airway) as well as a urinary catheter and a mucus extractor (to clear the baby's airway).

# Going into labour

With the onset of labour the midwife will be contacted. In the early stages, the mother will be at liberty to move around and relax in her own home.

When labour commences the midwife will be contacted. She will visit the mother at home and assess the contractions.

If the labour is still in the very early stages the midwife may leave, calling at regular intervals to check on progress.

*During the early stages of labour the midwife will monitor the mother's progress. The midwife may not be present at all times but she will visit regularly.*

*The mother may wish to move around as the contractions begin. This will ease the pain and may speed up the labour.*

### ESTABLISHED LABOUR

Once the mother is in established labour (when the cervix is dilated by four centimetres or more) the midwife will stay by her side in order to assist the birth.

The conduct of the birth will be very much the same as that for a hospital birth, with the exception that the mother will be more in control.

During the labour there is no reason why the mother should be confined to a bed or even one room, and she may wish to move around, have a bath, or even take a walk in the garden.

The act of standing may even speed up the labour as the force of gravity will cause the baby's head to push down, encouraging the cervix to soften and dilate more quickly.

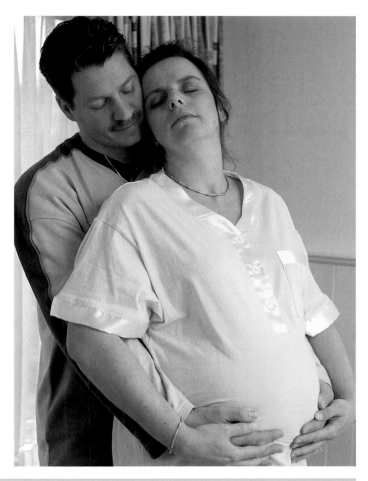

## Transfer to hospital

If a complication does arise during the course of a delivery at home, the midwife will contact the hospital immediately. Based upon the symptoms she reports, the registrar on duty may advise that the mother be transferred to hospital to receive urgent medical attention.

Community midwives are experienced in detecting abnormalities in labour.

### MONITORING

The mother's heart rate, temperature, pulse and blood pressure will be closely monitored. As will the baby's heart rate. The strength, length and frequency of uterine contractions will also be noted.

Regular checks will be made to assess cervical dilatation and the descent of the baby through the birth canal. Close observation will provide warning signs of any abnormalities, so that hospital transfer can be arranged before complications become hazardous.

### COMPLICATIONS

Transfer to hospital during or after birth will be recommended if the following complications arise:
- Meconium-stained liquor (green or black waters) – can indicate a baby in distress. Inhalation of the meconium may cause the baby severe breathing difficulties
- Fetal distress – if the labour is prolonged the baby may become distressed (indicated by an irregular heart beat)
- Haemorrhage – although some bleeding is common during pregnancy it can occasionally be a sign of placental abruption
- Maternal exhaustion – occasionally labour may be prolonged or difficult. The midwife may provide a certain degree of pain relief (gas and air) but transfer to hospital for an epidural (which anaesthetizes spinal nerves) may be necessary
- Excessive bleeding after birth – may occur if the uterus fails to contract after birth
- Retained placenta – this may need to be removed under general anaesthetic after birth
- Fetal respiratory problems – though the midwife will carry resuscitation equipment for such an event, an ambulance should be called immediately.

*If there are complications during labour, the mother will be transferred to hospital. The midwife will continue to monitor and check for any abnormalities.*

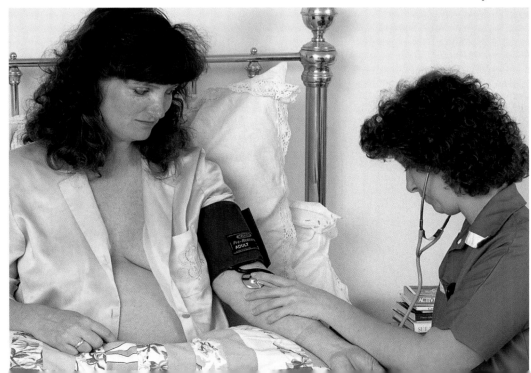

# Home birth step-by-step

Once the mother begins to experience the first signs of labour the midwife will be contacted. The midwife will intervene as little as possible, allowing the family to share a more private experience.

As with a normal hospital labour, the birth can be divided into three stages:
- Dilatation of the cervix
- Delivery of the baby
- Delivery of the placenta.

When the mother feels that the labour has begun (indicated by regular contractions or even the breaking of her waters) she will contact her midwife.

The midwife will arrive at the home, and will examine the mother in order to check her blood pressure and assess what stage the labour has reached.

### DILATATION

In most cases the first stage of labour takes between six and 12 hours so the midwife might not stay at first.

If the birth is still in the very early stages and she is satisfied that the mother is making good progress, the midwife may only the put in an appearance at regular intervals to check upon the family.

One of the advantages of a home birth is that, while a mother would normally be confined to a hospital ward at this stage, at home she is at liberty to move around the house. This generally means that the mother will be more relaxed, and it might help to take her mind off the pain experienced.

### DELIVERY

When the mother's cervix is almost fully dilated, the midwife will stay with her, monitoring progress, and giving encouragement.

Intervention from the midwife will be kept to a minimum to allow the mother and her partner, and perhaps even other members of the family, to share in the remarkable experience of birth together.

## Onset of labour

The midwife is called as the mother begins to experience the first signs of labour.

The midwife observes the frequency and strength of the uterine contractions, as well as the degree of cervical dilatation.

The mother's blood pressure is checked. Once the midwife is satisfied that the mother is making good progress, she departs, calling regularly to check on the mother's progress.

The father sits with his partner, reassuring her throughout the early stages of the labour.

*The midwife examines the mother, and monitors her blood pressure. As the labour is in the very early stages, the midwife does not stay, but checks on progress at regular intervals.*

*The mother's partner reassures her during the early stages of the birth. He holds her hand and tries to help her through the contractions.*

## Waters break

As labour progresses, the mother's contractions become more frequent and intense. She feels an immense sense of release as the amniotic sac surrounding the baby ruptures, and her waters break. (Plastic sheeting has been placed to protect the carpet.)

The midwife examines the waters, which look healthy; this is a good indication that the baby is not in any distress.

*Several hours into the labour the mother's waters break and a gush of fluid is released. The midwife examines the amniotic fluid, which appears healthy.*

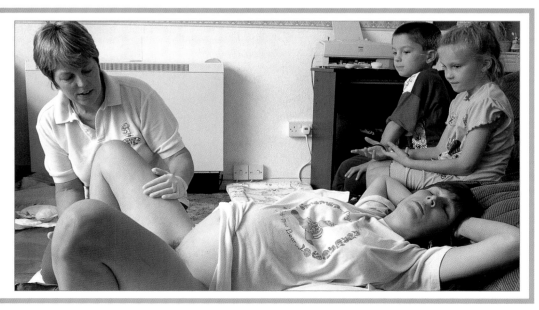

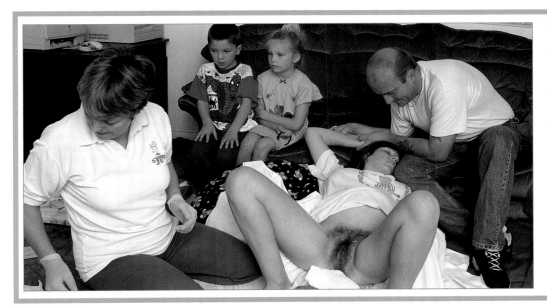

## Dilatation

The midwife is satisfied with the mother's progress. It is several hours into the labour and the cervix is almost fully dilated.

At this stage the contractions are frequent and very intense. The mother is encouraged by her partner to push, while the midwife explains to the children exactly what is happening. Fortunately they have been well prepared by their mother and father for the event.

*Once the cervix is fully dilated, the mother can begin to push the baby out. The midwife explains to the children that their sister will soon be arriving.*

## Crowning

As the mother pushes, the baby's head begins to emerge and the vagina distends to allow its passage.

The family watch as the mother gives a second push and the baby's shoulders follow.

The father helps to support the baby's head, and with one final push the baby is delivered.

After a quick check the baby is handed to her mother.

The midwife shows the father how to cut the cord. Minutes later the placenta is delivered and, after a routine check, is disposed of by the midwife.

Both mother and child are well.

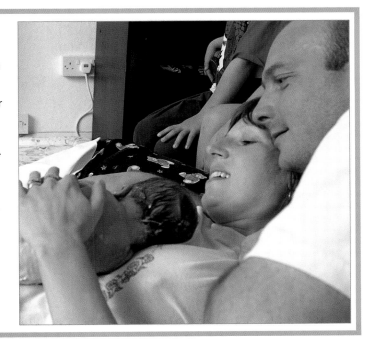

*Once the cervix is fully dilated the mother begins to push. As the baby's head emerges, the vagina distends and with a few more pushes from the mother, the child is delivered.*

*The midwife makes sure that the child is breathing well before passing her to her mother. Together the proud parents admire their newborn baby girl.*

## Post-natal recovery

The midwife examines the baby, checking its breathing rate and pulse. She inspects the umbilical cord very closely, as any abnormality, such as a missing artery, can be an indication of a cardiovascular disorder.

The placenta is examined to ensure that it has come away from the uterus fully. Once she is happy that it is complete the midwife carefully disposes of the placenta.

When the midwife is satisfied that both mother and child are

*Once the family have had time to bond and recover from the birth, the midwife returns. Both mother and baby are examined to ensure they are well.*

well, she leaves the family to bond with the child, and begins the task of clearing up.

While the mother rests, the midwife helps the father to bathe the child.

The family are then left alone until the midwife returns several hours later. Again the midwife examines mother and baby, and answers any questions that the couple may have.

The midwife visits daily for the first few days after the birth, and will continue to monitor the progress of both mother and child for up to a month.

Visits from friends and relatives are kept to a minimum at first in order to give mother and baby time to rest and recover.

# Water birth

Every year, around 20,000 babies worldwide are born in a birthing pool. The benefit of water for relaxation and pain relief during labour and birth mean that its popularity is increasing.

Some women choose to give birth as naturally as possible, without the use of drugs and outside the traditional hospital environment. One of the alternative birthing methods is the increasingly popular option of water birth.

A water birth is simply a normal birth carried out with the woman immersed in warm water. The availability of water pools provides women with an alternative form of pain relief, where the woman feels more relaxed and in control of the birth experience.

## NEW DEVELOPMENTS

Medically, water births are relatively new, having been first recognized in the 1960s, and only practised in a few hospitals since the late 1970s. In Britain, new health service guidelines introduced in the early 1990s recognized the importance of the mother's wishes regarding childbirth, and granted the right for any woman to 'choose where her babies are born'.

The change in guidelines now means that midwives are becoming increasingly aware of and practised in delivering water births, and many hospitals provide this choice of delivery as part of their normal service to women. Not all water births are carried out in hospital, however.

Studies in the USA have suggested that planned home births are actually safer than hospital deliveries (although this may be due to the high number of women who opt for Caesarean births), and a water birth at home is the natural progression. Specially designed water pools can now be hired for home use, and midwives are trained to deal with any special requirements the mother might have.

*During a water birth, a baby will not breathe in water if it is at the same temperature as the amniotic fluid. After leaving the water, however, the baby will begin to breathe air normally and should not be re-immersed.*

## Hydrotherapy – the benefits of water during labour

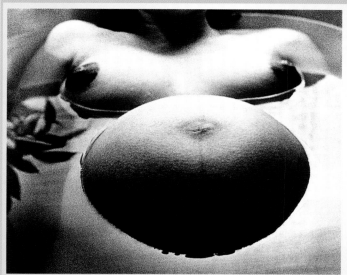

As well as providing a natural environment into which a baby can be born, water offers the mother a gentle form of pain relief. The various aches and pains associated with pregnancy – particularly lower back and buttock pains, and internal pressures – are eased by immersion in warm water, as the water supports the added weight, relieving the feeling of pressure.

Warm water also relaxes the mother, as the increased temperature slows the heart rate and increases the pressure within

the venous system. This is invaluable, as labour pains usually result in the mother tightening her muscles inward, which can prolong labour.

Water pools also give the mother the chance to try out various possible positions when it comes to the birth, as well as offering a gentle form of exercise. Options include kneeling, squatting, sitting or lying against the side of the pool, and the mother will be able to decide which birthing position is most comfortable. Partners can also enter the bath at this stage if they are planning to be in the bath on the day. This also gives partners the chance to help out with backache-relief exercises learned in antenatal classes.

*A warm bath is the best form of pain relief for mothers who choose a drug-free birth. During labour, the warm water also dilates the cervix, easing pain.*

# Recommending a water birth

Before a mother decides to have a water birth, she should be made aware of all the risks and benefits. These will be discussed with a trained midwife.

Many women choose to use alternative and self-help methods of pain relief at home and in hospital in order to avoid the use of drugs. One of their main choices is the use of the water pool for labour and delivery.

### BENEFITS OF WATER BIRTH
Because of the relative novelty of water births, there has been very little research into the advantages and disadvantages of delivering in this manner. For this reason, each case will be judged on its merits by the mother's midwife or birth centre, although there are certain

*A water birth can be a family affair. Because the mother is less stressed, families are more likely to join them in the pool, actively participating in the birth.*

complications that preclude a water birth (see box). However, there are also some definite benefits to delivering in water.

The main benefit is natural pain relief. The painkilling properties of warm water usually mean that no drugs are needed, hence the term 'aquadural'. Only about 10 per cent of mothers abandon a water birth to take painkilling drugs. The mother may take nitrous oxide and

oxygen ('gas and air') while in the pool, but to avoid any harm to the baby's respiratory system, no other drugs can be administered unless the mother leaves the pool.

### RELAXING EXPERIENCE
Another major benefit of water births is the relaxing effect on the vagina, vulva and perineum. This results in less stress to these parts of the body. The cervix is also dilated by warm water, and the pelvic floor muscles are relaxed, easing the passage of the baby.

Finally, a water birth encourages family involvement in the experience, improving the bond between the father and/or siblings and the newborn.

*A mother shows her daughter the placenta after a water birth. This is a good time for the newborn's brothers and sisters to learn about birth.*

---

## Water-birth criteria

There are various criteria that the mother and the fetus must meet before a water birth will be allowed by the midwife. Although the criteria vary depending on which maternity unit or midwife is overseeing the birth, the following points must be considered:

■ The pregnancy must be single – that is, twins and other multiple births must be done on 'dry land'

■ The pregnancy must also be between 37 and 42 weeks; premature or late births may be problematic, and should be carried out in a hospital

■ Breech births will probably also not be viable, for fear of

life-threatening complications

■ The mother should have had no more than four babies

■ Previous births must have been vaginal (that is, those who have had a Caesarean section will not be considered)

■ The results of screening for HIV and hepatitis B and C must be negative because of the potential risk of cross-infection to others involved in the birth

■ The baby's development must be normal, and fetal heart rate must be satisfactory during the final weeks of pregnancy

■ Mothers over a given weight – usually around 150 kg (330 lb) – are excluded.

---

## Preparations for a water birth

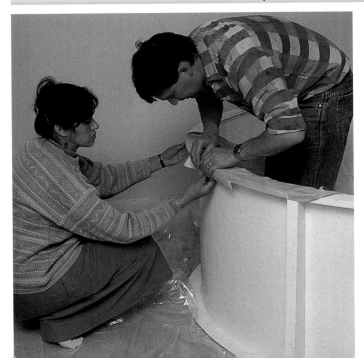

*Birthing pools can be hired, allowing mothers to deliver in their own homes. The birthing environment is important, and the pool – and the room it is in – must be carefully prepared.*

The water-birth decision will come after the mother has had discussions with her midwife. The mother will have to be aware of advantages and disadvantages, and also meet the criteria laid down by her midwife. Once the decision is made, the family can begin preparations.

■ If a pool is to be hired for a home birth, it should be set up well in advance to allow the mother to get used to moving around inside it. It should be big enough to allow her to stretch

out and move around, and allow room if a partner is to be present. The water, which should be maintained at 36.5–37.5 °C, must be level with the woman's breasts once she is in the pool

■ A good supply of towels should be at hand in order to dry off the newborn, as it will be susceptible to hypothermia if not dried straight away

■ The air will be very humid, and an air temperature of 21 °C should be maintained by an air-conditioning unit

■ A large kitchen sieve should be available to scoop out any faeces produced by the mother during labour

■ A waterproof pillow is useful for supporting the mother's neck.

■ Drinking water should be available for the mother.

# Water birth step-by-step

The stages of a water birth at home are exactly the same as those of a conventional delivery. Some of the procedures are slightly different and need the right timing if everything is to go smoothly.

A woman should only enter a pool to give birth when she has established labour and meets the following criteria:

■ Labour must not have been induced artificially

■ The mother must not have had any form of pain relief, the only exception being transcutaneous electrical nerve stimulation (TENS), the electrical stimulation of muscles tissue for pain relief

■ The membranes must have ruptured (the so-called breaking of the waters)

■ The cervix is effaced (thin) and dilated to more than 4 cm (1.6 in) in a primigravida (first birth) or 3 cm (1.2 in) in a multigravida (second or subsequent birth).

Entering the pool at this stage ensures the maximum analgesic effect from the water pool.

To ensure the baby's safety, regular fetal heart checks will be made. In some cases, the midwife will assess the heart beat for a full 20 minutes before the woman enters the pool.

### LEAVING THE POOL

Both mother and fetus are monitored throughout the birth, and if there are any problems, the woman will be asked to leave the pool.

Reasons for leaving include an increase in body temperature or blood pressure, evidence of baby distress, vaginal bleeding or the need for additional pain relief.

## First stage of labour

At the onset of labour, the woman gets into the pool, and her family gather around for support. The midwife is also on hand to monitor proceedings and perform regular checks on the mother and fetus.

Because the mother is more relaxed during a water birth than a normal hospital birth – and not as visibly distressed or affected by drugs – her family are more likely to join in the experience. Drinks can be provided, as can facecloths, massages and reassuring hugs. The keen father can also assist the midwife.

The mother will be supported by the water, and can move around freely. While waiting for the baby to be born, she can experiment with various positions to find the most comfortable for birth. These movements also help the descent of the baby.

Gravity is one of the best aids to birth, and a squatting or kneeling position is preferable, although any birthing position is feasible.

*The birthing pool should be constructed in a room than can be kept warm and not too bright. This will avoid too much shock to the newborn.*

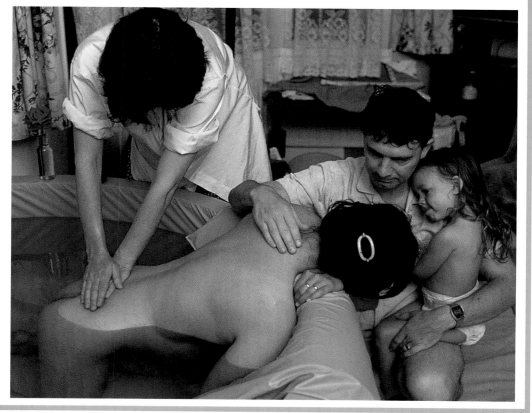

*The midwife, trained in water births, gently presses on the mother's sacrum, massaging away back pains. Meanwhile, her partner and daughter provide moral support.*

## Second stage of labour

Because of the warm water, the cervix dilates quickly. A vaginal examination by the midwife will confirm full dilatation, and the head of the baby will have begun its descent. The mother is allowed to push at her own rate.

Throughout the labour, the midwife will perform checks every 15 minutes on the baby's heart beat, half-hourly checks on the mother's pulse and hourly assessments of the mother's blood pressure and temperature. The water temperature will also be checked hourly.

*The final contractions push the baby out, guided gently by the midwife. It emerges totally immersed in the water, but then is carefully lifted into air.*

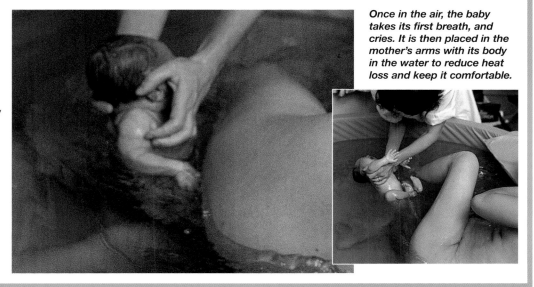

*Once in the air, the baby takes its first breath, and cries. It is then placed in the mother's arms with its body in the water to reduce heat loss and keep it comfortable.*

## Cutting the cord and postnatal checks

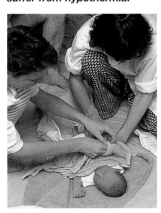

Once out of the water, the baby's physiological systems are triggered and the baby begins to breathe air. The baby is delivered to the mother's breast, and the umbilicus is cut. The procedure differs depending on the individual circumstances and midwives – often the cord is cut as soon as the baby leaves the water – but the postnatal checks are the same. The baby's temperature, heart rate and breathing will be measured (Apgar score) at one minute and again at five minutes after the birth.

*As soon as the baby emerges, the mother can put it to her breast. The midwife will cut and clamp the cord; usually 3–5 minutes after delivery.*

*The baby must be towel dried within minutes, as it will lose body heat rapidly and could suffer from hypothermia.*

## Third stage of labour

The final stage of the birthing process – the delivery of the placenta and membranes that surrounded the fetus – will usually be carried out once the mother has left the water. This is to ensure that any complications resulting in haemorrhaging will be noticed – the delivery of the placenta is messy and bloody, and blood owing to excess haemorrhaging may not be noticed if this occurs in the pool.

*The placenta and associated membranes will follow the birth of the baby, up to half an hour later. Drugs may be taken to ease delivery of the placenta if there is excessive bleeding.*

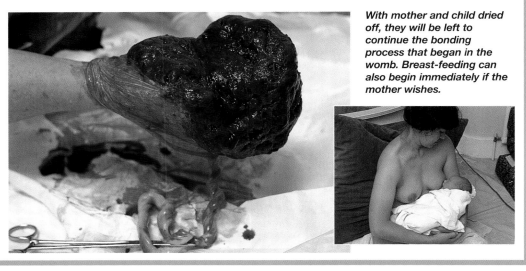

*With mother and child dried off, they will be left to continue the bonding process that began in the womb. Breast-feeding can also begin immediately if the mother wishes.*

# Pain relief in labour

The pain of labour and delivery is experienced differently by different women. And pain associated with the various stages of birth can be managed in a number of ways.

For some women, pain during childbirth is a positive experience – they consider it worthwhile when the end result is a live and healthy baby. Much of the pain experienced by women during labour is a result of the physical changes that take place in the uterus and cervix, and changes in hormone production. This pain is a natural part of birth, and such changes are necessary for the baby to be born.

■ **Uterine and cervical changes**
The contractions of the uterus at the onset of labour allow it to change shape in readiness for birth. The upper part becomes shorter and thicker and the lower part is taken up into the body of the uterus. As the contractions persist, the fundus – the top of the uterus – continues to press on the cervix, which dilates until the uterus and the cervix become a continuous birth canal.

■ **Hormonal changes**
Some women may experience discomfort because of increased hormone levels. The hormones act to relax the ligaments and muscles, allowing the uterus to grow in the abdomen. The joints also relax, and the spinal column tends to be fairly loose in pregnancy.

### PAIN THRESHOLD
Women experience pain in different ways. Some have a high threshold of pain; others have a low threshold and find labour intolerable. As each woman is unique in this respect, the basis for pain relief is asking about the pain and managing it on an individual basis.

### EXPECTATIONS OF PAIN
Before birth, a mother's expectations surrounding labour pain will often contrast with the reality. They may find that their ideas change considerably – that the pain is either much worse or not as bad as they thought.

Some women feel that if they have to ask for pain relief they have 'failed' because labour is supposed to be natural and they should be able to cope. This is not true as there are different types of labour. About 70–80 per cent of women go into labour spontaneously; others have long, complicated labour and some have their labour induced or accelerated. The pain associated with each is very different.

## Nerve supply of the uterus and cervix

*The uterus and cervix are served by a complex network of nerves. Pain will be experienced as the contractions of the first stage of labour begin. This will increase as the second stage of labour – the actual delivery – is underway.*

**Fundus**
Upper part of uterus

**Body of uterus**

**Cervix**
'Neck' of uterus; widens to accommodate passage of fetus

**Vagina**
Passage of fetus may result in stretching and tearing, causing pain

**10th, 11th and 12th thoracic vertebrae**
Nerves from this region serve the uterus; contraction pain is referred to this area of the back

**3rd and 4th lumbar vertebral border**
The level between the 3rd and 4th lumbar vertebrae is the usual site for epidural anaesthesia

**Cervical and upper vaginal nerves**
Pain results from cervical dilatation

**Nerves serving lower vagina and perineum**
Stretching of lower birth canal causes pain by putting pressure on the rectum and bladder

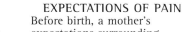

*Strong contractions begin in the early stages of labour. Although pain relief may not be necessary at this stage, emotional support for a woman is important.*

*As the cervix continues to dilate, the pain is often felt more strongly. This woman is attached to a cardiotocography machine, which monitors the baby's heart.*

# Coping with pain

The pain of each stage of labour is different because of the processes involved. The options for pain relief depend largely on a woman's wishes.

The pain of labour starts gradually and increases from a mild sensation that does not usually concern the woman, to very severe pain at the end of the first stage of labour.

In the second stage (the actual delivery), the pain is a constant but very different type of sensation. During this stage, as the woman is pushing, the contractions take on a kind of involuntary expulsive action which the woman is unable to control; the pain is constant and she feels the need to push the baby out.

It is usually the baby's head that causes this sensation because it is a firm, solid mass and as

such is distinct from the rest of the body. Once the baby's head is born, the mother's feeling of relief is extremely strong because she is over the most difficult part. However, the contractions continue and are still quite strong because the rest of the baby's body is yet to be born.

Once the baby is fully born, the placenta is delivered in the third stage of labour, and the contractions change yet again. These contractions are not quite as severe as during labour or the delivery of the child.

As soon as the baby and placenta have been delivered, the labour pains and contractions stop completely.

*The most difficult part of labour is the delivery of the baby's head, seen here just appearing. A woman's pain is usually at its most intense at this point.*

*During the first stage of labour, nitrous oxide is often inhaled for pain relief. This woman is holding a mask through which this is delivered.*

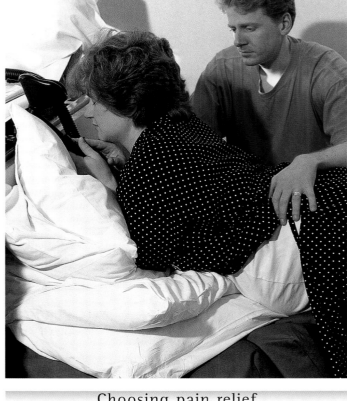

## Choosing pain relief

From the beginning of pregnancy, women are encouraged to attend antenatal parental classes in preparation for labour. At these classes, they are given an opportunity to discuss their wishes with regard to pain relief in labour. They are also able to discuss with their midwife the type of pain relief that they feel would be best suited for them.

In some maternity units, a woman can talk to an

anaesthetist about systemic (affecting the whole body) pain relief; this is the anaesthetist's area of expertise. The use of epidurals in labour is common, and the anaesthetist can provide information about the advantages and disadvantages of the various options.

*When pain is severe in the lower abdomen, the woman may find that squatting helps to ease some of the discomfort.*

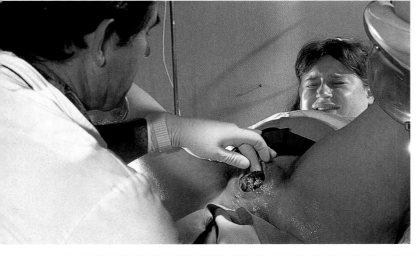

## Options for pain relief

The treatments available for pain relief in labour can be divided into two main categories: pharmacological and non-pharmacological.

### Pharmacological
Pharmacological pain relief involves the use of drugs. These include inhaled nitrous oxide ('gas and air'), which provides analgesia without inducing loss of consciousness, and pethidine, which is injected intramuscularly. The most popular form of this type of pain relief, however, is epidural anaesthesia.

### Non-pharmacological
These types of pain relief are drug-free, and include such methods as support and massage, positioning, mobility, relaxation and breathing, hydrotherapy (water therapy) and transcutaneous electrical nerve stimulation (TENS).

Complementary therapies are also used, such as homeopathy, aromatherapy, acupuncture, music, hypnosis, and sometimes yoga, which is increasingly being considered to be a form of complementary therapy. The aim of these alternatives is to enable a woman to cope with pain.

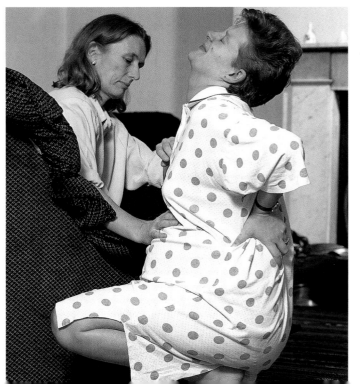

# Drug-free pain relief in labour

For women preferring not to use drugs for pain relief during labour, there is a variety of drug-free methods of pain control. These range from breathing techniques to complementary therapies.

Non-pharmacological methods can be used whether a woman is in labour in hospital or at home. Most methods of pain relief are means of distracting a woman from the pain of childbirth and do not actually reduce the pain. However, they help her to cope better with the labour pain, right up to the time of delivery. Drug-free methods of pain relief also tend to depend on the support given to the woman by her birthing partner.

### RELAXATION AND BREATHING

Techniques to calm and relax are generally taught in antenatal classes. Women and their partners are taught how to use breathing exercises and relaxation techniques to cope with the pain of labour; for example, the type of breathing that is most beneficial at the beginning of a contraction, while it lasts and as it ends.

Hydrotherapy (immersion in warm water) is also often used to relax the muscles during the first stage of labour, taking the edge off the pain.

### POSITION AND MOBILITY

Methods that allow a woman to take on a comfortable position work by using gravity to reduce

the impact of the pain on the uterus and the effect of the pain on the woman. If she is standing or squatting or even moving around, the contractions

tend to be much more effective and this encourages labour. This in turn may lead to more effective use of the contractions and possibly a shorter labour.

*Even if a woman has not opted for a water birth, she may well spend time in a water pool before the delivery. Warm water is an effective pain reliever.*

## Using electrical stimulation for pain relief

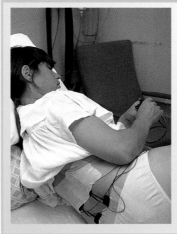

Transcutaneous electrical nerve stimulation (TENS) is a form of pain relief that is administered by a machine that generates low level electrical impulses. These are transmitted through electrodes placed on the woman's back.

Pain relief is achieved because the impulses stimulate nerves in the back and interfere with the pain signals transmitted to the brain. This encourages a build-up

*A great advantage of TENS is that a woman can control the signals herself. This form of pain relief is most effective in the earlier stages of labour.*

of the natural pain-relieving chemicals in the body (endorphins).

A woman is able to control the strength and rate of the pulses from the hand-held TENS machine. TENS can be used from week 37 of the pregnancy onwards and throughout the whole of labour, except when the woman is having a bath or shower. The machines are available in hospital or can be hired for home use. Often, women using TENS at home find it is particularly useful in the early stages of labour, as this is when it has the greatest effect.

*TENS equipment comprises a battery-powered unit with electrodes that attach to skin. It is usually used from the onset of the first stage of labour.*

# Choosing a drug-free birth

There is a bewildering choice of alternative pain-relief and pain-control
methods available to a pregnant woman; prospective parents should be aware
of the pros and cons of each type.

The advantages of non-pharmacological methods or self-help methods are that there are no clinical side effects, the women can use these methods themselves and their birthing partners play an important role. Furthermore, these methods can be used alongside other types of pain relief to make the pain easier to cope with.

*Often, simple measures, such as rubbing a sore back, help to make the pain of labour more bearable. This is where a birthing partner can assist.*

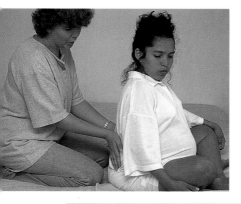

A further advantage of these methods is that they appear to be more natural and can be used in the home as well as in hospital. They are quite useful for distracting a woman from the pain, and she will feel more in control of her labour. They are also beneficial because fewer drugs need to be used for pain relief.

### DISADVANTAGES
One disadvantage of drug-free methods is that the pain itself is not actually reduced, and they only provide a distraction from the pain. The pain may be easier to cope with, but it is not actually reduced, as it would be with pharmacological methods. Relaxation and breathing techniques also need to be learnt and practised before labour begins, and this is not always possible for some women and their birthing partners.

*If a woman can move around during labour, she will feel more able to control the pain herself. Leaning forward over a chair may be beneficial.*

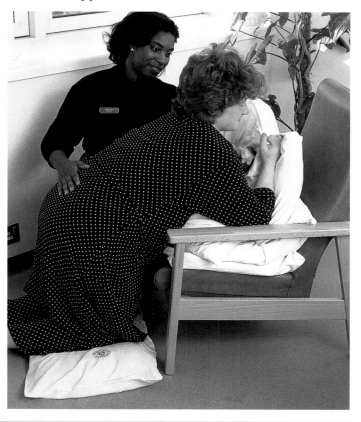

## Complementary methods

There are several complementary therapies that may be used by women during labour. Midwives can provide information on some of these therapies, their uses and their limited effects. Although their precise benefit is unproven, they are becoming more popular.

*Many women wish to have as natural a birth as possible. If a woman is healthy, and there is little risk of complications, most units will try to ensure this.*

### Acupuncture
This is the stimulation of particular points on the body, using special needles to enhance the flow of 'energy' along pathways called meridians. Some hospitals have midwives who are trained in acupuncture and who are able to offer help and advice, often in the antenatal period and in preparation for labour. Most units allow women to bring their acupuncturist in with them if they need treatment during labour.

*Acupuncture – using needles to stimulate nerve pathways – is believed by some to be beneficial in labour and birth. It also serves to calm the mother.*

### Acupressure
This is based on similar principles to those of acupuncture, and involves the application of pressure to increase the level of endorphins (natural pain-relieving chemicals) in the body.

### Aromatherapy
This involves massaging oils into the skin and inhaling their vapours to stimulate, refresh, sooth and heal. During labour, it reduces stress and pain.

### Homeopathy
The homeopathic remedies used in labour will depend on the physical and emotional state of the mother.

### Hypnotherapy
Self-hypnosis may be used to induce a state of concentration, combined with relaxation, to reduce the perception of pain.

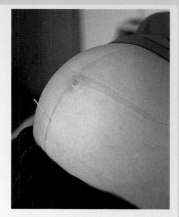

### Osteopathy
This involves the manipulation of the spine, joints and muscles by relaxing the woman, easing the process of birth.

### Reflexology
This is concerned with the reflex zones of the feet, as they are considered to correspond to different parts of the body. These zones are massaged in order to increase the circulation within the body, reduce tension and enhance relaxation.

# Episiotomy

Medical intervention by cutting the perineum is sometimes necessary during childbirth to assist delivery. This procedure – an episiotomy – involves careful surgical incision and repair.

An episiotomy is a surgical cut made in the perineum (tissues surrounding the vagina) during childbirth. Over 85 per cent of vaginal births involve some perineal trauma, which may be spontaneous (tearing) or intentional (an episiotomy). Tears and episiotomies can be categorized according to the degree of damage they cause:
■ First-degree tears – damage skin
■ Second-degree tears or episiotomies – involve perineal muscles
■ Third-degree tears or episiotomies – partially or totally disrupt the anal sphincter
■ Fourth-degree tears – completely disrupt the external and internal anal sphincters and epithelium.

Worldwide, episiotomy rates differ greatly. In the Netherlands it is performed in 8 per cent of vaginal births; in the UK, 26–67 per cent; and in some East European countries, 99 per cent.

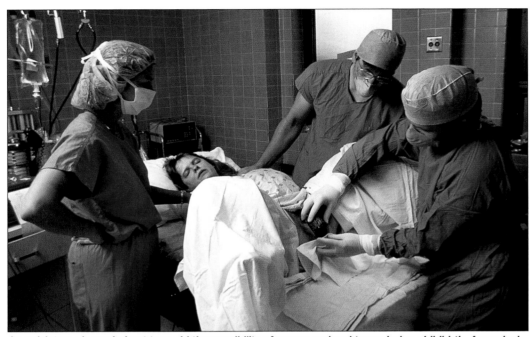

*An episiotomy is carried out to avoid the possibility of severe perineal tears during childbirth. A surgical cut widens the vaginal orifice.*

## Predisposing factors

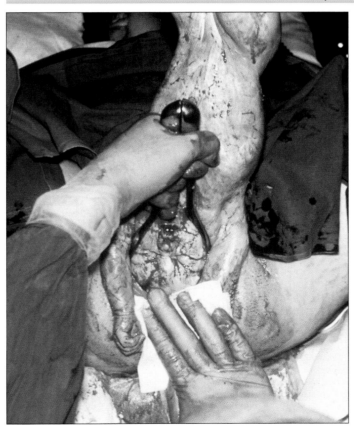

There are a number of circumstances and risk factors that increase the possibility of an episiotomy being performed.

### RISK FACTORS
An episiotomy is more likely if:
■ There is a delay in the second stage of labour due to a tight perineum. This is more likely if the baby is big, if the head is poorly flexed, or if it is a first baby. Delay in the second stage is also caused by shoulder dystocia (where the passage of the shoulders is obstructed)
■ The perineum is threatening to tear – there is, however, another school of thought which believes that tears heal better than episiotomies and that therefore the perineum should be allowed to tear
■ An instrumental delivery is to be performed
■ The presentation and position of the fetus requires more space within the pelvis. If the baby is in

*Assisted deliveries, such as those involving forceps, often require an episiotomy. This expands the vaginal orifice, allowing safer use of the instruments.*

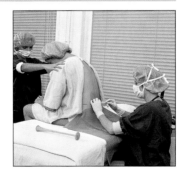

*An epidural is an anaesthetic delivered into the spinal column. Often administered during labour, it works effectively to prevent pain from an episiotomy.*

an unfavourable position, such as breech presentation (buttocks first), an episiotomy can help
■ The baby is premature – an elective episiotomy is performed to reduce trauma to the head.

### EPIDURALS
Epidural anaesthesia during labour is not in itself a risk factor for episiotomy, but it does increase the chance of an instrumental delivery, which in turn requires an episiotomy.

## Assisted delivery

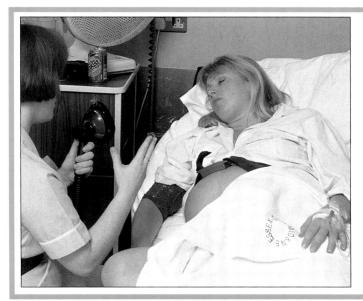

### First stage of labour

*While in early labour, the mother has a chance to wash and freshen up. She may also enjoy a short bath or shower.*

*The midwife carries out a number of checks on the mother and baby. She then talks through the birth plan with the patient and looks at options.*

As with a normal delivery, labour usually begins with the onset of regular painful contractions or a 'show', and the mother is admitted to the labour ward.

There, she is seen by a midwife who takes her medical history, examines her and checks blood pressure, pulse and urine. The midwife checks the abdomen for the baby's size, presentation, activity and heartbeat, and takes a cardiotocograph trace (electronic monitoring of the baby's heart rate). She assesses the state of the cervix and the presenting part of the baby by vaginal examination. She then goes through the mother's labour plan, reviewing the available options, and discussing any possible problems.

### Pain relief

The mother finds that some gas and air helps her to cope with the pain during the early stages of labour.

However, as the contractions increase in intensity and frequency, the gas and air does not adequately control the pain and she requests an epidural. This is an anaesthetic placed in the epidural layer of the spinal cavity, which blocks the nerves of the lower body. It provides very effective analgesia, but has the disadvantage of immobilizing the mother and may affect her ability to push during delivery.

*The mother is given a local anaesthetic into the lower spine. The anaesthetist then inserts an epidural catheter for introduction of the anaesthetic.*

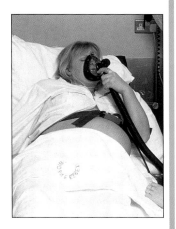

*As the contractions increase, the mother finds that some gas and air helps her to cope with the pain. The baby's heart rate is monitored constantly.*

### Early fetal distress

With effective analgesia in place, the obstetrician examines the mother again and looks at the cardiotocograph during contractions. He describes the risks of the hypoxic (oxygen depriving) effect of the contractions on the baby's brain and how, if inadequately managed, there is a risk of brain damage.

The obstetrician then explains that progress has slowed over the last hour and now, with signs of fetal distress, the best option is to assist the delivery by ventouse. suction. He describes how the procedure will help the baby's passage through the pelvic cavity.

▼ *The obstetrician explains the cardiotocograph to the mother. He tells her that the baby is beginning to show signs of early distress.*

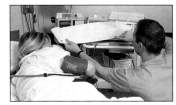

▶ *The birth management options are explained. The obstetrician recommends ventouse delivery and describes how this will be carried out.*

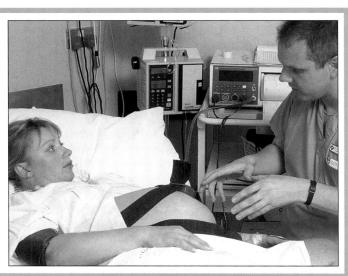

## Positioning the ventouse suction cup

The mother is informed about the risks of the procedure, and is told to expect the baby's head to appear slightly distorted by the suction cup. She is positioned in readiness for the procedure.

Some mothers have a urinary catheter inserted to drain any residual urine and prevent a full bladder from impeding progress. If time and circumstances allow, the effect of the epidural may be allowed to wear off a little, giving the patient better control during the actual delivery.

*The baby's head is palpated for position and lie. The ventouse suction cup is carefully positioned over the crown before it is applied.*

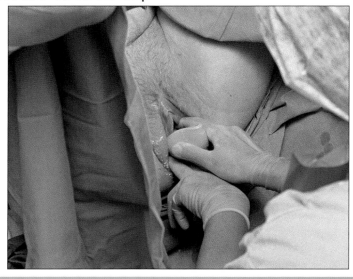

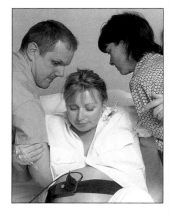

*The medical staff give physical and emotional support to the expectant mother. The support of a friend or partner is also very valuable at this time.*

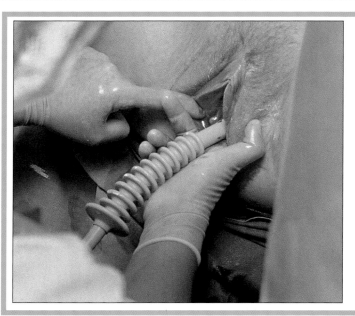

## Suction pressure

After checking the position of the cup on the head once more, the obstetrician slowly increases the suction pressure to provide a firm connection between ventouse and scalp. This will transmit the gentle pulling force from the obstetrician to assist the baby down through the birth canal.

The mother is asked to push with each contraction. Throughout the labour, she is constantly reassured to allay the inevitable high levels of anxiety about her baby's welfare.

*The position of the cup on the head is checked again. The doctor then slowly increases the suction pressure to assist the baby through the birth canal.*

*The patient pushes with each contraction, as in a normal delivery. Most of the force responsible for expelling the baby is due to the contractions.*

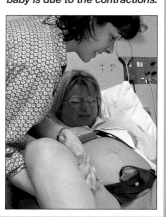

## Crowning

As the baby's head moves slowly down the canal and towards the perineum, its heartbeat is monitored on the cardiotocograph. If, at any point, there is concern that the ventouse is not proving effective, or that there is unacceptable fetal distress, the procedure may need to be reviewed and alternative options considered.

Once the baby's head has been delivered, the cord is checked for its position, as in a normal delivery. The baby's airway is also checked and cleared.

At this time, the mother may be able to put her hand down to feel the baby's head as it emerges.

▼ *As the baby's head appears, the ventouse cup will be seen attached to the scalp. The scalp may appear slightly distorted from the suction pressure.*

*As the baby's head is delivered, the umbilical cord is checked for its position. The baby's airway is then also checked and cleared at this time.*

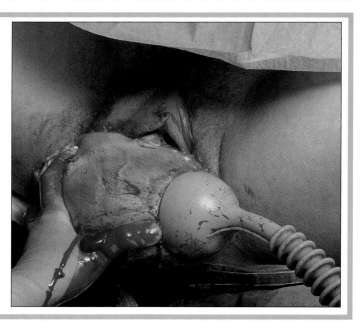

## Delivering the baby

As the anterior shoulder of the baby is delivered, the mother is given an intra-muscular injection of syntocinon or syntometrine. This drug contracts the uterus and helps the delivery of the placenta, reducing of the risk of haemorrhage. The ventouse cap is removed to allow the obstetrician greater access to assist in the delivery of the anterior shoulder. Depending on the lie of the presenting part, some minor manipulation may be required to deliver the shoulder.

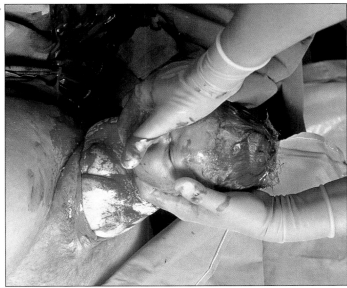

*The ventouse cap is removed from the baby's head to give the obstetrician room to manoeuvre. Some slight manipulation may be needed.*

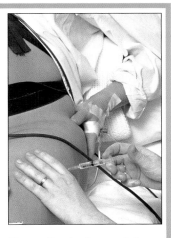

*The mother is given an intra-muscular injection of syntocinon or syntometrine. This assists with delivery of the placenta.*

## Cutting the cord

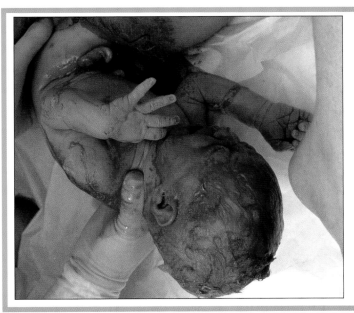

With the delivery of the shoulder, the widest diameter has been delivered and the rest of the body follows easily.

The baby is held while the cord is clamped and cut. The suction mark from the ventouse is clearly visible on the baby's scalp, but usually causes only minor damage and the swelling will subside over the next couple of days. Some bruising occasionally occurs.

The baby is passed to the paediatrician for assessment and the obstetrician can prepare for the delivery of the placenta.

*The widest diameter of the baby is across the shoulders. Once the shoulders have been delivered, the rest of the baby's body slides out easily.*

*A clamp is put on the baby's umbilical cord, which is then cut. Shortly afterwards, the placenta is delivered and is checked.*

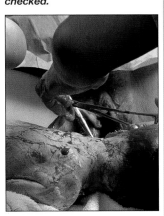

## Postnatal checks

The paediatrician checks the baby's condition using the APGAR score. This assessment is made one minute after delivery and again after five minutes. A score of 0-2 is given in each of five areas: activity (muscle tone), pulse rate, grimace (reflex irritability), appearance (skin colour) and respiration. A score of 7–10 is normal, 4–7 might indicate need for intervention and below 3 requires immediate resuscitation.

An identification tag is always applied to the baby's ankle at this stage.

▼ *The baby is checked using the APGAR score. This system of assessment is performed at one minute, and then five minutes, after delivery.*

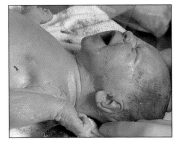

▶ *If the APGAR score is satisfactory, the baby is washed, wrapped in a blanket and given to the mother to hold. She may put the child to her breast.*

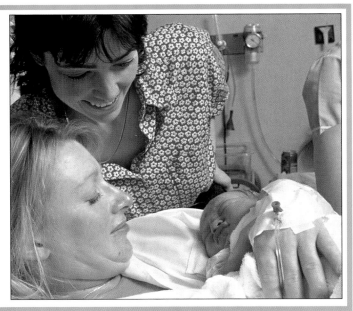

# Caesarean section

Caesarean section is now a very common method for delivering a baby, but it is still a major operative procedure. It is performed with the mother awake, except in certain emergencies.

Caesarean section is the delivery of a baby through an incision made in the front of the abdomen and the front of the uterus. About one in every five babies born in teaching hospitals in the UK is born by Caesarean operation, and about one in every six babies born in non-teaching units. This means that there are at least 100,000 Caesarean operations performed in the UK each year.

There are two classes of Caesarean; those that are planned, and those that are emergencies.

### PLANNED CAESAREAN
There is a range of conditions which may require an elective Caesarean delivery, including:

■ **Disproportion**
It may be obvious that the baby is too large for the mother's pelvis and will not be able to be delivered vaginally. This can often be predicted before labour. In the antenatal clinic, doctors estimate the relative size of the baby's head and the mother's pelvis; it should become clear that the baby's head will not pass through the pelvis easily. This test is also done if the buttocks are coming first (breech delivery).

'Trial of labour' is performed when it is not certain that there is disproportion. This is an

*A breech presentation is when the baby's buttocks – rather than head – engage in the pelvis. Although normal delivery may be possible, the need for a Caesarean must be considered.*

attempt to see whether, when labour has been properly established, the baby will come down in the mother's pelvis.

Often the trial is successful and a vaginal delivery is possible, but the trial fails if after a few hours the baby is not coming down properly, or if either the baby or the mother is becoming distressed.

■ **Placenta previa**
This is a condition in which the placenta lies over the birth canal, preceding the baby before

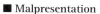

*Caesarean sections are performed for a number of reasons, most often if there are likely to be difficulties with a normal vaginal delivery.*

delivery. There could be marked and dangerous bleeding, and both the baby's life and the mother's life may be at risk.

Placenta previa can be diagnosed fairly early in the pregnancy by ultrasound. The mother can sometimes be told as

*Pregnant women are more prone to developing high blood pressure. If a normal delivery would be dangerous for mother or baby, a Caesarean section will be performed.*

early as the 30th week of the pregnancy that the placenta is in such a position and that the only safe delivery will be a Caesarean.

■ **Malpresentation**
This means that the baby is not lying correctly; for example, when the baby lies across the mother's uterus instead of coming out head first or buttocks first.

■ **Chronic medical conditions**
Certain conditions, such as heart disease, may be indications for a Caesarean operation. It is not always possible to know whether a woman with heart disease will be capable of labour, even if she wants to have a vaginal delivery.

## Emergency Caesarean

If there are sudden difficulties with the labour that cannot be foreseen, an emergency Caesarean may be undertaken. Conditions that warrant an emergency Caesarean include:

■ **'Fetal distress'**
The process of birth can be traumatic for the baby, sometimes resulting in a condition called fetal distress. It is most often diagnosed when the baby's heartbeat has become irregular.

■ **Prolapsed umbilical cord**
Sometimes when the membranes rupture (the 'waters' break) quite unexpectedly, the umbilical cord comes down as the waters rush out. This is an emergency and the only treatment is a rapid Caesarean, otherwise the baby will asphyxiate. The condition is seldom diagnosed before it happens, and it will not occur if the baby's head is fully engaged in the pelvis. A general anaesthetic may be needed.

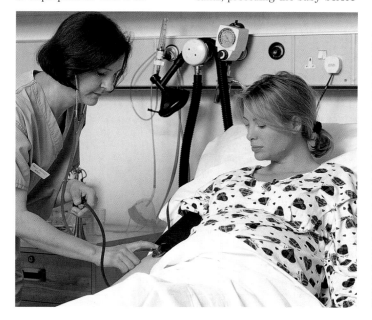

# The operation

The woman will be admitted into hospital and prepared as for any other operation. The procedure is fully explained to her and her partner, if present.

## Administering the anaesthetic

Caesareans may be performed with either a general or a spinal epidural anaesthetic. With the latter, the woman is conscious throughout the operation. For a spinal anaesthetic, a needle is placed in the lower spine, into the area where there is cerebrospinal fluid. For the epidural, the needle is not inserted so deeply into the spine and anaesthetic passes through a catheter which is placed in the spine where the nerve roots emerge. The two are often combined in a spino-epidural anaesthetic.

*Many anaesthetists prefer to have the woman lying on her side to receive the anaesthetic. This reduces the chance of postural hypotension (low blood pressure).*

It takes about 20 minutes to set up epidural anaesthesia. A catheter is inserted to empty the bladder to prevent any damage to it during the operation.

*This woman is sitting upright while having her anaesthetic commenced. The anaesthetist is preparing the site with a local anaesthetic injection.*

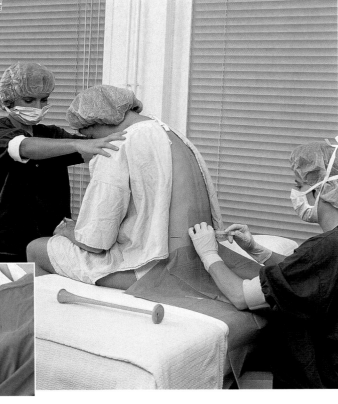

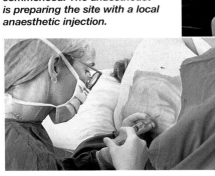

## The procedure

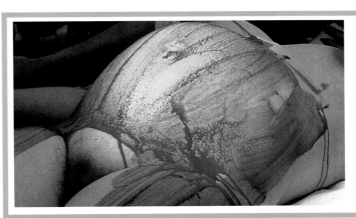

### Preparation

After the woman is anaesthetized and taken into the theatre, the skin over the whole of the lower half of her abdomen and the upper part of her thighs is prepared. The entire area is washed carefully with an antiseptic solution, usually containing an iodine preparation.

Towels or sterile drapes are placed over the woman with an aperture across the lower abdomen, over the operative site. The baby will normally be delivered through an incision just above or at the level of the upper part of the pubic hairline. This hair will have been shaved off before the operation, usually before the patient comes to the operating theatre.

*The whole of the lower part of the woman's abdomen is carefully cleaned with an antiseptic preparation, which is left on the skin for the duration of the operation.*

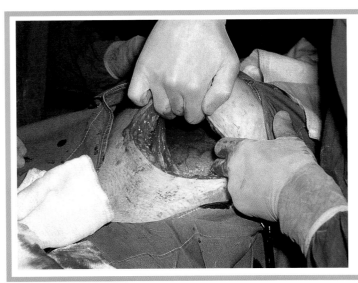

### Making the abdominal incision

The incision in the lower abdomen goes from side to side (transverse). Once the skin has been incised, blood vessels that may be bleeding are coagulated electrically to stop them oozing. The fat under the skin is then incised.

Next, a sheath of silver-coloured tissue is seen and this is cut across; muscle is found underneath it. The sheath is separated from the muscle by a few quick cuts with scissors. The muscles run vertically, and the surgeon must separate them sufficiently to allow the baby to pass through. The peritoneum is then reached, which is a membrane found over the whole of the abdominal cavity. This is cut either with scissors or a knife and direct access to the uterus is achieved. An instrument is then inserted to enable the surgeon to identify where the bladder is attached to the front of the uterus. The bladder is pushed down, so that the incision in the uterus can be made in the place that will be later covered by the bladder when it is allowed to fill up after the operation.

*The surgeon gently stretches the opening in the abdominal wall to make sure that there is good access to the uterus, and that the baby can be safely delivered through it.*

## Cutting the uterus

The cut across the lower part of the uterus is then made. It is now important to get the baby out as quickly as possible. Great care is taken to see that the baby is not damaged. The sac of amniotic fluid in which the baby lies is opened with scissors or with the tip of a knife.

The surgeon reaches beneath and behind the baby, so that if the head is in front, as it usually is, it can be brought out through the incision. If the baby is lying the other way round, the legs are brought out.

*The bladder is held down and protected by a retractor. Suction is used to remove blood and fluid when the uterus is opened.*

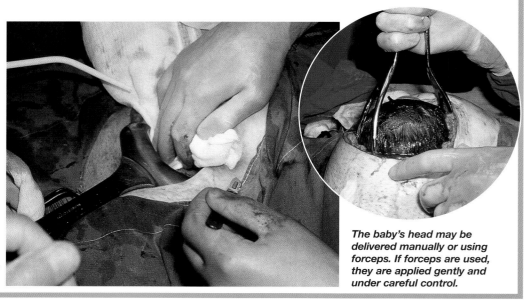

*The baby's head may be delivered manually or using forceps. If forceps are used, they are applied gently and under careful control.*

## Delivering the baby

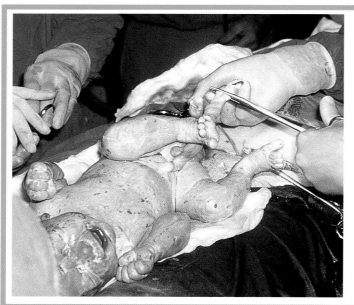

Often, the baby takes its first breath once its head is out and before the rest of the body has been delivered, as happens in a normal delivery. The rest of the baby is then delivered.

If the mother is awake, the baby is shown to her and her partner and they may be able to handle it. The surgeon then delivers the afterbirth after clamping the cord. The surgeon hands the placenta and sac to a nurse, who makes sure that they are complete.

*The baby often takes its first breath before the whole body is delivered, and may cry immediately after delivery.*

*Once the baby has been delivered, the placenta and membranes are slowly removed after giving a drug that contracts the uterus.*

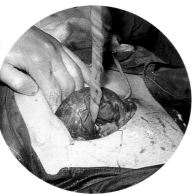

## Checking the baby and repairing the wound

The paediatrician or midwife responsible for the baby makes sure that it is breathing properly. If there is a breathing problem, the baby is put onto a resuscitation table and, if necessary, a tube is passed into its air passages so that its lungs can be inflated with oxygen. Sometimes, fluid or mucus has to be sucked out of the baby's air passages.

If the mother is awake, she (and her partner) can be handed the baby again or even put it to her breast.

Once the afterbirth has been delivered, the surgeon starts to repair the incision made in the uterus. He uses catgut or a similar absorbable material which will dissolve within a few weeks.

*After delivery, the baby may need to be placed on a resuscitation table so that mucus and other fluids can be cleared from the air passages.*

The uterus is sewn up in two layers to make sure that the scar is going to be firm, and perhaps allow the woman to have a labour in a subsequent pregnancy. The bladder is then lifted back up to cover the wound.

Next, the abdomen is closed by stitching the straight muscles together, and by carefully sewing up the sheath that was cut at the beginning of the operation. The skin is then stitched neatly.

The operation takes 20–45 minutes, depending on the experience of the surgeon and the difficulty of the procedure.

*The father is often present at the operation, and will be able to hold the baby a short time after it has been delivered.*

# After the operation

Although a Caesarean section is a major operation, the mother's recovery is usually uncomplicated. She will be able to leave the hospital within a few days.

Once the operation is finished, the woman is taken to the recovery room. From there, she is taken to the postnatal ward and closely monitored to ensure that all is well. Following Caesarean delivery, the uterus behaves in virtually the same way as it does after a normal delivery, namely reducing in size day by day, until after a few weeks it is almost back to the size it was at the beginning of the pregnancy.

### AFTERCARE OF MOTHER AND BABY

The baby's aftercare is no different from that after a normal delivery, because the drugs used for the spinal and epidural have no effect on it.

The epidural catheter used for administering anaesthetic during the operation can also be used to aid pain relief after the operation. It is quite usual now to inject a narcotic such as morphine into the epidural space before taking the epidural catheter out. The process of removing the catheter is completely painless.

An epidural is a very good anaesthetic for a Caesarean because the patients feel bright and are very rarely sick after an epidural. They have less pain in the following few days than with a general anaesthetic.

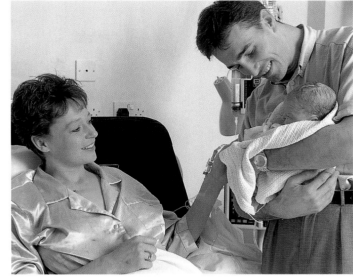

*Although the mother will have more abdominal discomfort after a Caesarean, she will be able to look after the baby as normal, including breast-feeding.*

General anaesthetics are given in cases of great hurry, because it takes 20 minutes or so to set up an epidural, whereas a general anaesthetic can be given in three minutes and this may be necessary if there is a lot of bleeding from a condition, such a placenta previa, or if there is a prolapsed umbilical cord.

Sometimes a catheter is passed into the woman's bladder, and this is usually left

*Once mother and baby have returned home, they will be visited in the normal way by the midwife or health visitor.*

in place for a day or so after the operation. It will be taken out after sensation has returned to her bladder. The mother should then be able to pass urine quite easily.

### GOING HOME

Most women are able to leave hospital within a few days of a Caesarean – sometimes as quickly as three days after the operation. It is then important that they have plenty of support at home, and the midwife or health visitor will usually visit mother and baby in the weeks following the birth.

Within a few weeks of the operation, there should be complete recovery for the mother. In some cases, patients are able to resume normal activities within 10 days of a Caesarean.

---

## History of Caesareans

Caesarean sections have been carried out for over 2,000 years, but the earliest were always post-mortem (after the mother had died). The word Caesarean probably comes from the Latin 'caesus', derived from 'caedere' (to cut out). Legend has it that Julius Caesar was born in this way, although this is doubtful. However, the operation may be named after an ancient law, restated by Caesar, which decreed that a woman dying during labour should be cut open in the hope of saving the unborn child.

In 1610, a Caesarean section was performed on a live woman, but she died from infection after 25 days. There was no anaesthetic and the wounds were left open.

The operation became much safer once it was decided to remove the baby from the lowest part of the uterus. With the development of techniques of anaesthesia and the discovery of effective antibiotics, the safety of the operation improved.

The popularity of the procedure has increased to such an extent that in some hospitals, the rate of Caesarean births is now around 20 per cent of all deliveries.

The increased use of epidural rather than general anaesthesia during the operation has meant that the mother is able to be involved in the operation, and can handle the baby shortly after the birth.

*It is becoming increasingly common for the father to be present during the operation. In this way, the parents can share in the birth experience.*

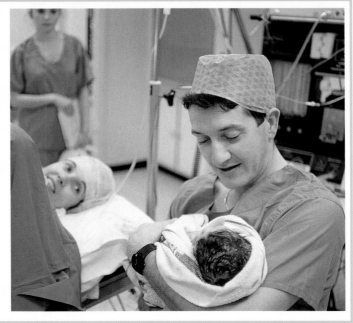

# Twin birth

While relatively common, twin births hold special dangers for both
the mother and babies. A specialist medical team is in attendance to
actively manage the birth, avoiding potential dangers.

A twin pregnancy may occur for two reasons:
■ Two eggs are released from the ovaries and are fertilized at the same time – resulting in non-identical (dizygotic) twins
■ A single fertilized egg splits in two, giving rise to two separate fetuses, which are genetically identical (monozygotic) twins.

### FREQUENCY

Natural twin pregnancies are relatively common. In 1980, an average of 1 in 50 children born in the UK was a twin. In 2001, this figure is 1 in 35, due to the increase in the number of pregnancies from assisted conception techniques such as IVF, and an increase in the number of women aged over 35 giving birth.

### PREGNANCY PROBLEMS

Most minor problems associated with pregnancy are more common in multiple pregnancies.

In the first trimester (the first three months of the pregnancy) the circulating levels of various pregnancy hormones are higher than average. This may cause marked nausea and vomiting,

sometimes to the point of requiring hospital admission and intravenous fluids.

A mother carrying twins is placing a high demand on her cardiovascular system and she is likely to need more rest. She may also need to take maternity leave much earlier.

As the pregnancy progresses, a mother carrying twins is increasingly likely to suffer from backache, indigestion, haemorrhoids and varicose veins due to the greater abdominal bulk and pressure on surrounding organs.

During the third trimester, the mother may be increasingly tired and will find that she requires more rest.

### MANAGEMENT

Multiple pregnancies need careful management, and ante-natal clinic visits are increased to allow close monitoring of the mother and babies.

*Twins represent a greater than normal amount of growing tissue within the uterus, placing the mother's body under increased pressure.*

## Complications

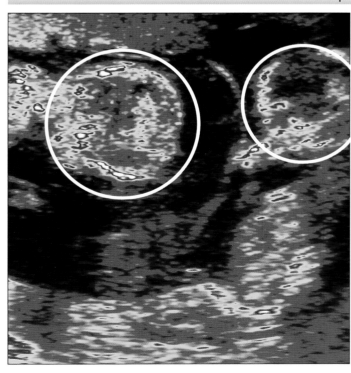

*This scan shows twins at 20 weeks' gestation (heads circled). The baby on the left is lying horizontally, while the twin on the right is in a vertical position.*

Almost every major complication is more common in multiple pregnancies, particularly:
■ Maternal anaemia (iron and folic acid deficiency)
■ Pre-eclampsia (pregnancy-induced high blood pressure) – this can lead to placental abruption (detachment of the placenta) or fatal maternal haemorrhage if left untreated
■ Malpresentation – the second twin may be displaced by the first into a transverse position
■ Placental insufficiency – where twins share one placenta there may be a deficiency of oxygen and nutrients
■ Placenta praevia – in which the placenta is positioned in the lower segment of the uterus
■ Premature rupture of the membranes and premature

labour – due to the overdistension of the uterus or malpresentation
■ Prolapsed cord – in which the umbilical cord lies beside or below the presenting part of the baby, causing hypoxia (oxygen starvation).

### MONITORING

Close ultrasound monitoring of fetal growth ensures the early identification of any problems.

Inevitably, twin babies are more prone to prematurity and low birth weight and are subsequently at higher risk of neonatal (newborn) problems. As a result, the mortality rate for twins is four times higher than that for singletons (single baby).

### LABOUR

Delivery of the first baby often proceeds naturally. However, cord prolapse or an unusual lie (positioning of the baby) may require a Caesarean section to deliver the second baby safely.

# Labour

Labour and delivery of the first twin proceeds as for a singleton. The potential problems of a twin birth most often actualize during delivery of the second baby.

As with a singleton pregnancy, the onset of normal labour may be heralded by several signs:
■ A 'show' as the cervical mucus plug is passed
■ The 'waters breaking' as the amniotic sac ruptures
■ Regular contractions, of at least one every 10 minutes.

Due to the size and pressure on the uterine wall, premature labour is relatively common in multiple pregnancies. Labour may be induced if there is evidence of placental-insufficiency or maternal complications, such as pre-eclampsia, arise.

The day before delivery, the mother makes a last antenatal visit to the hospital, where:
■ She is weighed and examined abdominally
■ She has her blood pressure, temperature and pulse rate taken
■ She is attached to a monitor to check the babies' heart rates
■ She has blood taken for cross-matching in case a transfusion is necessary.

Those women being induced or having an elective Caesarean would then stay overnight.

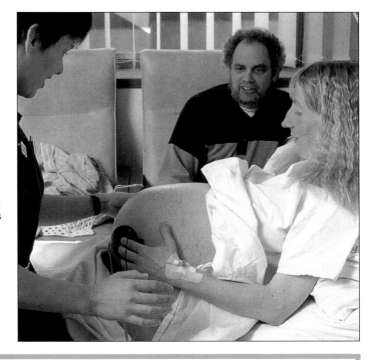

*Monitoring the babies' heartbeats is useful for the obstetrician and reassuring for the mother. Each baby is monitored individually.*

## Admission to hospital

The mother is admitted to hospital and assessed, often in the presence of a birth partner.

During the early part of the first stage of a twin labour, the onset of regular contractions shortens the cervical length and the forward-most fetus is pushed down against the dilating cervix.

At this time, the mother may choose to sit up, lie on her side or walk around, which may ease the pain. Mild analgesia may also be given if needed as the labour commences.

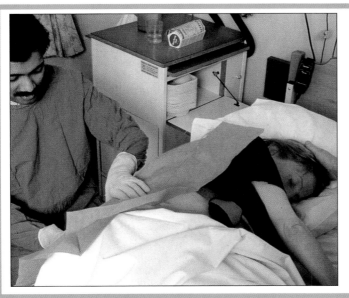

*In the early stages of labour the mother may find it helpful to move around. This will help to control pain and precipitate the birth.*

*As the contractions begin, the mother may require analgesia. It is a good idea for her to rest at this stage, conserving energy for the birth.*

## Epidural

An epidural is recommended for twin births since, after the delivery of the first twin, the second twin may need to be manipulated into a suitable position for delivery. If manipulation of the second twin is not possible, a Caesarian section may need to be performed.

The mother lies on her side as the anaesthetist inserts an epidural catheter into the epidural space and injects local anaesthetic.

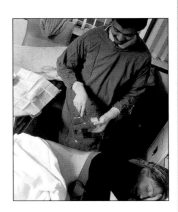

*The anaesthetist prepares the skin for an epidural. After sterilization, local anaesthetic is injected into the soft tissue over the intervertebral space.*

*Once the local anaesthetic has taken effect, the epidural can be given. A catheter is inserted into the epidural space and anaesthetic injected.*

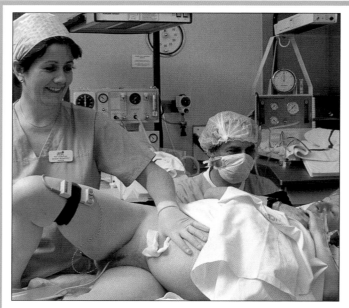

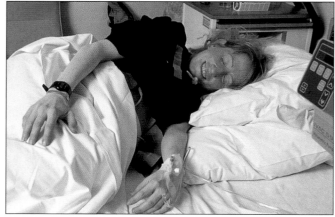

*As it is important to anticipate the potential problems of a twin delivery, monitoring of both fetal hearts by cardiotocography is essential from early on in labour.*

*The first stage of labour ends when the cervix is fully dilated. The delivery of the first twin will be managed similarly to a singleton birth.*

## First stage of labour

During labour both babies and the mother are monitored for signs of distress. Before the epidural was in place, a scalp clip was positioned on the presenting part of the first twin and an abdominal monitor was placed on the mother to monitor the heart of the second twin.

The rate and size of contractions, the progress of labour, and the mother's blood pressure, pulse and general condition are all constantly monitored to ensure her health throughout the birth.

Traces of the babies' hearts are observed between and during contractions. Any severe or prolonged slowing of the fetal heart rate with lack of beat-to-beat variation indicates fetal distress.

Active intervention is more likely than with a singleton delivery, because of the risks to the second twin in particular. The monitors will signal any persistent signs of hypoxia, which would require immediate intervention.

Although the mother has been given effective epidural analgesia, she is still working hard. Controlled breathing helps to maintain oxygenation of the maternal and fetal blood flow and helps her to feel in control.

The mother may find it that it helps to sit up in the intervals between contractions.

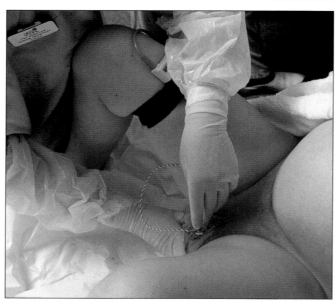

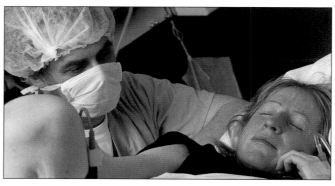

*It may be necessary to adjust the monitoring clip on the first baby's scalp as the head 'crowns'. Monitoring continues until the baby is completely delivered.*

*Twin deliveries may involve an obstetrician, anaesthetist, paediatrician and up to three midwives. However this varies according to the hospital.*

## Second stage of labour

As for a single delivery, the second stage of labour is heralded by the full dilation of the cervix.

The first baby's head has descended by this stage and is pressing the rectum against the lower spine. The soft tissues of the perineum begin to stretch and thin out as the head presses against it. As the head 'crowns', the perineum is assessed by the obstetrician in case an episiotomy is required. This is an incision in the perineum to accommodate the baby's head. The scalp monitor clip may be repositioned.

*Contractions build up, increasing in duration and intensity as labour progresses. They reach a crescendo as the first baby's head emerges.*

## Crowning

The first baby's head emerges and the mother is encouraged to push as the rest of its body is delivered. Mucus is cleared from the baby's nose and mouth to help it breathe freely. The cord must be clamped promptly to prevent one twin losing a significant amount of blood by bleeding into the circulation of the other. Both ends of the cord are given identity tags.

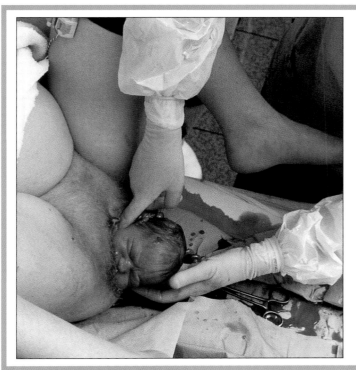

*Once the baby's head emerges the midwife runs a finger round the back of its head to check whether the umbilical cord has looped around its neck.*

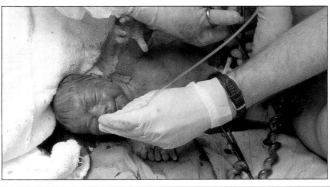

*Even following a straightforward delivery the baby's mouth and nasal passages may need to be cleared of mucus that has accumulated during delivery.*

## Mother and baby

In a single birth, the mother is injected with a stimulant drug such as syntometrine after the birth to make the uterus contract and expel the placenta. This is withheld in a twin delivery until the second baby has been born.

While the mother enjoys a few precious moments with her new baby, the obstetrician carries out an abdominal check to ascertain the position of the second baby. External manipulation may be attempted to correct an unusual lie. Occasionally this is not possible and an urgent Caesarean section is necessary for the safe delivery of the second twin.

*Once the first twin is born, the umbilical cord is clamped and cut. This prevents any blood passing between the twins' two circulations.*

*Following the birth of the first twin the contractions subside for a few minutes. This allows the mother a few precious moments with her baby.*

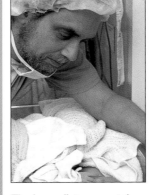

*The immediate neonatal care of the baby falls to the paediatrician. He or she must quickly assess any problems or special needs.*

## The Apgar score

Within five minutes of the birth, the paediatrician carries out an overall health check of the newborn baby using the Apgar score.

This is based on assessment of the baby's cardiorespiratory and neurological systems, by measuring the following:
- Colour (pale/blue, pink body with blue extremities or completely pink)
- Respiratory effort (absent, weak or strong cry)
- Heart rate per minute (absent, slow or fast)
- Muscle tone (limp or active motion)
- Reflex response (none, weak or strong).

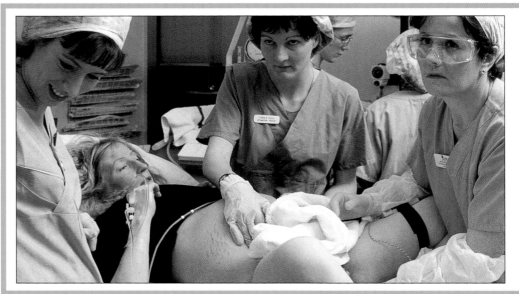

## The second twin

Provided the second baby is in a longitudinal position and the presenting part (usually the head) is engaged, a vaginal examination is carried out and then the membranes of the second baby are broken.

The obstetrician places her hand in the vagina to prevent cord prolapse and guides the presenting part of the second twin. A fetal monitor may be attached to the baby's scalp at this point to signal any distress as the amniotic fluid slowly drains out.

*Little time is lost between the delivery of the two babies. Any delay increases the possibility of complications, such as hypoxia.*

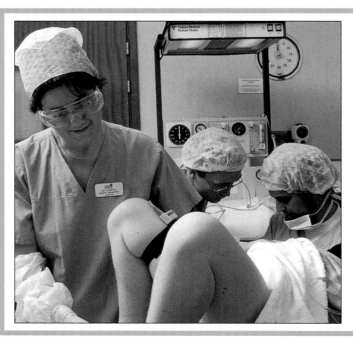

## Awaiting arrival

If the baby is presenting well, normal contractions will act to push the baby out.

Delivery of the second twin needs to be achieved quickly because this baby is at greater risk of hypoxia due to placental separation or contraction of the placental site.

If there is any delay in labour at this stage, intervention such as ventouse suction or forceps may be necessary to help the baby's descent. If the head is too high for forceps delivery, an external version may be carried out. This entails the obstetrician palpating the abdomen to move the baby.

*The obstetrician plays an active role in the birth of the second baby, holding the presenting part steady over the brim of the pelvis as the waters drain out.*

*Contractions subside slightly after the birth of the first baby. They then restart with great intensity before the birth of the second twin.*

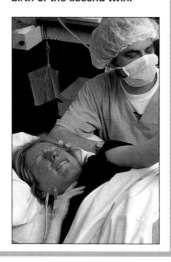

## Third stage

The second stage ends with the delivery of the second twin, who is passed to the waiting paediatrician.

In the third stage of labour the placenta is delivered. The uterine distension from a multiple pregnancy places the mother at greater risk of prolapse and haemorrhage as occasionally the uterus fails to contract. A muscle stimulant such as syntometrine is given as the second twin's shoulder is delivered, which should immediately cause the uterus to contract, separating the placenta.

*While the medical team check the second baby and ensure that placental delivery is complete, the mother can finally relax and cuddle her baby.*

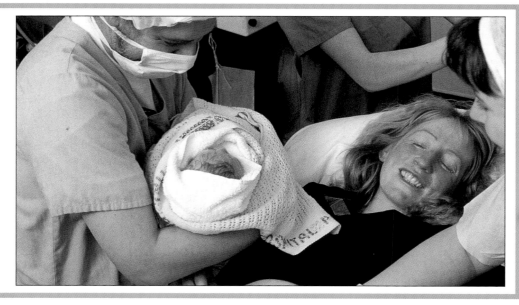

## Stretching the perineum

Normally the baby's head gradually stretches the tissues ahead of it, but in a breech birth the largest part of the baby comes last and there is less time for this to occur.

If an epidural is not used, local anaesthetic will be injected to anaesthetize the area beforehand.

*An episiotomy may need to be performed, whereby the skin and muscles of the perineum (between the vagina and anus) are cut to expand the entrance of the birth canal.*

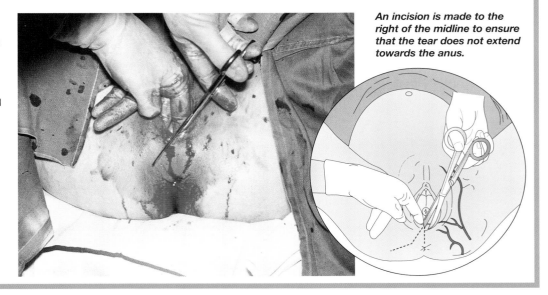

*An incision is made to the right of the midline to ensure that the tear does not extend towards the anus.*

## Delivering the buttocks and legs

The mother continues to push with the contractions and the baby's buttocks emerge from the vulva. At this stage it is very common for the baby to open its bowels and pass fetal stools, or meconium.

*As the baby's thighs appear, the obstetrician gently places a finger behind each knee to encourage the legs to deliver over the perineum.*

*The baby's pelvic bone rotates through 90 degrees, initially facing sideward and then eventually coming to lie so the back is facing upwards.*

If the legs do not appear spontaneously, a finger is placed behind the baby's knee and the legs are gently flexed bringing the knee toward the chest and then outwards, the foot being lifted over the perineum.

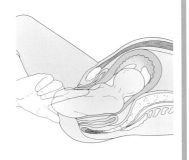

## Delivering the trunk

The obstetrician now finds the umbilical cord and pulls it down to create a free loop, ensuring it is not overstretched as the rest of the delivery is completed.

Further maternal effort leads to delivery of the baby's trunk to the level of the arms, which are usually lying across the chest and deliver spontaneously as the baby descends.

Sometimes one or both arms have risen above the baby's head, and can even lie so the hand is behind the head. This is called a nuchal arm and a further manoeuvre must be carried out to assist delivery if this happens.

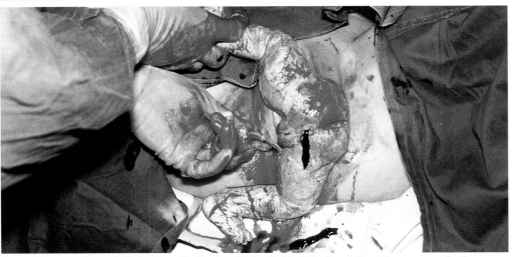

*One of the arms is nuchal, that is, with the hand lying behind the head. For this reason, a further manoeuvre must be carried out to assist delivery before the baby can descend any further.*

## Managing a nuchal arm

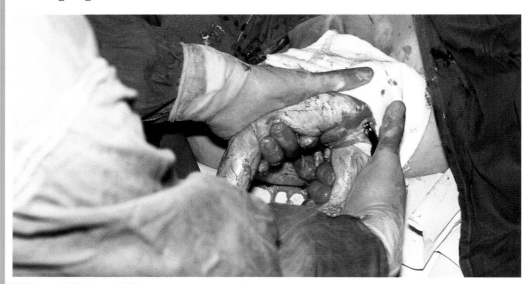

The obstetrician places a towel around the baby and only grips the baby's pelvis, avoiding the soft abdomen, which is easily damaged if handled excessively.

If a nuchal arm is discovered, the baby is gently rotated through 90 degrees. This allows the obstetrician to insert his finger in the angle of the baby's left elbow and sweep the arm downwards and across the chest.

*The obstetrician runs a finger over the back of the baby's neck and down over one shoulder to determine the position of the arms, before manipulating the baby through 90 degrees.*

## aRotation

If the other arm is also raised above the head the procedure is repeated in the opposite direction.

The entirety of this manoeuvre takes place between a single contraction and only lasts a couple of seconds. It is useful to have an epidural in place if these manipulations are needed, as otherwise the urge to push is very great.

*The baby is now rotated through 180 degrees from the position of delivery of the first arm. The baby has now delivered to the level of the shoulders, and no downward traction is used.*

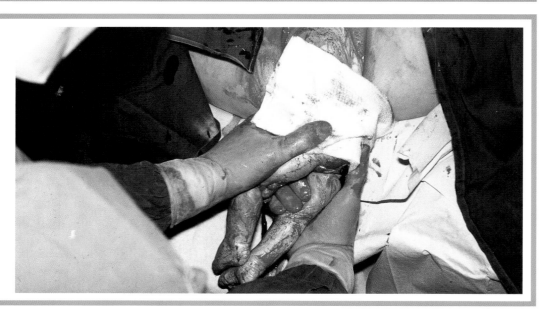

## The flexed head

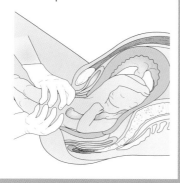

The baby's head has now entered the pelvis, with the chin well tucked into the chest. This is called a flexed head and it is essential for a safe delivery.

Some babies can be seen to have extended necks on the ultrasound scan carried out before birth. It is advisable for these 'star-gazing' babies to be delivered by Caesarean section, as there is a greater risk of injury to the cervical spine if the head is in this position.

*The obstetrician reaches over the baby's right shoulder in order to verify the position of the second arm.*

*The obstetrician must also check that the baby's head is flexed, which is essential before a safe delivery can be carried out.*

## Delivering the right arm

Now the baby has been rotated, delivery of the right arm is easily carried out. With the next contraction the baby's head will be delivered and a decision has to be made on how to assist this.

*The baby is rotated in an anti-clockwise direction. Once this manoeuvre has been carried out, delivery of the right arm is easily achieved.*

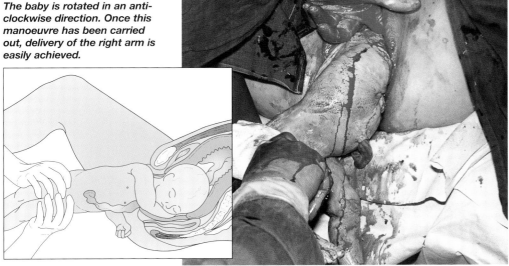

*Once both arms have descended, the head will be delivered. This is a crucial point in any breech birth, and the obstetrician must decide how delivery of the head should be assisted.*

## Delivering the head

Two methods are commonly used for delivery of the baby's head. The aim is to ensure that the head is delivered very slowly and in a controlled manner.

Some obstetricians use forceps to control the delivery, whereas others prefer to place a finger inside the baby's mouth to encourage flexion of the head. The head is supported by placing a hand behind the head, just under the mother's pubic bone.

*Forceps are applied and the baby is lifted upwards by an assistant. The delivery of the baby is completed with the mother's next contraction.*

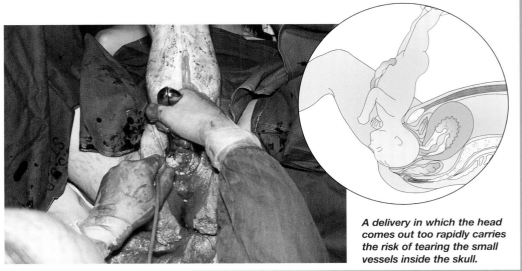

*A delivery in which the head comes out too rapidly carries the risk of tearing the small vessels inside the skull.*

## After the birth

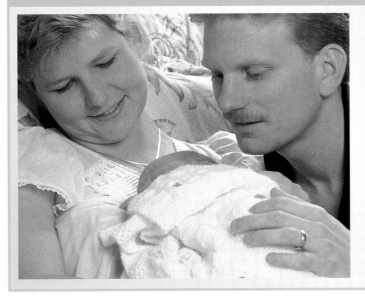

The final stage of labour is the delivery of the placenta and surrounding membranes, which were responsible for protecting and nourishing the fetus during pregnancy. This stage can last between five and 25 minutes.

**Post-natal examination**
After the initial moment of bonding with her child, the mother will be examined to ensure that her uterus is firm and well contracted. The episiotomy will then be carefully repaired by suturing.

*While the mother's episiotomy is repaired, the baby is checked thoroughly by a paediatrician. It is then returned to the parents' arms.*

The newborn will also be examined to check for any physical abnormalities, before being cleaned and returned to the mother.

As well as a preliminary examination by the midwife, it is also important for a paediatrician to examine the newborn before discharge home, as congenital hip problems are more common in babies born by breech delivery. If this is the case, it will occasionally require the use of a plaster-cast splint for a few months so that the baby's hip does not dislocate.

As with any birth, the mother will be visited in her home by a midwife in order to ensure that both she and her baby continue to thrive.

# Anatomy of the placenta

The placenta is the organ which provides the developing fetus with all the nutrients it needs. It is a temporary structure formed in the uterus during pregnancy from fetal and maternal tissues.

The placenta takes on the role of the lungs and the intestine for the developing fetus. It achieves this by bringing the blood of the fetus close to the maternal blood within its internal structure, allowing the fetus to take up oxygen and nutrients, while waste products are carried away.

The placenta becomes detached at birth and is delivered after the baby in what is known as the third stage of labour. It is then examined to check that it is complete and shows no evidence of abnormality or disease which may have affected the fetus.

### PLACENTAL APPEARANCE

At full term the placenta is a deep red, round or oval flattened organ. It normally weighs about 500 g (4.8 oz), or one sixth of the weight of the fetus it nourishes. There are two sides to the delivered placenta:

■ The maternal aspect (which is attached to the lining of the womb) – this shows subdivisions where the placental tissue is divided by fibrous bands (septa). It is deep red and feels spongy

■ The fetal aspect (from which the umbilical cord arises) – this is covered in fetal membranes. Its surface is shiny and smooth with large umbilical vessels.

**Fetal aspect of placenta**

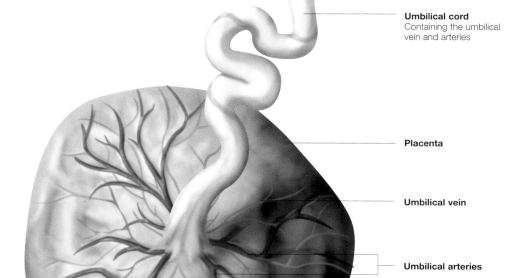

**Umbilical cord**
Containing the umbilical vein and arteries

**Placenta**

**Umbilical vein**

**Umbilical arteries**

*The placenta has two aspects: the maternal and the fetal. The fetal aspect of the placenta (shown here) is identifiable by the large umbilical vessels.*

## Variations in the placenta

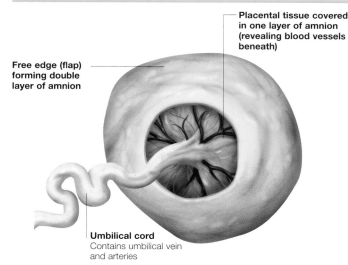

**Free edge (flap) forming double layer of amnion**

**Placental tissue covered in one layer of amnion (revealing blood vessels beneath)**

**Umbilical cord**
Contains umbilical vein and arteries

There are a number of variations that can occur in the form or arrangement of the placenta. These are usually of little clinical significance, posing no threat to mother or developing fetus, although occasionally they may present problems.

### PLACENTAL VARIATIONS

Possible variations include:

■ Succenturiate placenta – here there is an extra, or accessory, lobe of the placenta which lies within the fetal membranes a

*In a circumvallate placenta the amnion (the membranous sac containing the baby) folds in on itself, creating a double layer over most of the placenta.*

short distance away from the main placenta

■ Battledore placenta – this is the name given to a placenta in which the cord inserts at one edge rather than centrally, as is the normal situation

■ Velamentous insertion of the cord – this describes the unusual arrangement whereby the umbilical cord itself does not reach the placenta but inserts into the fetal membranes a little distance away. The umbilical vessels then divide on their way to the placenta

■ Circumvallate placenta – this occurs when there is extensive folding back of the membranes, which may be associated with bleeding during birth.

# Inside the placenta

As the placenta develops, the fetal blood vessels form chorionic villi (finger-like projections) within it, to absorb nutrients and oxygen from the incoming maternal blood vessels. Waste is also passed back to the maternal blood.

The placenta provides the means by which the growing fetus can receive oxygen and nutrients from the maternal blood circulation and, at the same time, dispose of its waste products. To allow these transfers to take place, the placenta has a very rich blood supply from both the mother and the fetus.

A cross-section of the placenta reveals that this organ is made up partly from maternal tissue and partly from fetal tissue. The spiral arteries that arise from the maternal uterine arteries bring blood into the base of the placenta. This blood then leaves the arteries and fills wide 'pools' (intervillous spaces) in which the fetal villi are suspended. The maternal blood then returns to her circulation through numerous veins.

The fetal villi are finger-like projections that contain blood vessels connected to the fetus through the umbilical cord. They branch again and again to create the maximum amount of surface area for the transfer of oxygen, nutrients and waste substances to and from the maternal blood.

Although the two circulations come close to each other, maternal and fetal blood do not

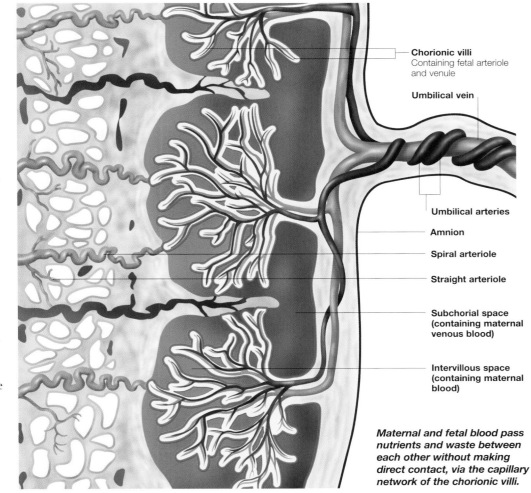

**Chorionic villi**
Containing fetal arteriole and venule

**Umbilical vein**

**Umbilical arteries**

**Amnion**

**Spiral arteriole**

**Straight arteriole**

**Subchorial space (containing maternal venous blood)**

**Intervillous space (containing maternal blood)**

*Maternal and fetal blood pass nutrients and waste between each other without making direct contact, via the capillary network of the chorionic villi.*

mix, being divided by the thin walls of the villi.

### FUNCTIONS OF THE PLACENTA

The placenta has a number of functions, which are vital to fetal growth and development:
■ Respiration – fetal blood is supplied with oxygen from the

maternal circulation via the placenta, which also carries away waste carbon dioxide
■ Nutrition – nutrients which circulate in the maternal bloodstream are passed to the fetus through the placenta
■ Excretion – waste products from the fetus are passed from the two umbilical arteries to the

villi, and ultimately the maternal circulation, for disposal
■ Hormone production – the placenta is an important source of hormones, especially oestrogen and progesterone. These hormones not only help to maintain the pregnancy, but also prepare the mother for the birth of her child.

## Abnormal conditions of the placenta

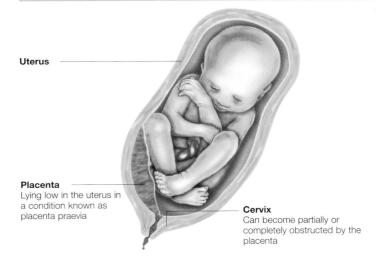

**Uterus**

**Placenta**
Lying low in the uterus in a condition known as placenta praevia

**Cervix**
Can become partially or completely obstructed by the placenta

There are several problems involving the placenta that may occur during pregnancy. One of the most well known is placenta praevia, a condition in which the placenta has implanted in an abnormally low position within the uterus.

Because of its low position, the placenta in these cases may actually come between the fetus and the cervix, making a vaginal delivery very difficult. Placenta praevia is often associated with

*When the placenta implants in the lower segment of the uterus, it is known as placenta praevia. Its position between the fetus and the cervix is problematic.*

bleeding in the later months of pregnancy.

### PLACENTAL ABRUPTION

Placental abruption refers to the separation (partial or complete) of the placenta from the uterine wall. This is potentially a very serious condition in which bleeding occurs between the placenta and the uterine wall.

This bleeding may remain within the uterus, or may track down through the cervix to present as vaginal bleeding. Placental abruption can usually be managed to give a safe outcome, but the lives of both mother and baby are at risk from this condition.

# After the birth

Even though prospective parents have spent nine months or more preparing, the arrival of the baby will inevitably lead to feelings of anxiety. In the immediate aftermath of birth, a couple will be exhausted and reactions to a new baby may be mixed.

Although parents often feel an intense and immediate love for their baby, it can take a period of time to adjust. Siblings may also present difficulties when the baby arrives, as they vie for attention.

However, new parents quickly develop parenting skills, while older children settle down. Importantly, for a father, his position now changes from a largely supportive role, to one in which he becomes physically and emotionally involved with his baby.

Left: New parents learn to interact with their baby from birth and the bond between child and parent quickly becomes established.

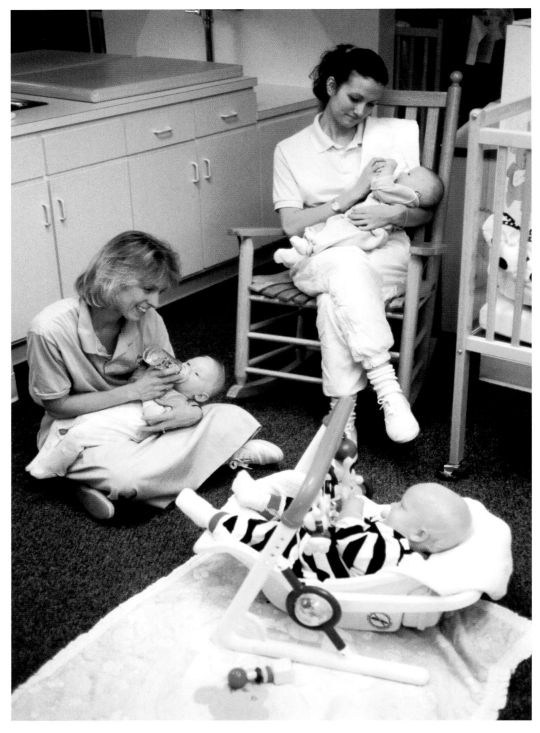

Day care centres are an invaluable resource for parents who have to balance work and family commitments.

yellowing of the skin and eyes, but this usually resolves spontaneously or after a course of simple treatment. Checks are carried out again just before the baby goes home from hospital and again at six days old, when a Guthrie blood test is used to check for two treatable causes of mental handicap. At six weeks, all babies have a full physical and developmental assessment, which is usually carried out by the GP.

### CHANGES AFTER BIRTH
As a woman's uterus begins to shrink back to its normal size, it sheds its lining as a blood stained vaginal discharge, known as lochia. This is perfectly normal and settles down after a few weeks. Mothers who have had birth interventions, such as an episiotomy or a caesarian section will have wounds that will quickly heal if kept clean and dry, although recovery from a caesarian section takes longer, and for a while it may be advisable not to lift or carry heavy objects or drive.

Psychologically, parents must make huge adjustments to cope with their new circumstances, and the baby's constant cycle of feeding, changing and sleeping. It is common to feel low for a few weeks after birth, and these 'baby

### CHECKING YOUR NEWBORN BABY
In the first few weeks of life, a baby undergoes an important series of health checks. The Apgar score, which measures breathing, heart rate, colour, muscle tone and reflexes, is used to assess the baby's condition immediately after birth. Even if the baby does

initially require some help with breathing from the midwife or doctor, there are usually no long-term effects. However, a few babies will have conditions such as heart defects that require medical treatment, and these are detected at an early stage and treated as soon as possible.

Many babies are born

with minor imperfections, particularly skin changes such as birth marks and Mongolian spots. Babies may also be temporarily affected by their mode of delivery, with forceps and vacuum extraction causing changes in the shape of the head or marks on the skin. Jaundice is a common condition that causes blues' may be exacerbated by disrupted sleep and the trauma of labour. If the mood becomes markedly low, a relatively rare condition known as postnatal depression may be diagnosed. It is important to recognize the symptoms of depression and to seek help and support quickly as it can interfere with the important bonding process between a mother and her child.

### BREAST FEEDING

Perhaps the most important decision to be made is how to feed your baby until solid foods are introduced at 4–6 months. In fact, this issue probably deserves some thought well before the birth. There are both practical and emotional advantages to breast-feeding, although it may not always be possible.

Initially the breasts produce colostrum, a thick yellowish liquid that is rich in protein and antibodies that support the newborn baby's immature immune system – even if you decide to bottle-feed, a mother should consider breast feeding for the first few days. After several days, the baby's sucking stimulates the production of normal breast milk. This milk is the perfect food for your baby, and contains all the nutrients necessary for his or her growth and development. At the same time, breast feeding is a chance to develop a very close, intimate bond. On a more practical note, breast feeding eliminates the need to carry bulky feeding and sterilising equipment when out of the house, although feeding in public can cause concern for some women.

### ADJUSTING TO FAMILY LIFE

Once a family has adjusted to the birth of a new baby, it is important to establish a routine, especially if there are other children. Tiredness may mean that initially, life seems like an interminable sequence of sleeping, feeding and bathing, so spending time with a partner is vital, especially if he or she is away from the home during the day. If the parent caring for the baby feels isolated, joining parent groups can prove helpful, although a careful balance between socialising and focusing on the family is important.

Babies undergo health and developmental checks at birth, six weeks, eight months and 18 months by either a health visitor or doctor.

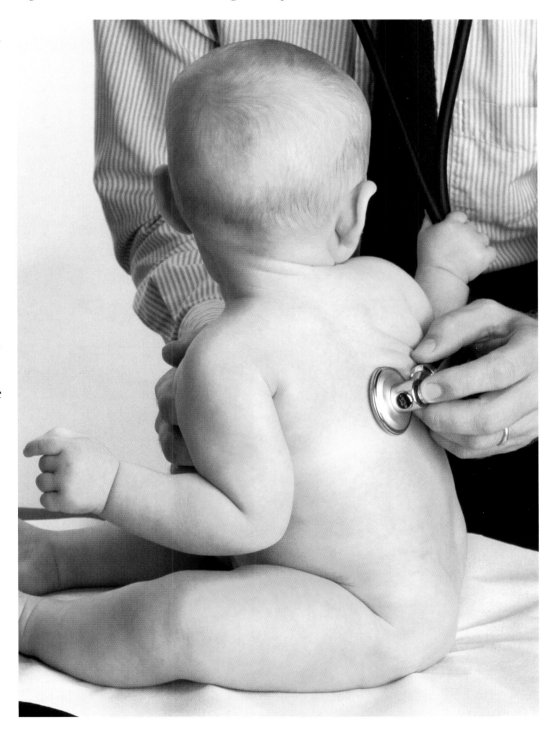

# Checking a newborn baby

Every baby has routine checks within minutes of birth to identify any life-threatening problem, to establish that the baby is healthy and to reassure the parents. Up to four sets of checks are carried out in the first week of life.

The first checks on a newborn are carried out by the midwife or doctor at delivery. Breathing must be properly established, and this and other functions are assessed in a standard way. Babies are given an Apgar score at one minute and then five minutes after birth.

### APGAR CHECKS

The five elements checked are breathing, heart rate, colour, muscle tone and reflexes. Each is given a score of 0, 1 or 2. The maximum Apgar score is 10 and seven or more is quite normal. Babies scoring five or less need to be given oxygen to help them establish their breathing.

When the baby is short of oxygen, breathing is irregular or absent, heart rate is below 100 and the skin is blue or pale.

### MEASUREMENTS

Shortly after birth, all babies are weighed, the circumference of the head is recorded, the baby's length is measured, and the midwife does a quick check for any obvious congenital abnormalities.

## The Apgar score

*The Apgar score was devised by an American paediatrician, Dr Virginia Apgar, to provide a standard way of monitoring a baby's condition.*

| Breathing | Regular, crying | 2 |
|---|---|---|
| | Slow, irregular | 1 |
| | Absent | 0 |
| **Heart rate** | Over 100 | 2 |
| | Slow, below 100 | 1 |
| | Absent | 0 |
| **Colour** | Pink | 2 |
| | Body pink, extremities blue | 1 |
| | Blue, pale | 0 |
| **Muscle tone** | Moving actively | 2 |
| | Moving extremities only | 1 |
| | Limp | 0 |
| **Reflexes** (often to a catheter in the nostril) | Cough or sneeze | 2 |
| | Grimace | 1 |
| | None | 0 |

*Placing his little finger in a baby's mouth, a doctor checks the baby's muscle tone.*

The baby's weight can indicate potential health problems. Any weight between 2,500 grams and 4,500 grams (5½-10 lbs) is normal. Low birthweight babies may need extra care. A very large baby may indicate that the mother has diabetes.

*Measuring the circumference of a baby's head. Head size depends on a baby's size but an average for a 3.4 kg (7.5 lb) baby would be about 35 cm (14 in). An abnormally small or large head may indicate brain problems.*

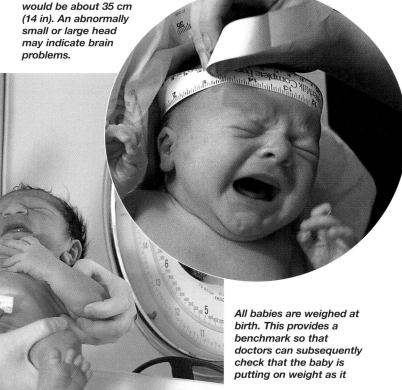

*All babies are weighed at birth. This provides a benchmark so that doctors can subsequently check that the baby is putting on weight as it*

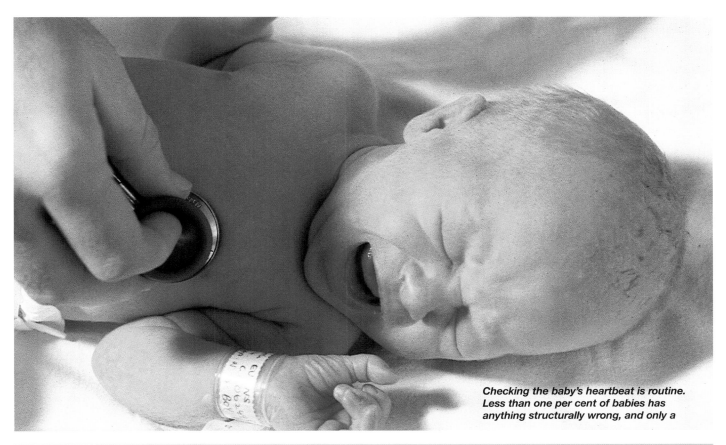

*Checking the baby's heartbeat is routine. Less than one per cent of babies has anything structurally wrong, and only a*

## First medical checks

A careful examination is made of every baby in the first 24 hours. Usually this is done by a member of the paediatric team, but it may be carried out by a midwife, particularly if the mother is to be discharged within six hours.

### MEDICAL HISTORY
The mother's medical notes are checked for any abnormalities discovered during pregnancy, and the mother is asked about any illnesses in the family. The baby is undressed and observed carefully from top to toe.

### HEART
Using a stethoscope, the heart is checked first, before the baby gets upset and starts crying – reactions that alter heart rate.

### BLOOD FLOW
The pulses in the groin are felt to make certain there is no blockage in the aorta, the main artery of the body – a condition that is known as coarctation of the aorta.

### JAUNDICE
Jaundice – now increasingly common – can damage the brain, so a check is made of the whites of the baby's eyes.

### ABNORMALITIES
Some congenital abnormalities – such as missing fingers – are obvious but some of the more dangerous problems are not. Cleft palate is often associated with a cleft lip, but it is easy to miss a cleft at the back of the palate. To have a thorough

look, the doctor will carefully depress the baby's tongue with a wooden spatula.

### BLOCKAGES
Any blockage in the digestive tract is a problem. Atresia of the bowel (blockage of the bowel) needs urgent surgery. Atresia of the oesophagus (blockage of the gullet) causes regurgitation of saliva. If the baby is showing this symptom, a tube is passed into the stomach to check that there is no block. Atresia further down the gut, such as duodenal atresia (just below the stomach), makes the baby vomit green bile. A blockage even further down the gut leads to a distension of the abdomen. The anus is inspected to make sure that it is present and open.

### HIPS
The hip is a ball-and-socket joint, and may be dislocated. It is relatively easy to treat early in life and is more common in girls, those with a family history of such things, and after breech delivery. All babies have a gentle examination to see if either of the hips can be dislocated. There are now ways of assessing the hip by ultrasound if there is thought to be any problem.

### GENITALS
The genitalia are carefully examined to make sure that the vagina is present in a girl and that the penis is normal and the testes have descended in a boy. Any abnormality may require surgery to correct it.

## Discharge examination

The baby is given a discharge examination before leaving hospital, but it may be done at home by the family practitioner. This checks that nothing has been missed and that no illness has developed.

Jaundice, for instance, caused by excess bilirubin (a bile pigment) in the blood, is extremely common in breast-fed or premature babies. A blood test may be needed to check the bilirubin level.

### UMBILICAL CORD
The umbilical cord separates from the baby at any time from three days to two weeks after birth. If the belly button (the umbilicus) becomes infected it will be very red and swollen with a discharge.

### FEEDING
It is important for the baby's growth that breast-feeding is properly established, and this is also assessed during the check.

## Guthrie test

All babies have a blood test after they are six days old. It is called the Guthrie test. The baby's heel is pricked and drops of blood are put on a special card. The test is to look for two treatable causes of mental handicap. An absent thyroid causes a high level of thyroid-stimulating hormone (TSH) in the blood. The other condition is phenylketonuria, where there is a block in the chemistry of phenylalanine, one of the amino acids in the body. Brain damage can be avoided by putting the baby on a special diet.

# Jaundice in newborns

A yellow discoloration of the skin (jaundice) often occurs in healthy newborn babies and it soon disappears. However, GPs examine jaundiced babies regularly to rule out any serious problems.

Jaundice is caused by an increase in blood levels of bilirubin, which is a waste product made when haemoglobin in red blood cells is broken down. Newborn babies have immature liver enzymes and are unable to chemically transform (metabolize) this bilirubin effectively for later excretion. Babies who are born underweight and those born to diabetic mothers are particularly likely to become jaundiced.

After a difficult delivery, babies sometimes develop a bruise-like haemorrhage under the scalp (cephalhaematoma), and may become jaundiced when the extra blood is re-absorbed. If the umbilical cord is not clamped early enough, too many red blood cells may pass to the baby (polycythaemia), and this can also lead to jaundice.

## PHYSIOLOGICAL JAUNDICE

A natural build up of unmetabolized bilirubin is termed physiological jaundice. It results from a natural decline in the number of red blood cells over the first few days of life and because a baby's liver enzymes are, initially, not fully unaccustomed to dealing with the broken down products.

Normal physiological jaundice always develops after the first 24 hours of life. Now that mothers and babies are discharged early

from hospital, most cases of jaundice appear after the baby comes home.

Mild jaundice looks like a slight suntan. It usually starts on the head and progresses to the feet. In more severe cases, the whites of the eyes become yellow.

Many GPs visit new mothers after they come home from

*Many newborns develop jaundice – it affects more than half of all full-term babies and over 80 per cent of babies that are delivered*

hospital. If the baby is jaundiced, the GP may examine the baby to look for anaemia or an enlarged liver. If the baby's urine is dark or the faeces pale, blood and urine tests are needed urgently.

Physiological jaundice usually disappears by the time the baby is two weeks old. The most important treatment is to make sure the baby is getting enough milk. If the mother is breast-feeding, she should be encouraged to continue or seek advice if there are difficulties. Weighing the baby regularly reveals whether there is an

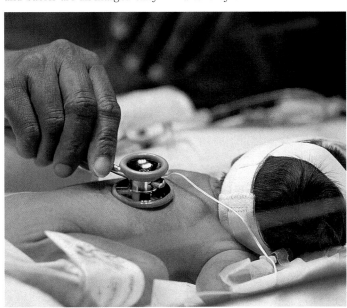

*A small percentage of newborns with jaundice may need treatment in an intensive care unit – ultraviolet light is one of*

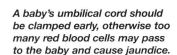

*A baby's umbilical cord should be clamped early, otherwise too many red blood cells may pass to the baby and cause jaundice.*

adequate fluid and calorie intake.

If the jaundice is severe, or the baby seems drowsy or has difficulty feeding, the midwife will take blood to measure the bilirubin level. Charts help the doctor decide whether phototherapy (light treatment) is needed to help break the bilirubin down.

# Causes of jaundice

Occasionally, prolonged jaundice in newborns can be caused by a serious illness, so further tests to establish the exact cause may be have to be carried out.

Jaundice occurring on the first day of life is always abnormal. It is usually due to breakdown of the baby's red blood cells by haemolysis. This can be confirmed by a blood test known as a Coombs' test.

Haemolytic disease of the newborn may occur if the mother has a different blood group to the baby and produces antibodies which cross the placenta (ABO or rhesus incompatibility). This is now rare because rhesus-negative mothers are given anti-D injections after childbirth to prevent them making these antibodies.

### RELATED FACTORS

Sometimes there will be a family history of jaundice. Most cases of prolonged jaundice occur in breast-fed babies, although the cause is still unknown. Breast milk jaundice affects 5 per cent of breast-fed babies and is not harmful, so mothers should continue breast-feeding. However, prolonged jaundice may be caused by serious illness, and investigations are needed.

### INVESTIGATIONS AND CAUSES

First, blood tests are done to determine whether the bilirubin is conjugated (with linked-up molecules) or unconjugated, and urine is tested. If the bilirubin is conjugated, further tests are needed. These may include an ultrasound scan of the liver or a liver biopsy.

Serious causes include liver disease and biliary atresia (blocked bile ducts). The latter must be diagnosed early because surgery may be life-saving if done within the first six weeks. Occasionally these babies need a liver transplant.

Chronic congenital infections such as cytomegalovirus and toxoplasmosis may cause prolonged jaundice. Jaundice may also be caused by hereditary metabolic diseases such as cystic fibrosis and galactosaemia.

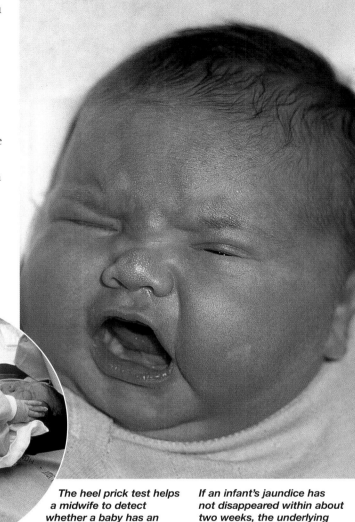

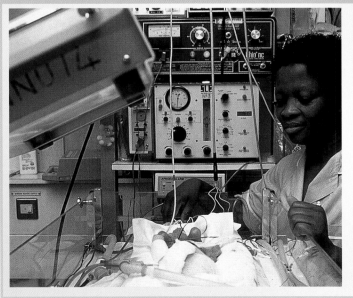

**The heel prick test helps a midwife to detect whether a baby has an underactive thyroid gland (hypothyroidism).**

**If an infant's jaundice has not disappeared within about two weeks, the underlying cause will need further investigation.**

## Treating jaundice in babies

Phototherapy lamps work on the principle that yellow bilirubin absorbs light of blue wavelengths, which changes it into non-toxic by-products. Phototherapy involves separating the baby from the mother and sometimes has side effects including dehydration and loose faeces, so extra fluids are needed.

A newer device is a body suit emitting blue light – this is worn under a baby's clothes and avoids separation problems.

Conjugated bilirubin that has been metabolized by the liver is

**Phototherapy means that a baby has to be separated from the mother during treatment, so this should only**

no longer harmful. However, if the level of unconjugated bilirubin becomes very high, a small amount may cross into the brain, where it is toxic (kernicterus). Kernicterus may cause deafness and/or cerebral palsy, but this can be prevented by prompt exchange transfusions of blood.

An exchange transfusion is a practical procedure used as a last resort to prevent kernicterus. Warmed rhesus-negative blood from a donor which has been cross-matched against the mother's blood and baby's blood is transfused into the baby's umbilical vein at the same rate that the baby's own blood is removed. This removes toxic unconjugated bilirubin and any antibodies present, and corrects any anaemia.

# First six weeks of life

It is a miracle that a newborn baby can be so calm, considering its dramatic change of environment. Yet the relatively helpless baby adapts quickly to the bombardment of sights, sounds and smells.

The newborn's senses are adapted to interact with other people. The baby's hearing is attuned to the human voice, and can recognize familiar voices, especially its mother's, from an early stage. The young baby soon learns its mother's smell too, especially if it is breast-fed.

In contrast to the surprisingly advanced sensory development of a newborn baby, its physical abilities are far less developed than those of other infant mammals, such as lambs and calves, which are able to stand and walk just a few hours after birth. A newborn human cannot even hold up its head at birth, and certainly cannot reach out for things with its arms.

### REFLEX ACTIONS
The baby does have certain reflexes (involuntary movements, such as the knee-jerk in adults), some of which will be lost by the time it is six months old if the child is developing normally.

Some reflexes are essential for survival. For example, the baby will automatically turn its head and open its mouth if someone touches its cheek (this is called the 'rooting' reflex) allowing it to find the nipple and feed. The newborn can also suck and swallow at the same time without needing to learn how to.

Some other reflexes are 'primitive', and their usefulness is less clear. One is the grasping

*Very young babies sleep for most of the day in two to three hour stretches. As they get older, sleeping periods lengthen.*

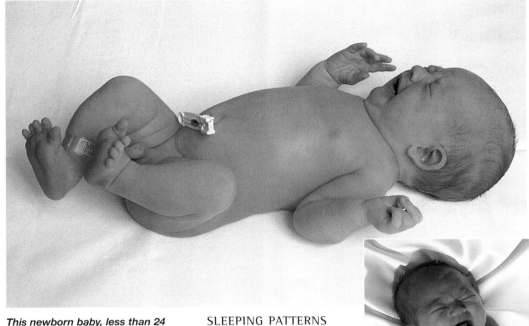

*This newborn baby, less than 24 hours old, still has the stump of the umbilical cord attached. The clamp prevents further bleeding.*

reflex, whereby a finger run across the baby's palm will cause it to close its fist so tightly around the finger that it is possible to pull the child. The baby will unfold the fingers if the back of the hand is stroked – this can be very useful if they become entangled in your hair, for example.

Although this is of no use to the baby, it is highly useful to baby monkeys clinging to their mothers back as she climbs, and presumably this reflex is a reflection of a shared evolutionary history.

### SLEEPING PATTERNS
After birth, the baby will spend most of its time asleep, although many exhausted parents would dispute this. This is because the baby will often only sleep for two or three hours at most before waking and crying until fed. The newborn does not distinguish between night and day initially, but as the weeks go by the baby gradually starts to sleep for longer intervals, with some only sleeping for perhaps eight hours a day while others will sleep for 22 hours. Very few babies will be sleeping through the night by six weeks, and some not until the end of the first year.

### REASONS FOR CRYING
At first, all the baby's cries will all sound similar. However, it is not long before the parents will be able to recognize the difference between the sudden, jolting cry of pain and the lilting, rhythmical cry of the hungry baby.

Babies cry to survive; it is the most obvious way to get the mother to attend to the baby's needs. A baby is unable to regulate its own temperature and may cry if too hot or too cold. Crying can also indicate tiredness, hunger, pain or discomfort. Sometimes, however, there seems to be no

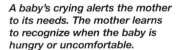

*A baby's crying alerts the mother to its needs. The mother learns to recognize when the baby is hungry or uncomfortable.*

explanation for their crying. A clean, well-fed and winded baby who keeps crying and will not sleep usually has colic (wind trapped in the intestine), the bane of a new parent's life.

Colic is usually apparent at around two weeks, and has often ceased by three months. Little is known about what causes colic, or what is the best way to ease it, but it always settles as the baby grows older.

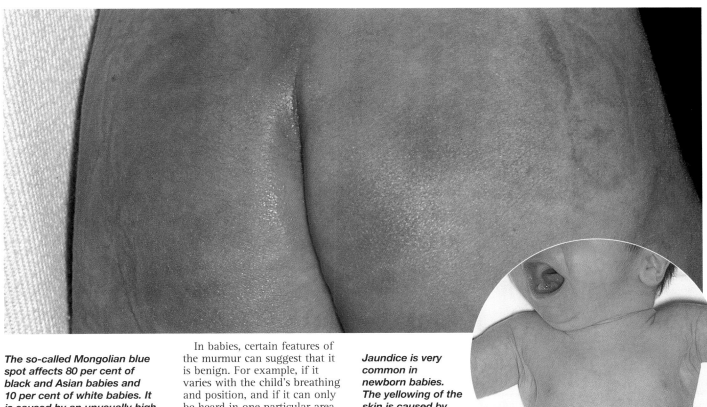

**The so-called Mongolian blue spot affects 80 per cent of black and Asian babies and 10 per cent of white babies. It is caused by an unusually high number of pigment-producing**

**Jaundice is very common in newborn babies. The yellowing of the skin is caused by bilirubin (a bile pigment) in the blood, which will be excreted by the liver after a few days. The baby may require UV treatment to restore the**

### HEART MURMURS

Minor abnormalities are not always visible, and are identified through medical examination. For example, heart murmurs are caused by turbulent blood flow through the heart valves. Informing a parent that their baby has a murmur causes profound worry.

Many murmurs are termed benign, or innocent. About one-third of children have a benign murmur during childhood, often when their blood flow increases, as in a fever or during exercise.

In babies, certain features of the murmur can suggest that it is benign. For example, if it varies with the child's breathing and position, and if it can only be heard in one particular area, and they have no other signs of heart disease, then it is usually benign. The baby will be regularly checked, and the parents can be reassured that there is unlikely to be anything seriously wrong.

### HOSPITAL TESTS

Parents are often convinced that their new baby has a squint. It is quite common for babies to have a 'pseudosquint', which happens because the bridge of the nose is slightly bigger than normal, making one eye appear to be squinting. Proper testing of the eyes will establish that there is no real squint.

### HEALTH CHECKS

The arrival of a new baby in the family is often a time of joy and celebration, but it is also the beginning of a lifetime of concern about the individual. Perfectly normal, healthy babies with small and self-limiting conditions, such as those described above, can cause parents unnecessary anxiety.

In the UK and most other developed countries, babies are formally checked after birth, both in hospital and at home, depending on where they were delivered, and are also at six weeks. This allow the doctor or health visitor to fully examine the child and it is also an ideal opportunity for the parents to air their concerns about their baby. As the infant grows, these anxieties generally subside.

## Forceps delivery

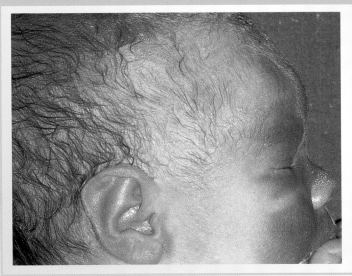

**If forceps have been used to assist delivery of a baby, swelling and bruising around the face can result. Although the baby's head looks deformed, it will regain its normal shape within a few days of the birth.**

Parents are often shocked at the first sight of their newborn babies. Unlike those born by Caesarean section, who often emerge a picture of perfection, many babies born vaginally look almost 'battered'.

Their skulls can be peculiarly dome-shaped from their slow, squeezed journey through the birth canal, and their faces are often swollen and bruised, particularly if they have been delivered with forceps, or if they have been delivered through the birth canal face-first. The swelling of the skull is called *caput succedaneum*, and goes away in the first few days after birth.

Sometimes forceps will cause not only bruising but temporary paralysis on one side of the baby's face, so that it looks lopsided. Occasionally, the baby will have such a traumatic delivery that a bump the size of a hen's egg forms on either side of the skull. Although this can be extremely alarming for the parents, the bruising is not permanent. However, it can take several months before the baby's head returns to its normal shape.

# Becoming parents

New parents soon discover that the arrival of a baby is a life-changing event. Many skills have to be learned, while relationships with family, friends and with each other undergo subtle changes.

After the birth of their first child, the lifestyle of both parents and their entire outlook on life will usually undergo marked changes. No babycare book can quite prepare them for the discovery that their own needs and desires must now give way to those of someone else – from now on, their baby will take priority.

## NEW SKILLS

The first few days of parenthood involve learning a whole set of new skills, such as changing nappies and bathing the baby.

So far as the mother is concerned, not only will she be involved in caring for the baby, but many of her thoughts and much of her emotional energy will be invested in the new arrival. Whenever they are apart, she will constantly be thinking and worrying about her child. A father needs to accept the strength of his partner's involvement with the baby and should not construe this as a rejection of himself.

## CONFUSION

It is quite common for mothers to pass through an identity crisis after the birth. One moment they may be career women with an independent income, and the next they are focused on their children, with their partner being the main breadwinner.

About two thirds of mothers

*Many mothers suffer some form of depression after the birth of a child. This is triggered by tiredness, the trauma of the birth and hormonal changes.*

are affected by the 'baby blues' in the first 10 days after birth. It is estimated that between 10 and 20 per cent of all new mothers experience the more serious postnatal (or puerperal) depression, when they feel weepy and sad and have no real optimism for the future.

Depressed mothers can become very isolated – they may be ashamed to admit exactly how they feel, and even scared that someone might take their baby from them.

*Having a baby is an exciting and joyful event. It is also a time of great adjustment, when the couple's outlook on life will often undergo radical change.*

## PERSONAL APPEARANCE

New mothers generally have little time to concern themselves with their appearance. They may make a concerted effort with clothes and make-up to look attractive, only to find that the baby then dribbles all over them; so it seems hardly worth the bother.

Sometimes, other people's reactions to a new mother's appearance can have an impact on her self-confidence and make her feel less attractive.

## SEX ISSUES

Tensions can be created in the relationship if the new mother believes that the father's lifestyle has barely changed at all. He is still going to work and may still expect a full sexual relationship.

After the birth, sex can be a problem for some women. Even after the six-week check, when they are usually given

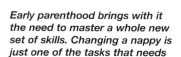

*Early parenthood brings with it the need to master a whole new set of skills. Changing a nappy is just one of the tasks that needs*

confirmation that sex can be resumed, many women still feel devoid of any libido. The cause is often a combination of chronic sleep deprivation and not feeling sexually attractive. At a time when the baby is making substantial claims on a mother's time and energy, the thought of having to accommodate another person's physical needs can be too much.

Lack of sex can be frustrating for many men, who may already feel sidelined by the arrival of the baby. If, as sometimes happens, a father has been used to being the centre of attention, he will be in for a shock as he finds that his partner's attention is now focused on the baby.

## COMMUNICATION

Some fathers may find it hard to adjust to their new role and may, in fact, have difficulties in accepting adult responsibility. They may continue the usual round of going to the pub or playing sport. Communication is

*After a baby is born, relationship problems can sometimes occur. Fathers may find it hard to adapt to their new role and may feel neglected by their partners.*

vital at this time as both parents may have fears and doubts that need to be worked through together.

Once people become parents, spontaneity can become a thing of the past. It becomes difficult to go out to dinner on the spur of the moment or to pop out to post a letter, for example, if they are in sole charge of a sleeping infant. Excursions require precise

planning – once the nappy has been changed, all the equipment assembled and the nappy changed yet again, it can sometimes seem hardly worth all the effort.

## FRIENDS AND RELATIVES

Once people have children, their social circles can undergo a radical change and they may find that they have more in common with other people who have children than with those who do not. New parents may find it difficult to talk about anything other than the baby, and may have to cut short social events to return home to relieve the babysitter. To their childless friends, this altered behaviour may be hard to understand and accept.

When people have children, their relationships with their own parents undergo a subtle change. The new parents now have their own family, which takes priority over any earlier ties. Yet they also realize, often for the first time, the sacrifices that their parents made for them and the strength of parental love. People who have nothing in common with their parents

*Having a child can change people's relationships with their own parents. New areas of communication often open up between the generations.*

can find that a new channel of communication has opened up, as their parents take pleasure in the arrival of their grandchildren.

Having children is also a time when many people who are adopted think about their birth families and try to trace them.

## FAMILY/WORK BALANCE

To support a growing family, parents have to divide their time between direct parental care and achieving the personal success that will allow them to make financial provision for their children.

Women, in particular, need to make important decisions about whether to return to work. The guiding principle here should be that a happy mother is a good mother; there are those who are not happy unless they are working, just as there are those who are only happy if they spend all their time in the company of their children.

## CAREER CHANGE?

Women who want to work may have to consider making a career change. Few women with babies or young children are able to work excessive and unpredictable hours and it can sometimes be easier to combine a career and motherhood in jobs where the management understands the needs and demands of a family.

*New mothers who return to work often have to juggle workplace demands with the responsibilities of motherhood. Long hours are rarely practical.*

# Physical changes after childbirth

The body undergoes many physiological changes during pregnancy. These are gradually reversed in the first six weeks after childbirth, during a period called the puerperium.

With the delivery of the fetus and placenta, the body experiences a change in the temporary hormonal balance maintained during pregnancy. The effects of the predominating hormones of pregnancy, such as oestrogen, progesterone and human placental lactogen (all produced by the placenta) begin to decline.

### PUERPERIUM

In the immediate post-natal period, most tissues revert to their pre-pregnant state, reversing physiological changes which had developed as a result of the pregnancy. The six weeks following the delivery, during which this reversal takes place and the uterus returns to its normal size, is known as the puerperium.

Throughout the puerperium, the new mother will be cared for by her post-natal primary care team: her doctor, midwife and health visitor.

*During the puerperium, the new mother is cared for by various members of the postnatal healthcare team. A midwife will visit the mother at home.*

*Immediately the baby is born, a woman's body begins to revert to its pre-pregnant state. Hormone levels that peaked during pregnancy now subside.*

## General effects

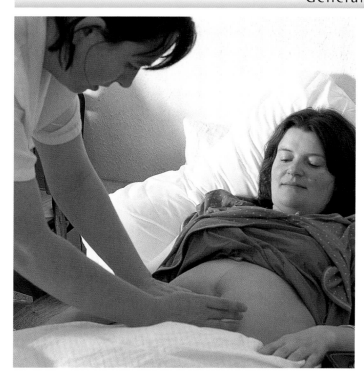

*After pregnancy, the muscle tone of the abdomen will be slightly lax. However, as time progresses, the muscles will*

Following childbirth, the general effects of pregnancy will begin to wear off, with the following results:

■ Soon after delivery, the effect of pregnancy hormones on the kidney cease and a rapid diuresis (increased urine output) occurs as the rate at which waste products are filtered from the blood through the kidneys increases

■ As a result of diuresis, the previously increased blood volume of pregnancy will return to normal, causing an apparent rise in the level of haemoglobin (pigment in red blood cells)

■ The leucocytosis (increased white blood cell count) of pregnancy will fade, resulting in a fall in the white blood cell count to normal levels

■ The blood temporarily thickens due to an increase in platelets (disc-shaped cell structures) and a rise in the level of fibrinogen (protein involved in coagulation of the blood). The development of clots within the blood vessels is therefore a risk during this period

■ The basal metabolic rate (minimum amount of bodily energy necessary to maintain vital processes) will rapidly return to its normal rate. In theory, weight should be dropping at this time, especially if the mother is breast-feeding

■ Hair and skin that was in such good condition in pregnancy will now appear dull, with hair falling out in large amounts as the follicles reach the end of their growth cycle

■ The large bowel (intestine) will gradually return to its normal activity, although constipation may be a long-term problem.

# Reproductive organs

The female organs of reproduction undergo rapid changes following delivery of the baby. The uterus and vagina shrink back to their normal size, menstruation returns and any damage sustained during the birth is repaired.

After delivery of the placenta, the circulating level of oestrogen rapidly falls. A natural breakdown of the excess uterine tissue causes the uterus to shrink back towards, though never quite reaching, its non-pregnant size. The blood vessels of the placental bed clot and shrink.

The remaining uterine muscle continues to contract intermittently throughout the puerperium, expelling debris. These contractions are most pronounced during feeding, as suckling stimulates the release of the hormone oxytocin.

### LOCHIA
The discharge and debris expelled after delivery and during the puerperium is known as the lochia. Initially, this consists mainly of blood and placental cells, but after the first week or two the lochia becomes paler and pinkish, eventually diminishing to a normal vaginal discharge.

### TRAUMA
During delivery, the mother often sustains trauma to the vagina and perineum (region between anus and urethral opening). This may range from minor bruising to lacerations and possibly an episiotomy incision, made during delivery to enlarge the vaginal opening.

### Uterus one week after childbirth

Thickened

Stretched

### Uterus six weeks

Contracted uterus

Vagina returned to normal size

*Immediately after birth, the uterus begins to shrink. After six weeks, the uterus has contracted, although it will never*

### SKIN HEALING
The injury may require immediate suturing or it may be sufficient to manage the tissue damage by simple local hygiene measures. Either way, skin healing should be complete by day six, with deep tissue taking some weeks to heal.

The vaginal walls will shrink, and the normal folds reappear. The cervical opening should also shrink but, again, it will never return to its pre-pregnant state. The commonly seen 'erosion of pregnancy', in which the inner lining of the cervix extends onto the outer surface, disappears.

### OVARIAN FUNCTION
If the mother breast-feeds, suckling stimulates production of the hormone prolactin. This suppresses re-growth of the uterine lining and delays the return of the menstrual cycle.

If the mother does not breast-feed, or when she discontinues feeding, prolactin levels fall and ovarian suppression wanes, allowing ovarian function to re-commence. The uterine lining will regenerate in the next six weeks, with the resumption of menstruation and fertility.

## Post-natal check-up

Most doctors provide a six-week post-natal check clinic to make sure that all new mothers have no remaining physical problems and that physiological changes have ensured their return to the normal, pre-pregnant, state.

At the check-up, the following problems are looked for:

■ Risk of thrombo-embolism
■ Difficulty in establishing breast-feeding, including poor technique, cracked nipples
■ Infections
■ Post-natal depression.
   Women who have experienced pregnancy-related illness, such as hypertension, should be carefully assessed.

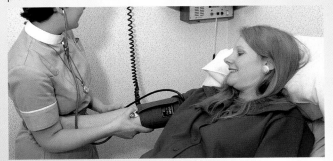

*Women who have had high blood pressure during pregnancy are carefully monitored after the birth.*

## Psychological effects

As up to 80 per cent of new mothers experience post-natal 'blues', this may be considered by some as a normal part of the changes that occur at this time.

It is true that the combination of fluctuating hormones, general pains, lack of sleep and awareness of the new burden of responsibility is enough to produce a period of emotional instability. This, however, should settle during the six weeks after delivery and should not be mistaken for the beginning of a puerperal depression.

### Cholesterol levels
Evidence exists that the rapid reduction in cholesterol levels that occurs during the puerperium may contribute to post-natal 'blues'. Adequate nutrition for the mother is therefore important.

*Many women experience post-natal blues due to a combination of factors. This emotional instability usually resolves after six weeks.*

173

# The female breast

The breast undergoes structural changes throughout the life of a woman. The most obvious changes occur during pregnancy as the breast prepares for its function as the source of milk for the baby.

Men and women both have breast tissue, but the breast is normally a well-developed structure only in women. The two female breasts are roughly hemispherical and are composed of fat and glandular tissue which overlie the muscle layer of the front of the chest wall on either side of the sternum (breastbone).

### BREAST STRUCTURE
The base of the breast is roughly circular in shape and extends from the level of the second rib above to the sixth rib below. In addition, there may be an extension of breast tissue towards the axilla (armpit), known as the 'axillary tail'.

Breast size varies greatly between women; this is mainly due to the amount of fatty tissue present, as there is generally the same amount of glandular tissue in every breast.

The mammary glands consist of 15 to 20 lobules – clusters of secretory tissue from which milk is produced. Milk is carried to the surface of the breast from each lobule by a tube known as a 'lactiferous duct', which has its opening at the nipple.

The nipple is a protruding structure surrounded by a circular, pigmented area, called the areola. The skin of the nipple is very thin and delicate and has no hair follicles or sweat glands.

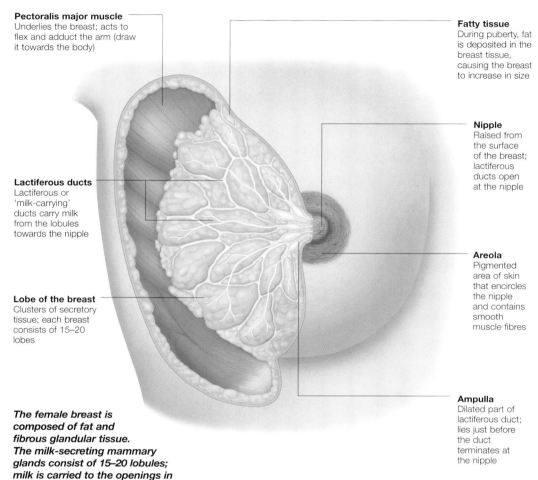

**Pectoralis major muscle**
Underlies the breast; acts to flex and adduct the arm (draw it towards the body)

**Lactiferous ducts**
Lactiferous or 'milk-carrying' ducts carry milk from the lobules towards the nipple

**Lobe of the breast**
Clusters of secretory tissue; each breast consists of 15–20 lobes

**Fatty tissue**
During puberty, fat is deposited in the breast tissue, causing the breast to increase in size

**Nipple**
Raised from the surface of the breast; lactiferous ducts open at the nipple

**Areola**
Pigmented area of skin that encircles the nipple and contains smooth muscle fibres

**Ampulla**
Dilated part of lactiferous duct; lies just before the duct terminates at the nipple

*The female breast is composed of fat and fibrous glandular tissue. The milk-secreting mammary glands consist of 15–20 lobules; milk is carried to the openings in*

## Blood vessels of the breast

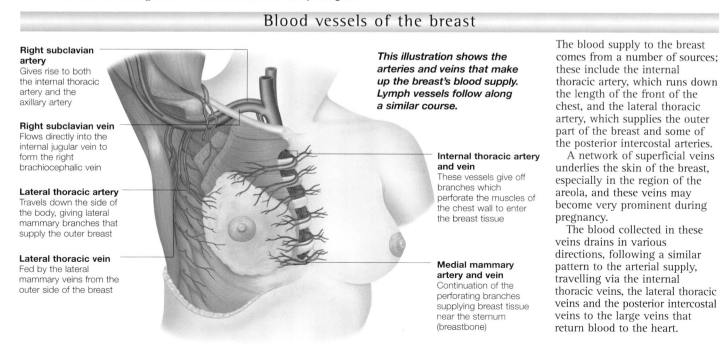

**Right subclavian artery**
Gives rise to both the internal thoracic artery and the axillary artery

**Right subclavian vein**
Flows directly into the internal jugular vein to form the right brachiocephalic vein

**Lateral thoracic artery**
Travels down the side of the body, giving lateral mammary branches that supply the outer breast

**Lateral thoracic vein**
Fed by the lateral mammary veins from the outer side of the breast

*This illustration shows the arteries and veins that make up the breast's blood supply. Lymph vessels follow along a similar course.*

**Internal thoracic artery and vein**
These vessels give off branches which perforate the muscles of the chest wall to enter the breast tissue

**Medial mammary artery and vein**
Continuation of the perforating branches supplying breast tissue near the sternum (breastbone)

The blood supply to the breast comes from a number of sources; these include the internal thoracic artery, which runs down the length of the front of the chest, and the lateral thoracic artery, which supplies the outer part of the breast and some of the posterior intercostal arteries.

A network of superficial veins underlies the skin of the breast, especially in the region of the areola, and these veins may become very prominent during pregnancy.

The blood collected in these veins drains in various directions, following a similar pattern to the arterial supply, travelling via the internal thoracic veins, the lateral thoracic veins and the posterior intercostal veins to the large veins that return blood to the heart.

# Lymphatic drainage of the breast

Lymph, the fluid which leaks out of blood vessels into the spaces between cells, is returned to the blood circulation by the lymphatic system. Lymph passes through a series of lymph nodes, which act as filters to remove bacteria, cells and other particles.

Tiny lymphatic vessels arise from the tissue spaces and converge to form larger vessels which carry the (usually) clear lymph away from the tissues and into the venous system.

Lymph drains from the nipple, areola and mammary gland lobules into a network of small lymphatic vessels, the 'subareolar lymphatic plexus'. From this plexus the lymph may be carried in several different directions.

### PATTERN OF DRAINAGE
About 75 per cent of the lymph from the subareolar plexus drains to the lymph nodes of the armpit, mostly from the outer quadrants of the breast. The lymph passes through a series of nodes in the region of the armpit draining into the subclavian lymph trunk, and ultimately into the right lymphatic trunk, which returns the lymph to the veins above the heart.

Most of the remaining lymph, mainly from the inner quadrants of the breast, is carried to the 'parasternal' lymph nodes, which lie towards the mid-line of the front of the chest. A small percentage of lymphatic vessels from the breast take another route and travel to the posterior intercostal nodes.

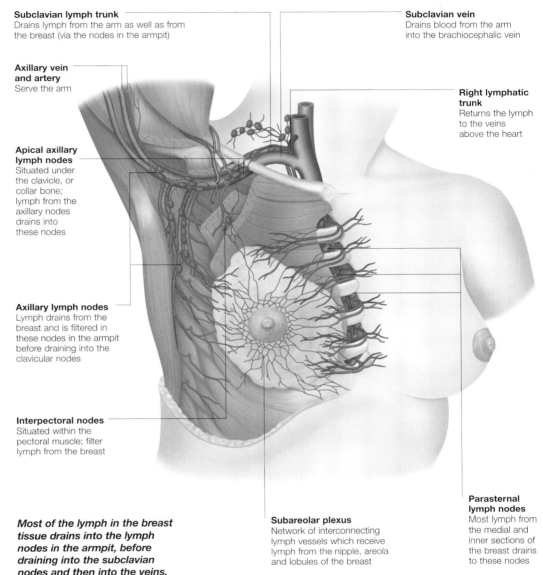

**Subclavian lymph trunk**
Drains lymph from the arm as well as from the breast (via the nodes in the armpit)

**Axillary vein and artery**
Serve the arm

**Apical axillary lymph nodes**
Situated under the clavicle, or collar bone; lymph from the axillary nodes drains into these nodes

**Axillary lymph nodes**
Lymph drains from the breast and is filtered in these nodes in the armpit before draining into the clavicular nodes

**Interpectoral nodes**
Situated within the pectoral muscle; filter lymph from the breast

**Subclavian vein**
Drains blood from the arm into the brachiocephalic vein

**Right lymphatic trunk**
Returns the lymph to the veins above the heart

**Parasternal lymph nodes**
Most lymph from the medial and inner sections of the breast drains to these nodes

**Subareolar plexus**
Network of interconnecting lymph vessels which receive lymph from the nipple, areola and lobules of the breast

*Most of the lymph in the breast tissue drains into the lymph nodes in the armpit, before draining into the subclavian nodes and then into the veins.*

## Lymphatic drainage and breast cancer

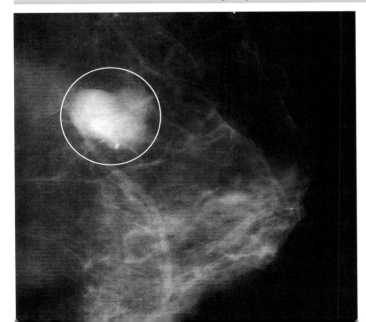

*This mammogram shows a malignant tumour in the breast. The tumour is apparent as the dense area (circled) within the breast tissue.*

Lymph fluid often contains particles such as cells which it has cleared from the tissue spaces. If the lymph has come from an area which contains a growing cancer, then it may contain cells which have broken off from that tumour. These cells will be filtered out by the lymph nodes where they may lodge and grow to form a secondary tumour, or 'metastasis'.

Knowledge of the pattern of lymph drainage of each area of the body, and especially of an area as prone to cancer as the breast, is therefore important to doctors. If a breast lump is found it is important for the doctor to check the associated lymph nodes for secondary spread of cancer cells.

### MAMMOGRAPHY
As well as examination of the breast by the doctor or the woman herself, mammography (X-ray examination of the breasts), can be used to check for breast cancer. Mammograms help to detect the presence of cancer of the breast at an early, and therefore more easily treatable, stage.

# Breast-feeding

Breast-feeding provides babies with a rich and reliable source
of food. When a baby feeds for the first time on breast milk, one of
the most intimate relationships between mother and child begins.

One immediate choice that every new mother has to face is how she intends to feed her baby – whether she is going to breast-feed or bottle-feed.

### BREAST CHANGES
The changes to the breasts that occur during pregnancy prepare the expectant mother for the production of milk, which begins in full shortly after childbirth.

During pregnancy, high levels of the hormones oestrogen, progesterone, and prolactin stimulate the breast glands to develop and produce colostrum, or 'pre-milk' shortly after birth. This is a yellowish liquid that is rich in proteins and antibodies, protecting the newborn from various infections. The protection lasts until the baby's own immune defences become more active.

### NOURISHMENT
After about three days the mother's breasts start to produce the true milk that will nourish and sustain the baby. Breast milk provides the best nourishment for babies because it is perfectly balanced, containing protein, fat, minerals and vitamins.

The real wonder of breast milk is that its composition changes within a feed, throughout the day and over the months. The milk is tailored to the exact requirements of the baby.

*Breast-feeding provides the child with an ideal balance of proteins and antibodies. The close contact brings the mother and child closer together.*

*Breast-feeding can be painful for the mother. But with time, both mother and child can benefit from this process.*

### A LEARNING PROCESS
Though breast-feeding might appear to be one of the most natural reflexes, for many women it can be fraught with anxiety.

Some mothers may not feel comfortable with the idea of their child feeding from their breast. Others, having made the decision to breast-feed their child, may find themselves physically unable to. This is usually due to the fact that the hormonal triggers that stimulate the 'let-down' reflex that brings forth the breast milk, are suppressed by factors such as stress and anxiety. Many mothers, particularly those breast-feeding for the first time, will need encouragement and reassurance from their partner.

Breast-feeding may be considered as a three-way combination of instinct, reflex and learning, and it may take some time before a mother feels confident and comfortable feeding her child.

*Milk produced by the mother's breasts changes in composition over time. This serves to meet the nutritional needs of the baby in the first few months of life.*

### MOTHER–BABY BONDING
As well as providing an optimum source of nutrition, breast-feeding is an invaluable part of the bonding process between mother and baby. Intimate moments spent nurturing her offspring help the mother form a deep psychological and physical bond with her child. Maternal instincts are magnified as the baby's smell, and the feel of its skin, become increasingly familiar.

### DISCOMFORT
Some mothers can find the first few days of breast-feeding extremely painful, but this is usually due to poor technique. It is worth persevering, as with time most mothers master the technique that works best for both them and their child.

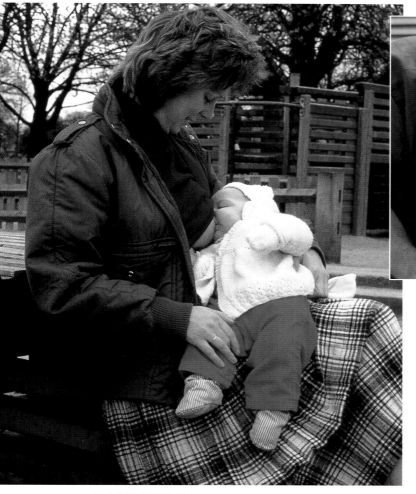

### ADVANTAGES OF BREAST-FEEDING
Breast-feeding satisfies many of the baby's immediate needs. This includes being fed, keeping warm and being held and touched by the mother.

Breast-feeding also offers many advantages to the mother. Many women appreciate the convenience of breast-feeding. The milk is always available and sterilization is not a problem. This can be particularly useful when the family is travelling since they do not need to worry about packing lots of equipment.

### PERCEPTIONS OF BREAST-FEEDING
Despite the many advantages not everyone is an advocate of breast-feeding.

Some women find the idea of using their breasts to feed their babies unpleasant or even offensive. Another problem is that other people can be offended by mothers feeding their babies in a public place. Nursing mothers are often

*A baby can be introduced to solid foods after around four to six months. Parents should ensure that solid foods are rich in vitamins and minerals.*

*Breast-feeding can be very convenient. It also offers the mother the chance to feed the child without worrying about hygiene and sterilization.*

expected to be as discreet as possible when in public, to uncover one breast at a time and to cover themselves up immediately as soon as the baby has finished.

This view is often engendered by men who find it hard to dissociate the sexual breast from the maternal breast. There are many examples of women who have been turned out of restaurants for feeding their babies in public.

### SEX-DRIVE
Many mothers become preoccupied with nurturing their child, and quite naturally their maternal feelings dominate.

The hormones responsible for stimulating the production of breast milk, also suppress the sex-drive and so it is quite common at this time for mothers to have a lower sex-drive.

In addition to a low libido, some mothers can find it difficult to reconcile being a mother as well as a sexual being. This can put a great deal of strain on the relationship between the mother and her partner.

### PHYSICAL ADVANTAGES
Breast-feeding does afford some physical advantages, however, as the presence of prolactin in the bloodstream (the hormone responsible for breast milk production) stops ovulation from occurring. The mother is able therefore to enjoy a break from her usual menstrual periods and the associated hormonal and emotional changes.

*The mother–baby relationship can be very intense and may exclude the father. An active approach can extend this intimacy to all family members.*

### FATHERS' ROLE
It is quite common for fathers to feel a senses of exclusion from the intimate relationship forged between the mother and child during breast-feeding.

A mother may feel that her attentions are torn between her loved ones; however, encouraging her partner to sit with her while she breast-feeds may help her partner to feel more involved in the process of caring for the baby.

### SOLID FOOD
Many mothers may worry about when to stop breast-feeding, as there is no set time to do so. Some mothers stop breast-feeding at four months and begin to introduce solid foods, while others may decide to stop much later.

The end of breast-feeding is usually a time of sadness for the mother, since it marks the end of a period of intense closeness between her and her child.

# Coping without breast milk

Newborn babies are adapted to drink their mother's milk. However, some babies cannot breast-feed, or have mothers who cannot produce milk, so the baby must rely on artificial nutrition in order to grow.

Parents who elect to feed their babies with artificial milk do so for a variety of reasons. Some mothers prefer bottle-feeding because they can see exactly how much milk their babies are getting. Bottle-feeding also allows the mother greater freedom, as she can share the feeding with others – especially useful if she has to return to work soon after the birth.

The prevailing opinion is that breast-feeding is best for newborn babies, but this does not mean that bottled milk is bad for them. Bottle-fed babies that are held close and cuddled while they are fed can – and do – bond early with their mothers (and fathers) in the same way that breast-fed babies do.

### DISADVANTAGES

The main disadvantage of milk formula is the increased risk of gastro-enteritis (inflammation of the stomach and intestine due to viral or bacterial infection). This emphasizes the need for sterilized equipment and fresh milk. It is also easy to overfeed bottle-fed babies, and obesity and vomiting is more common among them.

The total volume of milk given each day is based on the infant's weight. An average amount is 150 ml per kilogram, divided into five or six feeds.

*Although it is said that breast-feeding cements the bond between mother and baby, the contact involved with bottle-feeding also promotes bonding.*

*Gastro-enteritis is more common among bottle-fed babies. Sterilizing the equipment used to prepare feeds can reduce this risk.*

## Medical reasons for bottle-feeding

There are a variety of reasons why some babies are unable to breast-feed:

■ Maternal illness, such as active tuberculosis or HIV, may be present.

■ The mother may be taking medication or certain drugs which, if passed into the breast milk, could harm the baby.

■ Very premature babies are unable to feed normally, but can be given expressed breast milk or formula milk via a thin plastic tube into their stomachs.

■ Certain conditions, such as a cleft palate, make it difficult for the baby to suckle. In these cases, a specially designed bottle can be used with either breast milk that has been expressed by the mother, or with artificial formula milk.

■ Babies with inherited disorders of digestion or metabolism may not be able to tolerate human or formula milks, and, if so, they need to have special formulas.

*Premature babies are unable to feed effectively. Instead, a tube is passed through the nose and into the oesophagus, so that milk can pass into the stomach.*

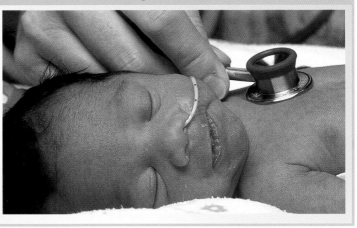

## MODIFIED COW'S MILK

Artificial or formula feeds have been modified over the years to be as similar to human breast milk as possible. This is because cow's milk contains too much curd protein, which forms a bulky mass in the baby's digestive tract and can lead to bowel obstruction. Cow's milk also contains too much sodium (salt) for a new baby, and has high levels of phosphorus, which can lead to low levels of calcium and can result in fits. Allergy to cow's milk also causes rashes, vomiting and bloody diarrhoea.

## FORMULA FEEDS

Since the 1970s, all brands of artificial milk in the UK have been modified. The 'living elements' of human milk, such as cells and enzymes, cannot be added, and this is where formula milk cannot match breast milk. Breast milk contains antibodies which protect the baby against infections, especially in the gut and respiratory tract.

## TYPES OF FORMULA

There are many different types of formula available. The whey-dominant milks have a whey-to-casein ratio similar to that of breast milk, and these are often marketed as 'first milks' for new babies.

The casein-dominant milks form a bulkier mass in the stomachs of babies and are supposed to be more satisfying for 'hungrier' babies. Casein-dominant milks can tend to cause constipation, and if a baby seems hungry, it is often better simply to increase the volume of the feed or to introduce solids if the baby is over four months old.

Sometimes, however, a baby under four months old will be on 250 g (9 oz) of formula every two to three hours, and, in such

a case, changing to a casein-dominant milk may help to fill up the baby more effectively.

All the formula milks have the essential vitamins A, C and D added, along with minerals such as iron. So long as the maternal diet is healthy, the breast-fed baby will receive these vitamins via breast milk.

## SOYA-BASED FORMULAS

There are also some highly specialized milks designed for specific medical conditions in babies. Soya-based milks do not contain any cow's milk protein. Therefore, they can be used in cases where the baby has an allergy to cow's milk protein, although this condition

*One advantage of bottle-feeding is that it involves the father in the baby's feeding. This provides an opportunity for early bonding.*

is uncommon. Although soya milks may be nutritionally adequate, some babies who have cow's milk intolerance may go on to develop an intolerance to soya-based milks, too.

Much more common is lactose intolerance, which may follow a bout of gastro-enteritis. In these cases, the gut is often temporarily unable to absorb the lactose in cow's milk. Soya-based formula can also be used in these cases.

*A baby's faeces can vary in colour from yellow to a deep green, depending on whether the baby is breast-fed or bottle-fed and if it is taking solid foods.*

## Special formula feeds

There are special formula milks for preterm babies which contain extra protein and calories to maximize their growth in the first few weeks of life. There are also special 'elemental milks' containing sugars, peptides and amino acids which are used in babies who have had to have part of their bowel removed due to disease and require a food which is easily absorbed. Hospital-based dieticians usually make up these milks for the specific needs of each baby.

Soya milk is available commercially and it is currently

fashionable among parents to change to soya milk if they are unhappy with their baby's behaviour, believing formula milk to be the cause of the problem.

Changing a baby's diet in the hope that it will improve its mood or make it sleep better is wishful thinking; special milk feeds should be used only to

*Soya-based milk formula is an alternative to cow's milk for babies with cow's milk allergies. A health worker should be consulted before changing a baby's diet.*

treat specific conditions. Exclusion diets in babies and toddlers can lead to the inadvertent slow starvation of

that child, and advice from a doctor or health visitor should always be sought before the milk is changed.

# Breast-feeding disorders

Breast-feeding is a natural reflex for both mother and baby. However, certain problems can arise, either physical or emotional, and instruction and treatment may be required to achieve success.

Providing nourishment through breast-feeding or breast milk substitutes is one of the most important tasks of caring for a newborn. While breast milk substitutes are an acceptable means of feeding, there is no denying the benefits that breast-feeding brings.

### BENEFITS

Not only is breast milk an optimum source of nutrition for the child, but it contains immune antibodies which serve to boost the child's immune system, making it less susceptible to illness, even in later life.

The physical act of breast-feeding also plays an invaluable role in the process of bonding between mother and child.

### PHYSIOLOGICAL CHANGES

During pregnancy the breasts develop considerably. Fat is deposited around the glandular parts of the breasts, and hormonal changes cause an increase in the number and size of ducts and alveoli (milk-producing sacs).

In late pregnancy the breasts secrete a creamy yellow fluid, known as colostrum, which is rich in antibodies. The

*The secretion of breast milk is triggered by the suckling action of the baby. This 'let-down' reflex is controlled by the hormone oxytocin.*

production of colostrum increases after the birth until it is replaced by breast milk.

In the 48 hours preceding childbirth, levels of oestrogen drop dramatically, triggering production of breast milk by the alveolar cells. Suckling of the breast by the baby results in a 'let down' reflex, whereby the mother's pituitary gland is triggered to produce oxytocin, which stimulates the myoepithelial cells surrounding the alveoli to contract, ejecting milk from the nipple.

### POSSIBLE PROBLEMS

Despite the fact that breast-feeding is a natural biological reflex, some mothers may not feel inclined to breast-feed their child. Of those mothers that do wish to breast-feed, some may encounter problems.

It is common for a mother to be anxious about breast-feeding, especially if it is her first time. This anxiety may result in the triggers of lactation being

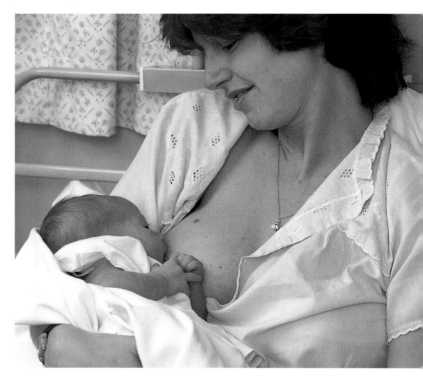

suppressed and the breasts fail to produce or 'let down' milk.

The mother will need encouragement from medical staff, so that she is confident and relaxed, before the normal

reflexes can occur. Many breast-feeding problems result from poor technique, and some mothers may require instruction as to how to breast-feed their child more effectively.

## Breast-feeding technique

### Incorrect nipple position

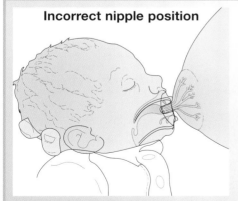

*It is important that the nipple is inserted correctly into the baby's mouth. If it is not inserted far enough, the baby will place its lips around the nipple, which can become very tender and sore as a result.*

### Ideal nipple position

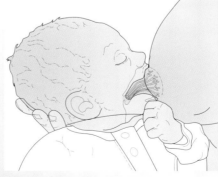

*The mother should hold the nipple so that it is prominent before inserting it into the baby's mouth. This enables the baby to suck the area surrounding the nipple (the areola) as opposed to the nipple itself.*

The mother should sit back so that she can support her child comfortably in her arms. At first she may need to be shown how to stroke the child's mouth with her nipple to induce the 'rooting' reflex, which causes the baby to open its mouth and search for the nipple.

**Helping the baby to feed**

The mother should hold her breast with the nipple between her forefinger and middle fingers, so that the nipple becomes more prominent. This will help the child to place its gums around the area surrounding the nipple (the areola) as opposed to the nipple itself, which can be very tender.

The mother should also be shown how to detach her child's mouth from the nipple without causing pain. This is done by the insertion of her little finger into the corner of the baby's mouth to break the suction, before detaching the baby.

# Physical problems

Some mothers may develop physical problems which make breast-feeding painful. The breasts can become inflamed or infected, requiring treatment.

Two to three days after the birth, the breasts become tender as increased milk production distends the glandular tissue within the breast.

### ENGORGED BREASTS
As it takes a few days for the milk ejection reflex to operate properly, some women's breasts may become painfully engorged around this time.

The alternate application of hot and cold towels to the breast may help in some cases, by stimulating bloodflow through the engorged areas of the breast. Another method is to stimulate the milk ejection reflex using an electric breast pump. Very severe engorgement which causes pain may be treated by prescribing small doses of the drug

bromocriptine for 24–48 hours.

The mother should be encouraged to continue breast-feeding if possible to stimulate the milk ejection reflex, and reduce the engorgement.

### CRACKED NIPPLES
In some cases suckling by the baby may lead to the nipples becoming cracked and inflamed. This is often as a result of the nipple not being inserted far enough into the child's mouth.

In such cases the nipple should be treated with chlorohexidine cream, and a nipple shield used to protect it during feeding. In more severe cases the child should not be fed from the affected breast, a pump being used to empty it manually to avoid engorgement.

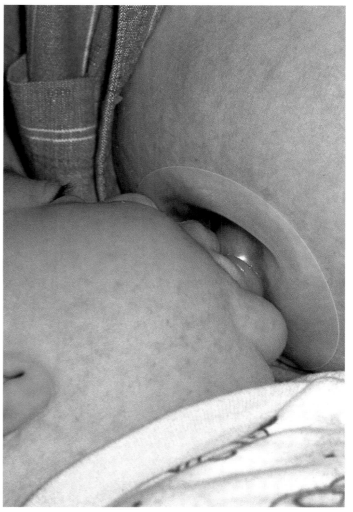

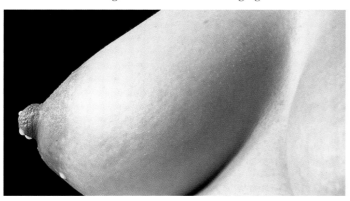

*Engorgement of the breasts often occurs three or four days after giving birth. The breasts can become very tender, causing painful breast-feeding.*

*Cracked nipples commonly occur due to incorrect breast-feeding technique. Application of a soothing cream and use of a nipple shield should help.*

## Inflammatory conditions

If the breasts become inflamed as a result of milk stasis or bacterial infection, the ability to breast-feed may be affected.
■ Milk stasis – this occurs when pressure within the engorged alveoli causes milk to seep into surrounding breast tissues, resulting in inflammation of the breasts. The mother should be encouraged to increase the number of feeds to the child, and empty the breasts manually with a pump after each feed.

■ Mastitis – this condition may occur when bacteria from the child's nasopharyngeal or umbilical areas are transferred to the mother's breast. Acute mastitis can occur a week after breast-feeding. Symptoms include a raised temperature and a hard, red area in one of the breasts.

Treatment consists of antibiotics to fight the infection and analgesics to reduce pain. If it is not too painful, the mother should be encouraged to continue breast-feeding.

In cases where pus accumulates and a breast abscess develops, surgical incision and drainage of the abscess will be required, followed by antibiotics.

*Mastitis occurs when the breasts become inflamed due to bacterial infection. If a breast abscess develops this will need to be drained surgically.*

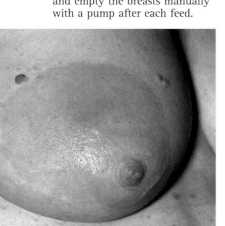

## Suppressing lactation

Mothers who make the decision not to breast-feed their child, or who decide that it is time to stop breast-feeding, may require treatment to stop their breasts from producing milk.

**Absence of suckling**
In most cases lactation will cease soon after birth if suckling does not occur, although the breasts may become engorged in this time.

**Easing pressure**
Some women may need to be prescribed a prolactin inhibitor (a drug that is used to stop the breasts producing milk). A supportive bra will also ease the pressure upon the breasts.

*Mothers who choose to bottle-feed their baby may require lactation to be suppressed. Drugs which inhibit prolactin production may be prescribed.*

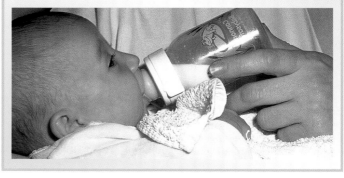

# Bonding with the child

Bonding between parents and children is vital for development in childhood. Unconditional parental love provides children with the security they need while going through transitional phases of life.

Bonding refers to the unique relationship that develops between parents and their children. It serves an important function – without bonding few parents could sustain the personal sacrifices that are required in caring for a child.

### EARLY AFFECTION
Some mothers report that they experience the first feelings of affection for their child when it is moving in their uterus. Others say that love comes suddenly when the child is born, while a third group says that emotions develop more slowly.

Contrary to popular belief it can take time for a mother to become emotionally attached to her baby – human relationships are not so mechanical that they can be switched on and off by a single event, such as birth.

So far as a child's later development is concerned, there are no apparent adverse consequences in the long term of failing to bond with the mother in the first few days of life.

### BONDING AFTER CHILDBIRTH
Most parents presented with a new baby follow an instinctive pattern of touching the baby's face, massaging the baby's trunk and gazing into its eyes. Babies for their part are surprisingly alert in the period immediately

*Communication between parent and child can start early. Some studies have shown babies imitating facial expressions at just two or three days old.*

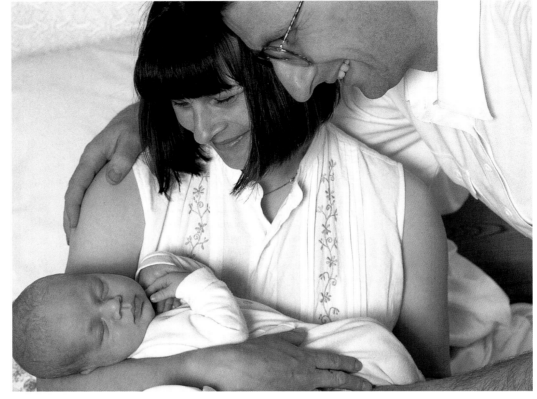

*Bonding between parents and a new baby is an instinctive process. Parents will tend to massage the baby's body and gaze into its eyes.*

following birth. Despite the exhaustion of having just been born, their eyes are open and they stare at the world around them. This action can facilitate the immediate bonding process between mother and child as the baby returns her gaze.

### EXCHANGING FACIAL EXPRESSIONS
Very young babies can imitate facial expressions, sticking out their tongues, opening their mouths wide and pursing their lips. In some studies they have been shown capable of matching happy, sad and surprised expressions at only two or three days old. It is believed that early imitation is one of the first efforts at communication between the baby and its mother.

### MATERNAL AND PATERNAL FEELINGS
Women – whether mothers or not – often produce the same emotional response to the sight of a baby. Their pupils display a marked enlargement. In men the response is less uniform: it is normally only those who already have children of their own who show this strong positive response.

Such research has been interpreted as suggesting that women are primed for maternal behaviour, while males need to have the protective, parental urges activated within them by the presence of their own babies. The positive side of this finding is that men who take little interest in other babies often become devoted fathers.

### LANGUAGE DEVELOPMENT
The baby-talk between a mother and her child not only provides an expression of her love, but is important for language development. The mother's high-pitched cooing places exaggerated stress on vowels, and communicates directly with the baby since its hearing is attuned to high frequencies.

### SIBLING RIVALRY
Babies also need to form relationships with their siblings. Rivalry is a natural response when two people are competing for the same prize – the attentions of the parents. Common responses can be regression and resentment from the older child. To help form a bond they should be included in the baby's care and activities, such as cuddling up to their parents and the baby, reading to the baby and playing.

### IMPORTANCE OF CARE-PROVIDERS

For the first three months of life, babies are not that particular about who looks after them. At between four and six months they are beginning to recognize their main care-provider and tend to settle down more quickly with them.

By seven months the baby has firmly bonded with its care-provider and can object vociferously to being handled by others. This bond develops into a close emotional relationship over a period of months and is a powerful influence on the child's emotional development.

### CARING FOR TODDLERS

During the toddler transitional stages, parents will need to tread a fine line between providing too much security and too little. A balance must be found between stifling the child's development by being over-protective and giving them the support that they need to grow.

### ENCOURAGING SELF-ESTEEM

For older children of around five and six, it is important for parents to give them a strong sense of self-esteem. A crucial factor in self-esteem is the quality of the parent–child relationship. A child must know,

*Comfort and security are vital to a toddler's healthy development. However, parents must take care not to inhibit the child by being over-protective.*

through the parents' words and actions, that he or she is loved unconditionally. When a child is naughty the deed should be criticized rather than the child. Children who enjoy unconditional love can learn to accept criticism and failure rather than be devastated by it.

### PARENTAL VALUES

Parents pass on their values to their offspring, not so much by talking about them as by applying them to everyday situations in family life. Children soon learn the kinds of behaviour of which their parents approve or disapprove. For example, parents who are relaxed about the untidiness of a child's bedroom, but firm about getting homework done on time are expressing the high value they place on education.

### GRANDPARENTS

Another valuable bonding relationship is that between grandparents and children. Grandparents give them another perspective on the world, and a sense of history and continuum that are important in handing down traditions and cultural and religious values to future generations. This is particularly valuable for immigrant families growing up in other cultures.

### DEALING WITH THE TEENAGE YEARS

An important goal for the parents of teenagers is to establish two-way communication; parents need to remember that communication is

*Older children can react with resentment to the arrival of a new baby. Involving them in the baby's care can help to overcome this problem.*

an exchange of ideas rather than a transmission of instructions. Parents should help their children through this sometimes difficult transitional phase by offering love and emotional warmth as well as a consistent moral code.

### IMPORTANCE OF PARENTAL CARE

Parental care is vital in a child's development. Infants forced to survive without a mother or father figure struggle to adapt, and accumulate problems in later years. They may find it difficult to make lasting attachments as adults and their trust may be affected.

*Parental care is extremely important to a child's development. An infant deprived of such affection can develop emotional problems in later life.*

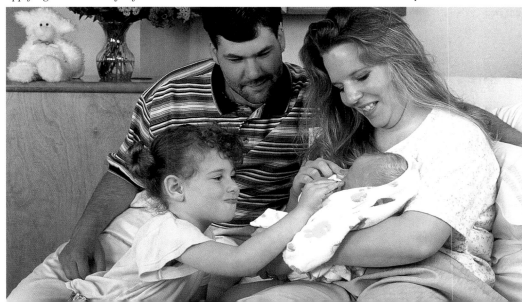

# Post-natal depression

### Pregnancy and childbirth are a time of profound physical and emotional change. However, 1 in 10 women develop some form of depression after childbirth.

The immediate post-natal period (the first few days after giving birth) is characterized by a number of physical and emotional changes, and can be a challenging time for mothers.

### POST-NATAL CHANGES

As hormone levels fluctuate, many women experience extremes of emotion, and may develop the 'baby blues' – a mild form of depression – for a few days after the birth.

Around 10 per cent of women, however, experience longer-lasting symptoms of depression. Most commonly this condition occurs between four and six weeks after childbirth.

Severe depression with suicidal ideas and psychotic symptoms (puerperal psychosis) is rare after childbirth.

### RISK FACTORS

Major risk factors for developing post-natal depression include:
■ History of psychiatric illness, especially depression
■ Mood disorder during the pregnancy
■ Relationship difficulties
■ Lack of support
■ Recent negative life event such as loss of a loved one.
   Minor risk factors include:
■ Low income
■ Complicated delivery
■ Severe 'maternity blues'
■ Physical problems in the baby.

### SYMPTOMS

Depressive symptoms include apathy, anxiety, low mood, and poor concentration.

Severe depression is often characterized by hostility toward the baby, or even psychosis, and must be actively treated with referral to the specialist mental health team. Mother and baby unit day-care or admission may be required.

*Post-natal depression may begin in the first six months after childbirth. Symptoms can affect a mother's ability to look after her baby.*

## Diagnosing post-natal depression

There is no definitive test to confirm the diagnosis of post-natal depression, which is made by clinical assessment.

### HORMONE LEVELS

The period after childbirth is dominated by changes in hormone levels, but there is no evidence that the hormone profiles of post-natally depressed women are any different from those women who do not develop depression. Research has, however, suggested a small increased risk in women who test positive for autoimmune thyroid disorders.

### POST-NATAL CHECKS

As well as general monitoring during the post-natal period, the post-natal check at six weeks gives the doctor or health visitor an ideal opportunity to assess the mother's mental state.

*The six-week post-natal check may include a questionnaire and a clinical interview. This enables doctors to identify women at risk of severe depression.*

# Treating depression

In most cases, post-natal depression lasts only a few months. Symptoms are managed by psychological support, with or without drug therapy.

As well as community care support, a variety of psychological interventions prove beneficial to women with post-natal depression. These include:
■ Community-based non-directive counselling
■ Cognitive behavioural therapy
■ Psychotherapy.

### DRUG THERAPY

While psychological intervention is effective in the management of mild to moderate post-natal depression, greater benefit can be gained from the simultaneous use of drug therapy.

In those who do not respond to psychological measures and patients with moderate to severe depression, anti-depressants may be prescribed. The few who develop psychotic symptoms will need further treatment with, for example, tranquillizers.

A dilemma arises for many women who may wish to breast-feed their baby while being treated. The advantages of medication for the mother must be balanced against the possible effect on the baby, especially in women on high dose regimens.

### HORMONE THERAPY

Following the pattern of hormonal change in the six weeks after childbirth, both progestogens and oestrogen have been suggested for use in post-natal depression.

As yet, there is no evidence to suggest that progestogens are effective. Oestrogen use is unlicensed and is therefore only given as part of clinical trials. It may, however, eventually have a beneficial role for some women.

*Antidepressants may relieve symptoms of severe post-natal depression. The drugs take effect within several weeks; full recovery may take up to a year.*

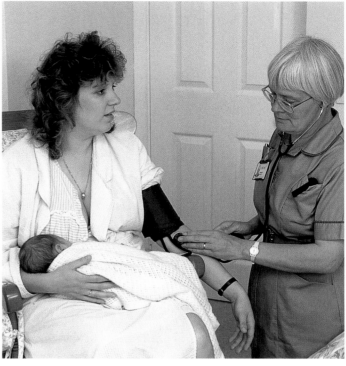

*Regular checks by a health visitor ensures that affected mothers receive extra support. The mother's mental health will be monitored.*

### MEDICAL SUPPORT

While most women will benefit from the community support offered by the community care team, for some a dedicated mother and baby day unit would be preferable. Unfortunately there are very few in the UK and for many, the only alternative is out-patient psychiatric care or even admission.

Involving the community psychiatric nurse at an early stage offers the patient and her family extra support as well as specialist monitoring of her progress.

### RECOVERY

The majority of women, even if left untreated, will recover within three to six months. Ten per cent of women who develop post-natal depression will still be symptomatic a year later, with a smaller percentage continuing with a chronic relapsing mood disorder. Depression can recur in subsequent pregnancies.

## Prevention strategies

Awareness of the risks, with prevention plans where possible, can reduce the incidence of depression.

**Recognizing the symptoms**
Antenatal education, covering the emotional pressures of parenthood, the temporary nature of 'maternity blues' and the risk of post-natal depression, will help women and their partners recognize early symptoms and reduce some of the associated guilt and anxiety.

Antenatal appointments should be used to promote a supportive relationship between the patient and the community care team, identifying those women who lack

*Women who are at risk of post-natal depression can receive extra support during pregnancy. Parenting classes help to prepare for the arrival of a baby.*

support from their own family and who have few friends.

**Depression in pregnancy**
If depression develops during pregnancy, it can be managed effectively with general support, psychotherapy and, if indicated, antidepressant therapy.

Although many women want to avoid taking any medication during pregnancy, the use of antidepressants and some newer selective serotonin re-uptake inhibitors (SSRIs) has not been shown to cause any congenital abnormalities in babies. In pregnant mothers with symptoms, the use of drug therapy is essential as the risk of relapse is high.

During the birth itself and in the immediate weeks following, the mother identified as high risk will benefit from extra support and reassurance.

# Returning to work after childbirth

Most working mothers have to decide whether to return to work after having a baby. For those who do, combining a career with the requirements of motherhood makes for a demanding life.

The decision about whether or not to return to work – and, if so, when – after having a baby is one that needs to be taken by most working mothers.

Nowadays, around half of mothers return to work before their children start school. Many find that holding down a job and raising children is a constant balancing act that requires discipline and stamina.

### NEW MOTHERS

For first-time mothers, one of the difficulties is that it is almost impossible to know in advance until they have had their baby whether or not they will want to go back to work.

Some women find looking after young children completely fulfilling and exciting, and feel that they cannot possibly be parted from them.

Others, however, miss the challenge of work and the contact with other people – it is important to them to spend time outside the home being something other than a wife or partner and mother.

Many working women feel that 'keeping a foot in the door', perhaps by returning to work on a part-time basis, may be necessary for their long-term career prospects. Taking time off while children are young may

*Working women may worry about how their children will cope in their absence. However, most children soon settle down happily with their carers.*

mean that when women are ready to return to work they have lost touch with the working environment and their skills may need updating.

### MAINTAINING LIFESTYLE

Financial reasons are another important motivating factor for returning to work. Many families today need two incomes and do not want their lifestyle to suffer when they have children.

Childcare is, however, expensive (and, in the UK, not tax-deductible), which means that some women on low wages may, in effect, be barred from the work economy. Once other expenses are paid, they may find that there is no financial advantage in working.

### FEELINGS OF GUILT

Most working parents experience some anxiety and guilt about balancing the equation of time spent with children and time spent earning the money to provide for them.

However, studies show that, all other things being equal, children whose mothers work do not suffer any more emotional problems or tend to be any less well-adjusted than the children of mothers who stay at home. The children of working mothers and those of full-time mothers perform equally well, both socially and academically.

Women returning to work may find that they miss their children more than they anticipated. They can sometimes

find it painful that, in their absence, their children achieve major milestones such as taking their first steps and uttering their first words.

### BONDING WITH A CARER

Mothers can also feel jealous of the affection felt by their child for its carer and do not want their children diverting love on to someone else.

It should be acknowledged, however, that, although their child may be spending the working day with someone else, this will not affect the child's love for them.

*Women return to work after childbirth for a number of reasons. Some mothers miss the stimulation offered by the working environment.*

*The majority of mothers today need to make a decision about returning to work. Around 50 per cent of mothers go back to work before their child starts school.*

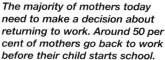

# Picture Credits

Apart from those images listed below, all of the pictures contained in this book were originally sourced for the part-work *Inside the Human Body*, produced by Bright Star Publishing plc.